League Park

League Park

Historic Home of Cleveland Baseball, 1891–1946

Ken Krsolovic *and* Bryan Fritz

McFarland & Company, Inc., Publishers
Jefferson, North Carolina, and London

LIBRARY OF CONGRESS CATALOGUING-IN-PUBLICATION DATA

Krsolovic, Ken, 1958–
      League park : historic home of Cleveland baseball, 1891–
1946 / Ken Krsolovic and Bryan Fritz.
          p.   cm.
      Includes bibliographical references and index.

      ISBN 978-0-7864-6826-3
      softcover : acid free paper ♾

      1. League Park (Cleveland, Ohio)—History.   2. Baseball
fields—Ohio—Cleveland—History.   3. Baseball—Ohio—
Cleveland—History.   I. Fritz, Bryan, 1954–   II. Title.
GV879.5.K77 2013
796.3570977132—dc23   2013001096

BRITISH LIBRARY CATALOGUING DATA ARE AVAILABLE

On the front cover: "League Park ca. 1920," © Jeff Suntala,
gouache on illustration board

Manufactured in the United States of America

McFarland & Company, Inc., Publishers
  Box 611, Jefferson, North Carolina 28640
    www.mcfarlandpub.com

Table of Contents

Acknowledgments

On March 3, 1979, *Cleveland Plain Dealer* sports editor Hal Lebovitz wrote, "Undoubtedly a more definitive work will be — and should be — done some day about the old park." This book is meant to be just that. It is for Hal and all of the others who played or cheered there, as well as for those who just wish that they had. Here's to ballparks being about watching games and sharing times with our community, friends and families. Here's to League Park ... may its stories and memories never fade!

The number of people who contributed to this project is staggering. Thanks to all of the librarians, researchers, friends and family members who contributed to, supported or inspired this effort. We tried to incorporate all of your input, thoughts and memories. It has taken much longer than anticipated, but we feel that we have cleared up many prior inconsistencies and that the extra time spent has only improved the result. Thanks especially to Rita Fritz and Lisa Krsolovic, whose support and understanding of our love and passion for sports and sporting venues allowed this volume to be completed.

Our thanks go out to many, including the Cleveland Public Library, Western Reserve Historical Society, Burton Historical Society at Detroit Public Library, John Carroll and Case Western Reserve University archives, baseball-reference.com, Pat Kelly of the National Baseball Hall of Fame in Cooperstown, Bob DiBiasio, Les Levine, Karl Fritz, Lindsey Lowman, Charles O'Neill, William Mullee, Stanley Kawecki, Tony Ursich, Tim Dembowski and Fred Weisman.

Preface

One of the great things about baseball is that it allows for time to talk. Not just before or after games, but even during games. And there's time even when you're playing. In 1981, a couple of guys on the same slow-pitch softball team in the eastern suburbs of Cleveland started to talk. While conversing on the bench, waiting for their turns to bat, one of them happened to mention his collection of stadium postcards.

It turned out that both had such a collection, along with a keen interest in comparing, visiting and talking about the places where baseball games and other sports were played.

For about the next 25 years, around jobs, moves, wives and kids (and more baseball games), the two continued to talk about ballparks, especially about Cleveland's ballparks. During that time, Cleveland Stadium, well-chronicled, was demolished. Jacobs (now Progressive) Field was constructed and quickly became adored. The pair occasionally visited other ballparks and continued to share their interest and observations.

But most of all, these two guys were fascinated by a plot of ground on Cleveland's East Side where Major League Baseball used to be played ... League Park. Mere remnants of a ballpark were standing there, along with a declining playing field. These two guys talked about writing a book about the place. They talked a lot.

Finally, in 2006, while taking a ride downstate to see a game at the then-new ballpark in Dayton, the talk started to get more serious. Bryan, a prosecutor for the city of Cleveland, began to spend lunch hours combing the newspaper archives at the Cleveland Public Library. In early 2008, Bryan met Ken for lunch at the legendary Slyman's restaurant on the near East Side of the city. Bryan handed Ken a rough draft. And rough it was—a series of stories and anecdotes that he had compiled and uncovered. But what a compilation to begin with! A former college sports information director and now an athletic director, Ken began to build a body on the skeleton.

Little did they realize how much work was still left to be done. Whenever it seemed that completion was nearing, more new sources and information would seem to appear. Questions arose from conflicting sources. More clarifications or additions from previous writings were addressed.

The goal of the book became to be as comprehensive as possible, although this meant relying almost entirely upon published sources, some well over a hundred years old. There just weren't the people around anymore to check facts with or confirm anything with any real credibility. As such, the research at times was painstaking. Many individuals were, in fact, found with memories of having attended games there. And those shared memories became parts of the bits and pieces that seemed, at times, to be overwhelming. But the further the project went, the more clear it became that the story of the ballpark needed to be told. That confirmation is what kept the project going.

In late 2010, Bryan came across a series of articles about the ballpark from the *Cleveland Press* in 1953. Those served as a perfect cross check to the project. In 2011, a fitting end to the project was provided by the city of Cleveland, as it approved a plan to resurrect the grounds after decades of failed attempts.

And so a long-standing goal has been fulfilled for a couple of friends. To future researchers, the hope is that much has been added here. And it's likely that further finds will be made. But perhaps, at least, the tales and events described here will show why League Park deserves to be remembered.

Introduction

To many baseball fans, America's ballparks have come to be as revered as the athletes who play in them and as important as the actual games that occur inside their walls. Whether it's a venerable park from the early 20th century concrete-and-steel era or some multi-purpose stadium from the latter half of that century, sports fans of this nation have come to revel in the nostalgia of these places where their memories were made.

Reverence for ballparks is a phenomenon that seemingly began in the late 1960s and has continued to gain momentum into the new millennium. Unfortunately, places like Ebbets Field and the Polo Grounds were not largely celebrated when their histories ended. Their passing was certainly noted, but their demise was not marketed by the teams that called them home. By the time that edifices such as Shibe Park and Forbes Field had reached their end in the early 1970s, however, fans had become interested in that one last look. In turn, teams began to realize that celebrating the old venue could be as much of an attraction as the opening of the new site.

League Park in Cleveland was hardly recognized as its major league days wound down after World War II for two primary reasons. First, the facility was not going away. Secondly, League Park had been on the brink of replacement for some 15 years. And indeed its run as a ballpark never really ended. Cleveland's legendary field is unique in that the site was used for baseball well before places like Shibe, Forbes and the rest ... and its usefulness was extended for many decades after the big leaguers left. Unlike most of those from the "classic" era of baseball diamonds, Cleveland's hallowed space has died the slowest death of any major league site. No wrecking ball or dynamite implosion would end its use. And it may still survive as a ballpark long into the future as the result of a modern miracle cure. Only because it had managed to hold on for so long does it have the opportunity to yet be reborn.

Built upon the site of its wooden predecessor of the same name, League Park's small capacity nearly cost it its life when it fell behind the times. But the ahead-of-its-time concept of a multi-purpose behemoth, Cleveland Municipal Stadium, allowed League Park to survive for much longer as the

3

primary home of the Cleveland Indians. After the inevitable move to Municipal Stadium finally occurred, League Park became a city property and was slowly and excruciatingly dismantled over the next six decades.

Even the casual fan knows of the legends of Yankee Stadium, Fenway Park and Wrigley Field. But the stories and happenings from League Park certainly compare, and arguably exceed, the tales from those more chronicled and famous fields of play. Ruth's 500th, DiMaggio's 56th, Cy Young's dominance, Wamby's triple play, Joss's perfection, Feller's debut, and many, many more key events (and obscure facts) are part of the story of League Park. So let us now learn of the fabulous venue and the events that entitle Cleveland's corner of East 66th and Lexington to a place of honor in the history of the National Pastime...

1

The Wooden Era

Teams played in wooden ballparks hastily erected on empty lots. Even more important than a park's characteristics was its location, as entrepreneurs scrambled to erect ballparks along the trolley and streetcar lines that sprang up in urban areas — Eric Enders, *Ballparks Then and Now*

Before League Park

Professional baseball came to Cleveland in 1869 when the idea of pro sports was a brand-new part of American life. So it was that on June 2, 1869, the already-famous Cincinnati Red Stockings, the first openly paid team, took on the Cleveland Forest Citys at Case Commons, located along Putnam Avenue (now East 38th Street) between Scovill (now known as Community College Avenue) and Garden Street (which has become Central Avenue) on the near East Side of the city.

The nine-member Forest City team had Al Pratt as pitcher and Jim White as the catcher. The second baseman was L.C. Hanna, who was the brother of Senator Mark Hanna. A gathering of about 2,000 Clevelanders was on hand to witness the event. The Forest City team proved to be gracious hosts for their opponents as the Red Stockings hit their way to a 25–6 win. A home run by center fielder Art Burt was the brightest moment for the home team. All in all, the crowd got its money's worth, staying behind ropes at the open grounds and paying 25 cents per ticket or 50 cents per carriage to watch.

By 1871, the Forest Citys had joined nine other teams to form the National Association of Professional Base Ball Players, the first major league. Playing at a new location further east along Garden Street from Case Commons at Willson Street (now East 55th Street), the team began the practice of selling season tickets at the new site, identified simply as National Association Grounds.

Wearing monogrammed white shirts with blue trim, the Forest Citys met Chicago on May 11 to open the home season. The Chicago contingent won the game, 18–10, in a contest marred by controversial decisions by the

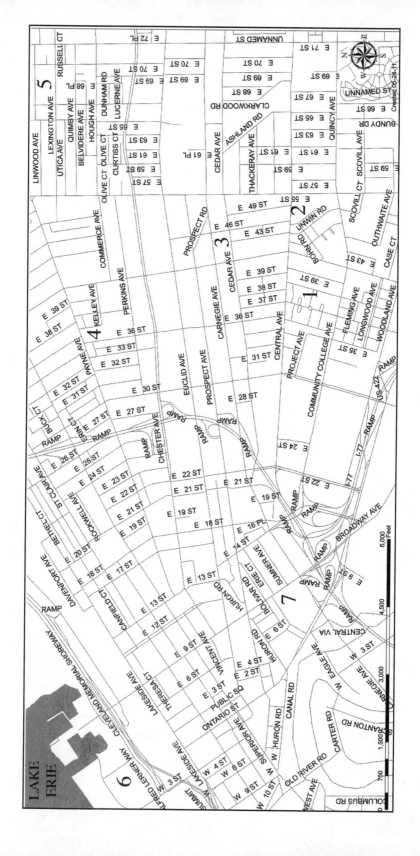

umpire. The Cleveland team left the field after eight innings in protest. The largest crowd at that site, 3,000, saw Cleveland host Fort Wayne on May 26. The Forest Citys lasted just one more season, playing their last game on August 19, 1872.

Pro ball returned in 1878, when Cleveland established the site for its third professional baseball home, this time along Kennard (now E. 46th Street), between Silby Street (now Carnegie Avenue) and Cedar Avenue. The Cleveland "Blues" joined the National League for the 1879 season, so locals called the location National League Park. An odd configuration, there were trees in play in the outfield during this site's early days. In addition, the left field fence was so short that fly balls hit over it were scored as ground rule doubles in 1880 and 1881.

Cleveland was involved in several historic pitching performances during this era, though all occurred on the road. First, the Blues were victims of the first-ever perfect game, as Lee Richmond retired 27 straight Cleveland batters at Worcester in 1880. (Five days later, John Montgomery Ward matched the feat for Providence against Buffalo; a perfect game would not occur again until 1904.) Charles Radbourn no-hit the Blues on July 25, 1883 at Providence. Seven weeks later, Cleveland got its first-ever no-hitter when Hugh Daily, a one-armed pitcher, shut down the Phillies in Philadelphia on September 13. By the time the 1884 season concluded, however, a general lack of success on the field caused the Blues to withdraw from the league.

Major league baseball returned to the city in 1887 when another version of the Blues entered the American Association. Frank DeHass Robison was the team's owner and a new baseball ground was built on the south side of Payne Avenue along Douglas Street (later East 35th Street) to East 39th Street. This larger plot featured an outfield fence of 400 feet or farther from home plate. In addition to its larger size, this location was chosen because one of the two streetcar lines owned by Robison went right past the park along Payne Avenue.[1] Unfortunately, a new owner and the new location did not translate into much success on the field, as the team struggled to a last-place finish with a 39–91 record. The 1888 team improved to 50–82 but still placed 6th in the eight-team league.

Cleveland rejoined the National League for the 1889 season, staying at the same locale as the former American Association team. The club earned a roughhouse reputation, but only posted a mediocre record of 61–72. At least

Opposite Page: Primary Cleveland ballpark locations through the years. 1. Case Commons (1869–1870); 2. National Association Grounds (1871–1872); 3. National League Park (1879–1884); 4. Spider Park (1887–1890); 5. League Park/Dunn Field (1891–1946); 6. Cleveland Stadium (1932–1993); 7. Jacobs/Progressive Field (1994–present).

two of the new players, however, would become noteworthy in Cleveland baseball history. One was a burly right-handed pitcher named Denton Young who would be forever known as "Cy" because he hurled the ball with the speed of a cyclone. The other was Charles "Chief" Zimmer, a catcher who would play a total of 13 years in Cleveland. It was also at this time that the team began to be known as the Spiders. Legend has it that one of the team's stockholders, George Howe, saw them in practice and remarked on how skinny and spindly they were, resembling the insects. Likewise, the field became known at Spider Park, which was noted for the excellent quality of its grass playing surface.

In 1890, Cleveland actually had two teams, the Spiders in the National League and the "Infants" in the new Players' League, a rival major league formed with hopes of improving player salaries and putting an end to the reserve clause. The new team played its games at Brotherhood Park, on land a few blocks south of the 1871–72 National Association grounds, bordered by Willson (East 55th), Kinsman Road, Diamond Street (nearest to home plate) and railroad tracks along the first base side. That league lasted just that one season and Cleveland placed 7th with a record of 55–77, averaging 927 fans at home. Cleveland player Pete Browning did lead the league with 40 doubles and a .373 batting average.

The Spiders also had a poor 1890 season at the Payne Avenue site, winning only 44 games that year, while losing 88. Pitcher Ed Beatin started 54 games for the team, completing all but one, and posting a 22–31 record. It has been said that the ballpark suffered irreparable damage following a fire from a lightning storm during a game with the Chicago Colts late that season, but documentation from that time remains elusive.[2] There is record of a game on June 5 with Chicago that got underway but was then abandoned because of a fierce storm. However, the only lightning strike reported that day took place at the Brotherhood Park game between the Infants and Buffalo. Neither team moved from their home field after that date, so if there was damage it must not have been extensive enough to force relocation.

League Park Debuts

Whether or not lightning was a factor, the Spiders headed to a new locale for the next season. On February 12, 1891, the city issued a building permit for construction of a brand-new park for the team that was farther yet to the east. As was the case with the Payne Avenue site, team owner Robison also owned the streetcar line that passed by the new venue and it is most likely that his transportation business would be helped more by the new park's location than the old. This new ground was bordered by Dunham (later East 66th

The original main gate and ticket booths for League Park were at the northwest corner of the grounds, behind home plate at the corner of East 66th Street and Linwood. Note the trolley tracks in the foreground running up East 66th. This line was owned by team owner Frank Robison, which was the main reason for the selection of this site in 1890 (Library of Congress, Prints & Photographs Division, Detroit Publishing Company Collection, LC-D4–36531).

Street) on the west, Lexington Avenue on the south, Beecher Avenue (later Linwood) to the north and residential properties that filled out the block to Russell (later East 70th Street) to the east. Home plate and the main entrance were to be at the northwest corner of the block, nearest to Dunham and Beecher. Officially, it was called National League Park, but the locals shortened it to League Park right away.

The total capacity for the new wooden park was estimated at 9,000 with dimensions of 375 feet to left, 420 to center and just 240 feet to right. The short right field fence was the result of a corner saloon and two adjacent houses whose owners refused to sell their properties along Lexington Avenue, as well as a single residence behind those three parcels that faced Dunham. City property maps show that eventually the property on Dunham was

The Cleveland Spiders' team picture in 1892 provides one of the best available looks at the original wood grandstand after it was constructed in early 1891. This shot would have been taken with the photographer's back just in front of the original right-field wall, which was located just 240 feet from home plate down the right-field line. The original grandstand had two boxes located on the roof, one on the third-base side for the owner and the other on the first-base side for the press (Cleveland Public Library).

acquired and the distance was lengthened to 290 feet down the right field line.

The ballpark featured a covered single deck grandstand behind home plate, with additional uncovered sections along each foul line and a bleacher section in left field. According to the *Plain Dealer*, the grandstand behind home plate, which seated 1,600, was designed by architect Walter Rice and cost $5,000 to construct. A wooden fence separated right field from the sidewalk along Lexington, where knotholes would "appear" overnight, allowing fans a peek inside during the games. Meanwhile, it was reported that Brotherhood Park would no longer be used for baseball. In 1891 it hosted Wild West exhibitions and tent shows.

Opening day at the new park was scheduled for May 1, 1891, against Cincinnati. The Cleveland team had come home from its season-opening road trip with a 5–3 record. The forecast for the home opener was for fair weather with occasional light rain. The schedule called for the players to leave

Here is a look toward home plate from over the center fielder's shoulder during League Park's wooden era, before 1910. The team had extensive screening built on the roof to keep foul balls from leaving the park and breaking adjacent windows. The smokestack behind home plate is from the building at the opposite corner of East 66th Street and Linwood. Note that the grandstand down the third-base line has been expanded and covered, placing this photograph in 1903 or later (Library of Congress, Prints & Photographs Division, Detroit Publishing Company Collection, LC-D4–70783).

the downtown Hollenden Hotel at 1:00 P.M., with the game to start at 3:45. They were paraded to the park on one of Robison's trolleys, accompanied by balloons, circus animals and a 16-piece band.

There were just two ticket windows, which were located near the home plate grandstand and only some 20 feet from Robison's trolley stop. But there were so many fans wanting tickets that the crowd waited in lines of up to 400 feet long in order to witness history. More delays meant that it was not until 4:08 P.M. that major league baseball was played on this site for the first time. The park was heralded by the *Cleveland Plain Dealer* as "the prettiest and best field in America."[3] The overflow crowd filled the site to its capacity, spilling out of the stands and onto the field. But the spectators were generally good-natured and did not require the presence of many police officers, according to reports of the day.[4]

Cy Young had been pegged by manager Bob Leadley to christen the new ballpark as its first pitcher. Wearing a white uniform with "Cleveland" in black letters across the front of the shirt and standing 55 feet from his target (the distance at that time), Young threw a fastball over the plate to start the game. Cincinnati's Biddy McPhee watched the ball sail past him. Umpire Phil Powers called it a strike.

The Spiders went on to win the game, 12–3. Young pitched effectively, giving up a total of ten hits but no runs until the 8th inning when Cleveland had already amassed an 8–0 lead. Arlie Latham of Cincinnati hit the first home run at the new park while Cupid Childs drove in four runs for Cleveland in a contest that lasted one hour and 58 minutes. Under an overcast sky the next day, Cleveland lost to Cincinnati, 7–4, as 4,000 attended. A week later, on May 9, the first college game was played at League Park as Adelbert scored eight runs in the last three innings to outlast Case Tech, 10–7.

Cy Young went on to have an excellent year as part of his legendary career. He pitched in 55 games, finishing with a record of 27–20. Childs scored 120 runs that year, third best in the league. George Davis's 35 doubles ranked second in the NL but the Spiders were only able to finish fifth of eight teams with a mark of 65–74. The team attracted a total of 132,000 fans, good for sixth in the league.

The Temple Cup

After expanding to 12 teams in 1892, the National League began experimenting with formats for a post-season championship playoff. By 1894, the series began being played for the Temple Cup, which was named for Pittsburgh businessman and former Pittsburgh Pirates owner William Temple. The trophy was a silver cup that Temple had donated.

In 1892, however, the NL opted for a split-season format. This enabled Cleveland to win its first-ever title by taking first place during the second half of the 1892 season. Overall, Cleveland's 93–56 record was second-best in the league. With the success, total attendance for the season improved to 139,928. Cy Young had finished second in the league in wins with a 36–11 mark and a league-best nine shutouts. Second baseman Cupid Childs was the hitting star for the Spiders, leading the league in runs scored.

The Boston Beaneaters had been the first-half champions and the two teams began the championship series at League Park on October 17. Some 6,000 fans came to see Young do battle with Jack Stivetts. It was a classic pitcher's duel as neither team scored through eleven innings, at which point the game ended in a tie due to darkness. Young had struck out six and yielded only five hits.

Boston defeated the home team, 5–4, in the second game before 6,700. John Clarkson, who had come to Cleveland from Boston during the season, pitched for the Spiders. Game three again matched Young and Stivetts. Once again it was a pitcher's duel, but this time Boston prevailed, 3–2. The teams traveled to Boston and the Beaneaters showed their dominance by winning the next three games there for a 5–0 series sweep. It was another good year for the Spiders in 1893 but the team fell to third place behind Boston and Pittsburgh. Childs and shortstop Ed McKean were the hitting leaders. Cy Young had another remarkable season with a 34–16 record. Attendance dropped slightly to 130,000, only good enough for ninth-best in the league.

In a disappointing 1894 season, in which Cleveland fell to sixth place, the highlight likely was a three-game set with Pittsburgh in late May. Nearly 7,500 fans saw Cy Young lose a tight one in the opener, 6–5, before the Spiders came back with a 5–2 victory in game two, while stealing 13 bases with Connie Mack playing catcher for the visitors. Pittsburgh won the deciding game 12–3 before 8,000 frustrated partisans, many of whom poured onto the field, forcing the umpire to call the game before the final out was recorded. Total attendance plummeted to just 82,000 for the season, 11th in the 12-team league.

There was great improvement in 1895. Outfielder Jesse Burkett topped the league in hitting with a .423 mark and Cy Young went 35–10. Nig Cuppy turned out to be more than an adequate second starter behind Young, posting a 26–14 mark. Attendance jumped to 143,000, but that still ranked only 11th for a team that finished second to Baltimore. That standing qualified Cleveland for the seven-game Temple Cup series, which was now between the first- and second-place finishers. The Orioles featured Wee Willie Keeler, just 5'4" and 140 pounds, but one of baseball's biggest stars.

Game One was played on October 2 at League Park. With Young on the mound for Cleveland, the game entered the ninth inning tied 3–3. John McGraw drove in Wilbert Robinson to give the visitors a one-run lead in the top of the inning. Reports listed attendance at 6,000 to 7,000 fans.[5] They saw the Spiders tie the game and then take the victory when Childs scored on a Chief Zimmer RBI, giving Cleveland a 5–4 win.

The next day, a crowd of 10,000 packed League Park as Cuppy pitched the Spiders to a 7–2 win and a 2–0 series lead. After an off day, Young took the mound again for the Cleveland and dominated Baltimore's hitters in a 7–1 win. This time, an incredible crowd of 12,000 somehow squeezed in to see the action, as the Spiders went ahead three games to none.

The series moved to Baltimore, where Cleveland dropped a 5–0 decision. The Spiders were subjected to abuse from vegetable- and rock-throwing fans ... not only at the game, but while going to and from the park as well. With

Cleveland up three games to one, manager Patsy Tebeau sent Cy Young to the mound again to try to clinch the series. Young held down the Orioles and Cleveland claimed the Temple Cup with a 5–2 victory, the first professional baseball championship for the city.

In 1896 the Spiders finished second to Baltimore again, setting up a Temple Cup rematch. Attendance did improve to 152,000, but that total ranked last in the league. Burkett repeated as batting champ as well with a stellar .410 mark and Childs posted a .355 batting average. Young won 28 games and tallied a league-high 140 strikeouts. He had come within one out of a no-hitter at League Park on July 23 in a 2–0 win against Philadelphia, but Ed Delahanty broke it up with a single.

This time, the series opened in Baltimore, where the Orioles won three in a row. The crowds in Baltimore were smaller than what Cleveland had drawn a year before. With Cleveland trailing in the series 3–0 when the teams shifted to League Park, attendance was also down there. After a postponement on October 7, Baltimore ended the series the next day with a 5–0 win in front of just 2000 fans.

Sunday Showdown

The Spiders fell to fifth place in the 1897 season with a 69–62 record and attendance dipped to 115,520. Burkett still hit an impressive .383 and Young, who had turned thirty years old, won "just" 21 games. The highlight of the year came in a game he pitched at League Park on September 18. Facing Cincinnati, Young tossed the first no-hitter at the site as he struck out three and walked only one. A changed scorer's decision on a ball hit to third baseman Bobby Wallace kept the no-hitter intact. The Spiders won the game, 6–0, and also took the second game of the doubleheader that day, 4–3.

The 1897 season also witnessed controversy over the "blue law" that prohibited baseball on the Sabbath in Cleveland. The sport was struggling with this issue in many cities but Robison was especially frustrated by his team's lackluster attendance and saw Sunday ball as the solution. At last, Robison decided to test the law and on May 16 the first Sunday game to be played in Cleveland in a decade was scheduled. With a packed house of 10,000 fans, ticket sales were cut off at 2:30 for the 3:00 game. Reportedly, there were at least as many people outside the park who were unable to get in.

When the Spiders went to bat in the second inning, the Cleveland police captain and owner Robison approached umpire Tim Hurst to stop the game. The nine players in the lineup for both the Spiders and Washington, as well as Hurst, were arrested and taken straight downtown to be booked. Robison had fully expected to be the one arrested for allowing the game to be played. Instead, he paid the $100 bail for each player. Spider Jack Powell was the only player to be tried, as a representative of the group. He was found guilty that week.

Robison then cancelled the game that was scheduled for the next Sunday, May 23, against Baltimore. On July 9, however, Powell's guilty verdict was overturned on appeal by Judge Walter Ong and the next day's *Cleveland Plain Dealer* headline proclaimed "Base Ball Playing Not A Crime."[6] Sunday games returned for the final weeks of the 1897 season.

In a curious twist, the "Liquor League," an association of saloon owners, had teamed with various clergy to lobby against Sunday baseball in Cleveland. Sunday was the busiest day of the week at the bars and their owners knew that competition from baseball would hurt their businesses.[7]

That season also marked the arrival of a player whose later significance in Cleveland baseball would far surpass his contributions during three partial seasons with the team. Louis Sockalexis, a Native American from the Penobscot tribe in Maine, was signed by Cleveland after showing considerable skill playing college ball for Holy Cross and Notre Dame. Big and strong, he was also the fastest man on the team. He impressed Spiders manager Patsy Tebeau in spring training and earned a starting spot in the Cleveland outfield, becoming the first prominent Native American in major league baseball.

With a .400 batting average by mid-season, Sockalexis was becoming a folk hero in Cleveland. But the 25-year-old had a lingering alcohol problem and his batting average began to plummet. Tebeau finally sent him down to the minors. In 1898, he briefly returned to the team, getting 15 hits in 21 games played. Once again he was banished to the minors following an alcohol-related incident. He had another brief appearance with the team in 1899, and was seemingly set to fade into baseball history.[8]

The Spiders again finished in fifth place in 1898. Young (25–14) and Burkett (.341) once again starred for the team, but attendance for the year dropped to a total of just 70,496. Less than a thousand had attended the home opener. Worse, the schedule had to be revised when Judge Ong's appellate decision was overturned by the Ohio Supreme Court on April 19, restoring the ban on Sunday baseball in Cleveland. If the club wanted to play on Sundays, it would have to go outside the city limits.

Back in 1888, Robison had experimented with four Sunday games outside the city at Beyerle's Park in the Geauga Lake amusement area. The owner decided to try this approach again. After considering Cedar Point, some 70 miles to the west, he decided on Euclid Beach Park, just east of the city limits in Collinwood, and at that time separate from Cleveland. The location was already open on Sundays as an amusement park and was only about ten miles from League Park.

On Sunday, June 12, the Spiders hosted Pittsburgh at Euclid Beach as

6,000 attended. The crowd would have been larger if it had not been for the rainy weather that day. The experiment came to an end a week later, again against Pittsburgh, as Collinwood police stopped the game in the eighth inning with 3,000 fans watching and Cleveland having just taken a 4–3 lead. Players were again arrested, this time after changing into their street clothes. Robison next tried to place games in Newburgh Heights, just south of the city limits, but was blocked. One late–August weekend, out of frustration, he even moved two games against Brooklyn (one on a Sunday, of course) to Culver Field in Rochester, N.Y. with little success. He was now fed up, and threatened to move the team out of Cleveland over this issue.

The Worst Team ... Ever

Robison didn't move the team, but he found another way to show his displeasure. Just before the season began, Robison purchased the St. Louis team, which had finished last in the National League in 1898 with a miserable record of 39–111. The teams were then reshuffled through a series of "trades" intended to place the best possible team in St. Louis while leaving the rest for Cleveland. Cy Young and the other top players were gone for Missouri. Robison's disgust with Cleveland was summed up when he told the *Cleveland Leader*, "The business arrangements by which I have transferred my interests to St. Louis would not interest the public, and I do not care to discuss them."[9]

The 1899 team was already being referred to as the "misfits" in the newspapers as the start of the season approached. An unfortunate tragedy occurred when Robison's 20-year-old daughter died of heart complications on April 26. As a result, the home opener at League Park was postponed until Monday, May 1. The Spiders split a doubleheader with Louisville that day, winning the first game, 5–4, and losing the second, 2–1, before a "crowd" of 500. The first game took 14 innings as Chief Zimmer drove in player-manager Lave Cross with the winning run. In game two, a questionable call led to Louisville's game-winning unearned run in the 9th inning. As a result, "Umpire Brennan left the field with a howling mob at his heels," according to the *Cleveland Leader*.[10] The split put the Spiders' record at 2–8.

Fewer than 1,500 fans showed up a week later at League Park as Cleveland took on St. Louis, stocked with the former Spider players. The strange contest saw the crowd cheer on both teams. Cy Young, now with St. Louis, took the win by an 8–1 score.

Then things really began to spin out of control for the Spiders. On May 15, Cleveland lost its 11th game in a row, 3–2 to Cincinnati in front of 150 fans on a cold, late spring day. Rain and cold then forced cancellations for four straight days before the Spiders hosted Philadelphia on Saturday, May

20. With Zimmer hitting a home run, the first of the year for Cleveland, the well-rested Spiders broke the losing streak with a 10–4 win.

In June, with the team 8–30, Lave Cross was dispatched to St. Louis by Robison. The 13-year veteran had been one of the only bright spots for Cleveland, with a batting average of .286. Joe Quinn took over the daunting task of trying to manage the Spiders to victory. He picked up his first win on June 15 with a 6–2 decision over Pittsburgh before 100 people at League Park.

Losses continued to mount and, with the Cleveland fans completely uninterested, many home games were switched to away contests. The team began being referred to by names such as the Exiles, Forsakens, Wanderers and Nomads. They returned home on July 1 to split a doubleheader with Boston in front of 1,500 ... the largest crowd of the season. The first game win, the highlight of the year, came in dramatic fashion. Down 7–0 in the ninth inning, Cleveland rallied to tie the game and send it into extra innings. Once again the Spiders fell behind, but Suter Sullivan's base hit drove in Quinn to give Cleveland a stunning 11-inning 10–9 victory. In the second game, however, it was back to normal as Boston won, 14–0.

The ineptitude on the field provided plenty of good material for Cleveland newspapers. Late in July, one headline blared, "Forsakens Drop a Doubleheader to the Colonels."[11] A doubleheader loss to New York that dropped the Spiders record to 17–84 was described as "The Daily Downfall."[12] The descriptions of the losses also contained increasing amounts of sarcasm. The Spiders fell to 18–92 on August 22 when they lost to Louisville 15–6. The *Cleveland Plain Dealer* noted that "The aggregation from Cleveland stumbled all over the diamond, and even failed to do that well."[13] The *Cleveland Leader* countered with "The Cleveland alleged baseball team yesterday again fully sustained the reputation it has been establishing for itself this season."[14]

The few games played at League Park at the end of August drew little interest from Cleveland baseball fans. On the 24th, the Spiders lost to New York 6–2 and the *Plain Dealer* noted, "There were at least 100 persons at League Park yesterday when the wandering aggregation of barnstormers called the Clevelands appeared on what used to be their home grounds."[15] A four-game series, two single games and a doubleheader, against Boston during the last week of the month drew a total of 700 fans. Reportedly, the team drew a total of just over 6,000 fans in 36 home dates for the year. That would mean that, excluding the two crowds of around 1,500, the team averaged only about 100 fans for its other home contests.

The season mercifully ended on October 15. The Spiders had lost 40 of their last 41 games and finished the year with a 20–134 record, a mark for major league futility unlikely ever to be surpassed. Washington, which finished in 11th place, won 54 games, 34 more than Cleveland. Shortstop

Robert Lochhead had batted just .238 and committed 81 errors in 146 games. Jim Hughey and Charlie Knepper tied for the most wins on the team with four, but Hughey lost 30 games and Knepper 22. Not surprisingly, Cleveland was one of four teams dropped from the National League when it downsized for the 1900 season.[16]

The American League

With the Cleveland market and League Park now open, the minor Western League seized the opportunity. The league, with eight Midwestern clubs from Buffalo to Kansas City, was to be renamed the American League for 1900 and had designs on becoming a second major league. Western League president Ban Johnson had tried to recruit former Spider executive Davis Hawley for the new venture. Hawley passed on the opportunity but arranged for young Cleveland businessmen Jack Kilfoyl and Charley Somers to meet Johnson at the Hotel Hollenden. Johnson convinced Somers, a prosperous coach dealer, and Kilfoyl, who owned a men's clothing store on Public Square, to purchase the Grand Rapids team and move it to Cleveland. The NL was asking for $15,000 for League Park and an assurance that the American League would remain as a minor league. So the new owners turned their attention farther east to a potential new ballpark at Cedar Road and East Madison (now East 79th Street). Baseball-savvy Connie Mack, who was taking over the AL Milwaukee team, stepped in to help negotiate for Cleveland.[17] The *Plain Dealer* reported that the NL settled for just over $10,000 for the park and its equipment, and League Park was officially transferred on March 23. Former Cleveland owner Robison, certainly still bitter at the city, had agreed to the sale. After all, he still owned the streetcar lines that passed by the park.

The new team was known primarily as the Cleveland "Lake Shores" and sometimes as the "Babes." The new owners wound up hiring the former Spider groundskeeper, Harry Hamilton, to prepare the field for their new club.

The *Cleveland Press* reported on April 4 that "The intruding right field fence at the Dunham Avenue ground will be removed back to its former position" once the corner property owner, Mr. Killacky, gave his permission.[18] Also, a new scoreboard was erected in right field.

After the debacle of 1899, interest in the new team was high. Hundreds of fans came out to watch practice before the team traveled to Indiana for its opener against the Indianapolis Hoosiers. On April 26, 1900, the Indianapolis team came to Cleveland for opening day at League Park. Mayor John Farley threw out the first ball as 6,500 (5,500 paid) turned out and saw Cleveland win, 5–4. Many fans were skeptical of the minor league squad and attendance did not stay high. The team finished in sixth place with a 63–73 mark.

In 1901, the American League followed through on its plans to challenge the 25-year old NL, declaring itself a major league and invading several eastern cities. Cleveland was joined in the eight-team circuit by Baltimore, Boston, Chicago, Detroit, Milwaukee, Philadelphia, and Washington. Cleveland met Chicago in the first-ever American League game, April 24 at Chicago, an 8–2 White Sox win. The team's League Park debut was a 4–3 win over the Milwaukee Brewers on Monday, April 29.

The Blues nickname was revived but the initial major league season in the American League was not very successful. Cleveland finished in seventh place and drew only 131,380 fans, last in the league. The team had "stolen" a name player, third baseman Bill Bradley, from the NL's Chicago team. However, not a single Cleveland player ranked among the league leaders in any major statistical category for manager Jimmy McAleer, a former Cleveland Spiders player, who had also guided the minor league squad the year before.

It didn't take long for League Park to once again host some notable moments, however. On May 9, it hosted the new league's first extra-inning game as Earl Moore threw nine innings of no-hit ball, only to lose to the White Sox, 4–2, in ten. Two weeks later, Cleveland rallied for the greatest last-out win in baseball history, scoring nine runs with two out in the bottom of the ninth to defeat Washington, 14–13. Another significant day at the park that season came when a rainstorm inspired the bleacher crowd to rush for the covered grandstand. A riot followed which engulfed players from both teams. In the off-season, there was a failed attempt at creating embankments and setting up an ice skating surface on the playing field in order to generate income during the winter.

Numerous changes took place before for the 1902 season. Management again attempted to schedule Sunday games in Newburgh Heights, but local ministers banded together to help block the games. Now called the Bronchos, the club was managed by Bill Armour. In addition, a 22-year-old rookie pitcher named Addie Joss joined the club along with former National League star Napoleon "Larry" Lajoie. The 26-year-old Lajoie's acquisition came as a compromise after a Pennsylvania judge blocked the player's further participation with the American League's Philadelphia Athletics after having "jumped" from the National League's Philadelphia Phillies.

Another player, pitcher Otto Hess, was signed from an open tryout at League Park during the season. In his first start, Washington tried to rattle the rookie, bunting 17 times. Hess made four errors but still won the game. Later that year, Armour, still short on pitching, learned of a top amateur in the bleachers before a game. He invited Charlie Smith to try out and wound up signing him. Smith went on to a nine-year career with four teams.

A key game that year took place at League Park on Saturday, June 7 against Baltimore. The Bronchos won, 7–3, with a packed house of 12,753 on hand. It was the largest crowd ever to see a baseball game in Cleveland, surpassing the record set during the 1895 Temple Cup. Many fans stood in the outfield or at the back of the grandstand. The next day, Cleveland played at Fairview Park in Dayton due to the Sunday ban, losing to Baltimore, 6–2, before a crowd of 4,876. The following weekend, another 10,000 fans turned out on Saturday at League Park as Cleveland beat Philadelphia, 6–3. On Sunday, June 15, some 6,000 fans showed up at 2,000-seat Mahaffey Park in Canton as Boston beat Cleveland, 5–2. The umpire had a difficult time making some calls as fans interfered with play. There were no ropes to hold back the overflow in the outfield and the standees also converged on the baselines. Cleveland utilized the Jailhouse Flats ballpark in Fort Wayne, Indiana, for Sunday games on June 22 versus Washington and August 31 against Boston, as well as Neil Park in Columbus for a game on August 3.

The batting star for Cleveland in 1902 was third baseman Bill Bradley. He hit .340 and also added 11 home runs, a huge number for the era. The team improved to a fifth place finish with a 69–67 record. Interest soared as attendance had more than doubled to 275,395, fourth best in the league.

The first World Series between the American League and National League was still a year away, but there was post-season play in 1902. The National League champion Pittsburgh Pirates accepted an offer to play against a team of American League all-stars. The Pirates had probably the best player in the game in Honus Wagner. The series was to be a best-of-five set, which opened in Pittsburgh's Exposition Park. Pittsburgh won the first game as Sam Leever bested Cy Young, who was now playing for the Boston American League team, by a 4–3 count. The next day, the Pirates won again in Pittsburgh, 2–0, as Deacon Phillippe threw a three-hit shutout. Cleveland ace Addie Joss took the loss.

Game three came to League Park as Leever matched up against another Cleveland hurler, Bill Bernhard, who had won 17 of 22 decisions that year. Each pitcher allowed just four hits before darkness ended things after eleven innings in a 0–0 tie. An agreement was then reached to play just one more game, also at League Park. On October 11, Cy Young pitched for the American Leaguers, shutting out the Pirates, 1–0.

In 1903, the Cleveland team changed its nickname to the Naps to honor Napoleon Lajoie, who had become the city's most beloved player ever after his transfer from Philadelphia. The *Cleveland Press* newspaper had campaigned for a new team nickname, and this tribute to the popular superstar beat out suggestions such as Buckeyes, Emperors, Metropolitans and Giants. The renamed squad moved up to fourth place in the league standings that year.

Attendance rose again to 311,280 (still 4th in the league) with an average

This is a view down the third-base line after the 1903 expansion of the baseline grandstands. The Bennett & Fish Clothing store avoided paying the ballclub for advertising space by placing ads on the roof of an adjacent house and garage, a tactic known today as ambush marketing. While those homeowners benefited at that time, many area residents would profit during the park's ensuing years by charging fans to park their cars on their property (National Baseball Hall of Fame Library, Cooperstown, N.Y.).

of more than 4,000 per game showing up at League Park, which had undergone extensive renovations. The baseline grandstands were rebuilt and enlarged. Carpenters extended the stands down the lines and added seven rows, bringing the grandstand seating capacity to 9,050. The seating area became continuous from behind first base, wrapping behind home plate and all the way down to the left field corner. A screen was added in front of the seats behind home plate, according to the *Cleveland Leader*.[19] Temporary "circus seats" were also installed beyond first base farther out toward the right field foul pole, making a potential for some 12,000 seats.

For the opener against Detroit, one source reported that 19,867 fans somehow jammed their way in, a figure that does not seem to have received official recognition, since smaller crowds later in the decade were reported as records. However, crowds sometimes were reported as the "largest ever" without consideration of previously announced attendances. Suffice to say that the crowd for the 1903 opener was over capacity because of the use of the circus seats and standing room about the edges of the field. At one point, the players formed a human rope to push the fans back. (Just weeks later, two fans were injured when some of those temporary stands collapsed.)

A footnote to the 1903 season happened one day with Bullet Jack Thomes in center field. He threw home in an attempt to put out a runner on a short hit to center but the throw went some 40 feet above home plate, nearly striking co-owner Jack Kilfoyl atop the grandstand roof. It was Thomes' last game in Cleveland as the owner ordered him dispatched to the minors the next day.

Lajoie led the league with a .344 batting average that year and Charles "Piano Legs" Hickman hit 12 home runs, second most in the league. Joss won 19 games. One of his wins was a shutout of Philadelphia on August 24 at League Park. He completed a rare feat by setting down the side on just three pitches in the second inning that day. Neutral Sunday games continued in 1903 with sites again including Canton (May 10 and June 21) and Columbus (May 17). Sometimes a Sunday game would be moved to the opponents' home park, where legal, and when the logistics and costs of travel allowed. But this was the final year of the neutral-site games for the Cleveland club.

The following year, 1904, Lajoie continued to excel, leading the league again in batting with a .376 average. He also led the league in hits, doubles, total bases and runs batted in. Elmer Flick batted .306 and Bill Bradley hit .300. Cleveland scored the most runs in the league and had the highest combined batting average. Addie Joss had the lowest earned run average of any pitcher at 1.59. While the National League champion New York Giants and manager John McGraw refused to meet the AL champs in what would have been the second World Series, the NL's Pittsburgh Pirates did agree to meet Cleveland in a five-game postseason series. The teams had each finished just fourth in their respective leagues, but fan interest was expected to be high because of the match-up of the two premier hitters in baseball, Pittsburgh's Wagner and Cleveland's Lajoie. Regular season attendance in Cleveland had fallen from a year earlier to 264,749 (again 5th in the league) and this was a chance for some additional income.

The series opened October 10 at League Park. A crowd of almost 4,000 saw Wagner hit a rare homer over the distant left field fence for two of the runs in a five-inning, rain-shortened affair that ended in a 2–2 tie. Game two, also at League Park the next day, saw the Pirates claim a 7–4 triumph. The series moved to Pittsburgh a day later and the teams battled to a 3–3 tie in 14 innings before it was called due to darkness. Cleveland won the next game 3–2 to tie the series at 1–1–2 and the teams agreed that the next day's winner would claim the series. Cleveland took the game, 4–1. Wagner went 6-for-21 (.286) at the plate to win the ballyhooed duel with Lajoie, who went 5-for-19 (.263).

Cleveland's 1905 season was scheduled to open on April 14 at League Park but snow caused a postponement until the following day. The Naps beat Detroit 6–2 to start what was expected to be a promising year. On June 30, however, Lajoie suffered a severe spike wound and blood poisoning resulted, which shortened his season to 65 games played. Cleveland faded to a fifth-place finish. Nap outfielder Elmer Flick did lead the league with a .306 batting average.

Flick had come to Cleveland during the 1902 season and been reunited with Lajoie, against whom he had won a legendary 1900 clubhouse brawl while they were playing for Philadelphia's National League team. At 5–9 and 165 pounds, Flick had gained a great deal of respect as a result of the tussle. Flick's acquisition by owner Charles Somers brought the Bedford, Ohio, native home and he wound up making headlines with three triples in a game against Washington on July 6, 1902, at League Park.

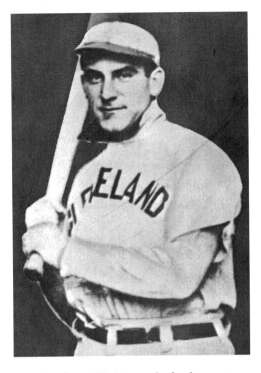

Napoleon "Larry" Lajoie was by far the most popular athlete in Cleveland after his acquisition from Philadelphia in 1902. The Cleveland team was called the Naps in his honor from 1903–1915, before taking on the moniker of Indians (Cleveland Public Library).

Late that 1905 season, injuries and the team's disappointing play led the Naps to call upon the services of Emil Leber in a move that would be unthinkable today. Leber was an amateur third baseman in Cleveland, playing for the local Forest City Parks team, and was considered one of the best amateurs in the city, both at the bat and in the field. A mail carrier by trade, he was given permission by the postmaster to have the afternoon off one day to show his skills in a tryout at League Park. He was signed, most likely in an effort to increase local interest in the struggling squad. In his first at bat, Leber drew a walk and scored. He appeared in just two games without getting a hit before returning to his postal route.

After the season, extensive improvements were made to the League Park playing field. Attendance in 1905 again had ranked fifth in the league, but had grown to a Cleveland record of 316,306. A state-of-the-art drainage system was installed. In addition, the stands were spruced up and painted and the press box was enlarged for 1906. Newspaper photos show that left field bleachers were also added some time during this decade. They had a separate entrance and were not contiguous to the main grandstand, which ended at the left field fence.

The hitting of Flick and Lajoie helped the Naps greatly in 1906. The team led the American League in hitting and runs scored. Robert Rhoads and Addie Joss each won 21 games as Cleveland moved up to third place, only five games behind first-place Chicago. The team had a strong finish and was particularly successful at League Park, going 25–7 down the stretch on their home field as attendance rose again to 325,733.

One bizarre moment in park history occurred on July 3 that year. It began to rain during the fourth inning of Detroit's 5–0 loss to Cleveland and the Tigers second baseman Germany Schafer donned a raincoat while playing his position. Ace pitcher Bill Donovan used an umbrella while serving as a base coach. The umpires must have gotten the message — the game was shortened to just six innings.

Now in his third year managing the team, Lajoie saw his batting average drop to .299 in 1907. Flick batted .302 and led the league with 18 triples. He also stole 41 bases. Cleveland had kept the hometown hero despite a spring training offer from Detroit to swap Ty Cobb for Flick straight up. The Tigers were displeased with Cobb's demeanor and temper. Somers passed on the offer, which turned out to be a huge mistake, as Flick's career essentially ended after the 1907 season. A stomach ailment sidelined him for all but nine games in 1908 and he also saw limited action the following two years before retiring.

The star pitcher of the 1907 team was Addie Joss, who led the league with 27 wins and had an earned run average of 1.83. He won ten games in a row early in the season. When Detroit came to Cleveland for a doubleheader on May 30, a record crowd of 17,316 jammed into every possible space in League Park to see if Joss could win his eleventh straight. Cleveland had won the opener, but Detroit got to Joss in the second game. Ty Cobb blasted a home run over the right field wall onto Lexington Avenue and Joss and the Naps lost, 6–0. Cleveland faltered to a fourth-place finish, eight games behind the pennant-winning Tigers but attendance increased again to 382,046. Joss did finish with a 27–11 record, second only to Detroit's Donovan in winning percentage.

In a League of Her Own

With just a handful of games left in the 1907 big league season, another League Park oddity took place on October 2. With the Naps in Philadelphia, a semi-professional team from Vermilion, about 40 miles west of Cleveland, was booked to take on a Cleveland amateur All-Star team. The hook was the appearance of 18-year-old Vermilion pitcher, Miss Alta Weiss.

A crowd of 3,184 turned out to see the light brown hair and blue eyes of the "mighty pretty" female hurler with hands as "big and tough as a man's," according to the *Cleveland Leader*.[20] She was outfitted in a cap and a dark blue serge dress that came down just below her knees with "Vermilion" in white across her chest. With her father and brother watching from the dugout, Weiss gained the respect and support of the crowd, striking out five and allowing just two walks and eight hits. An error led to a four-run fourth inning for "Vacha's All-Stars," while another miscue aided two runs in the eighth.

Weiss even got a hit of her own in the game and her team scored four runs in the eighth inning to take a 7–6 lead into the final frame. After the All-Stars scored three runs in the top of the ninth, the game was called due to darkness. As a result, the score reverted to the 7–6 final, although Umpire Abbner, perhaps in fear of an All-Star retaliation, declared that the game should be a 7–7 tie.

The *Cleveland Plain Dealer* followed the rules of baseball and posted the result as a 7–6 Vermilion win. The *Leader*, which ran its game story in the news section, compared the cheers she received to those usually reserved at League Park for Napoleon Lajoie and described her pitching motion as identical to that of Addie Joss.

The Greatest Game

The 1908 season featured pennant races that have never been duplicated, as both leagues had teams in the hunt until the final days of the regular season. Those circumstances added to what became known as "The Greatest Game." League Park later hosted contests that arguably had more significance in the history of baseball, but for sheer drama and importance, this single game still stands out.

On September 11, the tight race had the Naps in fourth place, but with only three fewer wins than league-leading Detroit. Sandwiched in between were Chicago and St. Louis. Now with a chance for a pennant, the Cleveland fans, who had largely avoided League Park most of the year, found renewed interest. By September 17, the red-hot Naps had climbed into second place and had a match-up with Boston. Addie Joss tossed a shutout to defeat the Red Sox and Cy Young, 1–0. The next day Robert Rhoads pitched the park's second no-hitter in a 2–1 win over the Red Sox. It was Cleveland's fifth straight victory and the race got even tighter. Detroit stood at 78–57, Cleveland a game back at 79–60, followed by Chicago at 77–61 and St. Louis at 77–62.

Ed Walsh and Addie Joss posed together prior to their incredible pitching duel of October 2, 1908, in the heat of the pennant race. Cleveland's Joss won the battle with a perfect game that day but tragically died barely two and a half years later of tubercular meningitis (National Baseball Hall of Fame Library, Cooperstown, N.Y.).

On September 22, Joss won his fifth straight game and now had allowed only one run in 27 innings. Cleveland, at 82–60, was now in first place by slim margins over Chicago (81–61), Detroit (79–60) and St. Louis (77–62). When Washington came to town on September 24, the team had won nine in a row and 14 of its previous 15 outings to go from 5½ games out of first place to a one-and-a-half-game lead in the standings.

The Naps' success was happening with Flick sidelined and Lajoie hitting only .289, the lowest mark of his 13-year major league career. And outfielder Joe Birmingham batted just .213. The team was capable of impressive hitting, however, having pulled off an amazing feat earlier in the summer when all nine Naps had hit safely and scored in the fifth inning of a 15–6 win over Boston at League Park.

By the end of September, Cleveland trailed Detroit by a half game with Chicago a game and a half behind the Tigers. After a Thursday off day, Cleveland hosted Chicago on Friday afternoon, October 2. There were five games left in the season.

Baseball fever had taken over the City of Cleveland. Joss, at 6'3", was even bigger than his 6'1" opponent "Big" Ed Walsh, a spitballer en route to a 40–15 season. A front-page *Cleveland Press* headline screamed "Fans Storm Grounds, Joss vs. Walsh."[21] The game had been moved up a half hour to 2:30 P.M. to help ensure that darkness would not play a part in the outcome. Nearly 11,000 fans crammed into the park. The weather was fair with the temperature hovering around 50 degrees.

Despite the tension and excitement of the race, and with the game featuring the two best pitchers in the league, the pre-game featured a couple of odd happenings. Joss had finished warming up when he went by Walsh and sat down. A photographer captured the two opponents in a calm moment before they did battle. Also prior to the game, the firemen of Cleveland Engine House #1 presented a loving cup to their neighbor who lived across the street from the firehouse, umpire Tommy Connolly.

In the first inning, Chicago's leadoff batter, Ed Hahn, knocked the ball in front of the plate. Joss fielded it and threw to first base for out number one. Player–manager Fielder Jones then popped out and Frank Isbell flied out to end the inning. Walsh set down the Naps in order in the bottom of the inning.

Joss retired the side without difficulty in the second and Walsh came to the plate with two out in the third. Walsh hit a grounder just past Joss's reach but Lajoie was able to scoop up the ball and throw him out at first. Joe Birmingham led off the third for the Naps and singled to right field. Walsh tried to pick off Birmingham, who had a long lead, but the runner raced to second on the throw to first. Isbell's throw to second hit Birmingham and ricocheted into right field. Birmingham continued to third base where he stood with no outs.

Walsh was able to get rookie shortstop George Perring on a groundout before striking out Joss, leaving Birmingham at third with two down. Right fielder Wilbur Good was up next. With two strikes, Walsh let loose a pitch that catcher Ossie Schreckengost could not corral. It was ruled a wild pitch and Birmingham came in to score. Walsh's mistake had given Joss and Cleveland the lead, 1–0.

In the fourth inning, Lajoie made every defensive play, throwing out two batters and then catching a short fly in right field. Joss got his first strikeout in the fifth when Patsy Dougherty went down swinging. George Davis then grounded back to Joss for an easy out. Joss again demonstrated his fielding ability with Freddy Parent at bat. Parent's grounder near the third base line was picked up by Joss, whose throw barely beat Parent to the bag.

As the seventh inning started, the crowd began to sense the drama of the moment. Walsh had given up only two hits and had struck out eleven but

An overflow crowd from 1909, the final season for the original park, shows fans lining the front of the enlarged third-base line grandstand. Capacity crowds with fans on the field, along with the dawn of the era of steel-and-concrete ballparks led to the demolition and rebuilding of League Park at the conclusion of the season (Cleveland Public Library/Stanley L. McMichael).

was losing, 1–0. Joss had retired all 18 batters in a row as he again took the mound. With one out in the bottom of the seventh inning, Chicago's Jones worked the count to 3–0 before taking two called strikes. With the count full, Joss hurled a low sinker that Jones let go by. Umpire Connolly called strike three. Isbell then grounded out to end the seventh.

In the bottom of the inning, Walsh breezed through the Naps' order with two strikeouts and a popout. The fans had grown eerily silent. Lajoie turned a bad-hop grounder into an out to start the top of the eighth. Another popout and easy fly ball to left followed. Cleveland threatened to score in the bottom of the eighth when Birmingham got his second hit and George Perring followed with a single to center. A double steal put the runners on second and third with nobody out. Schreckengost, whose finger had been injured on the run-scoring wild pitch in the third, was now replaced by Al Shaw in this key situation. Walsh then bore down to strike out Joss and Good. The inning ended as Bill Bradley grounded out. Walsh had wiggled out of the jam and the game remained 1–0, Cleveland.

Fielder Jones elected to use three straight pinch hitters against Joss in the ninth inning. Doc White had two strikes on him before grounding out to Lajoie. Jiggs Donahue became Joss's third strikeout victim for out number two. Jones then sent to the plate John Anderson, a .290 lifetime hitter in his 14th and final year in the majors. Joss had two strikes, one on a line drive foul past third, before Anderson hit a hard grounder to third baseman Bill Bradley. His throw to first was low but first baseman George Stovall dug it out in time for Umpire Silk O'Laughlin to raise his right arm to signify the out and complete the perfect game. Only the former Cleveland hurler, the great Cy Young, had previously pitched a perfect game in the American League. Young's had come for Boston in 1904.

Joss, who had thrown only 74 pitches, raced to the clubhouse to avoid the crowd. Walsh had been nearly as brilliant, allowing just the one run on four hits with 15 strikeouts. He had walked only one batter. The game took just one hour and twenty-nine minutes. League Park's unique, remote control, magnet-operated scoreboard told the story. The next day, newspapers proclaimed it the greatest game in baseball history. Joss would finish the year with some incredible statistics: a 24–11 record and a 1.16 earned run average with just 30 walks in 325 innings pitched. The pair ranks one-two in baseball history in career ERA, Walsh at 1.82 and Joss at 1.89.[22]

The two teams met again the next day at League Park. There were extra bleachers on the roof of the grandstand and swarms of people standing. The park was filled way above and beyond capacity. Attendance was announced at 20,729, perhaps exaggerated, but still the largest crowd ever in the park's wooden configuration with thousands located around the edges of the playing field. The White Sox prevailed, 3–2, as Walsh came in to pitch in relief and preserve the win. Home attendance reached 422,262 for the year, another record.

The Naps headed off to play the St. Louis Browns in the season-ending series while Detroit faced Chicago. When the dust settled, Detroit and Cleveland each finished the season with 90 wins, but the Tigers were awarded the pennant. Thanks to rainouts that weren't made up, Detroit finished with 63 losses while the Naps had 64. The next year, the rules were changed so that such an outcome couldn't happen again.

Many years later, Naps first baseman George Stovall reminisced about another hindrance to the team's pennant chase that year. He recalled that there was an advertising sign from a local shoe store that offered a free pair of shoes to any player hitting a triple in League Park. "I can clearly remember 17 instances when the fellows on our team were out trying to stretch hits into triples," Stovall recollected. "It was that darn sign staring them in the face ... they were all trying to get themselves another pair of shoes."[23]

Ballpark Evolution Begins

There had been tinkering with League Park's outfield seating, dimensions and the location of the diamond since the baseline grandstand had been reconstructed in 1903, but this was nothing compared to what was on the horizon.

Philadelphia's Shibe Park had opened in 1909 as home of the American League's Athletics, a double-decked, steel-framed structure. Advances in reinforced concrete had allowed for this new era in stadium design. Baseball's popularity was continuing to grow and this would allow for the construction of larger facilities to accommodate bigger crowds. Less wood also meant that the new edifices would be much safer from the fires that were always a threat in the older ballparks.

Shibe Park, with a seating capacity of 30,000, had columns, arched windows and a domed tower at the intersection behind the home plate grandstand. Just days later, 18,000-seat Sportsman's Park in St. Louis debuted and on June 30, 25,000-seat Forbes Field in Pittsburgh opened. Three days after that, minor league Swayne Field in Toledo became the fourth concrete-and-steel park. Both the Pittsburgh and Toledo plants were designed by Osborn Engineering of Cleveland.

Meanwhile, player-manager Nap Lajoie resigned from his managerial role in Cleveland during the 1909 season with the team's record at 57–57 in order to concentrate on his hitting. Deacon McGuire took the helm of the Naps (as they continued to be known), and the team went just 14–25 the rest of the way to finish in sixth place. After four years of growth, attendance dropped to 354,627.

One more major individual feat had taken place in that final year of the park's wooden configuration. It came in the second inning of the first game of a doubleheader against Boston on July 19, with Cy Young on the mound. After the runners on first and second had taken off with the pitch, Naps shortstop Neal Ball caught a line drive off the bat of Amby McConnell behind second base, stepped on the bag to double off Heinie Wagner and then tagged Jake Stahl, who was running from first. A full house of 10,000 had seen the first unassisted triple play in major league history! To top it off, Ball came to bat in the bottom of the inning to a huge ovation and promptly drove a ball over center fielder Tris Speaker's head and scampered around the bases for an inside-the-park home run. He added a double for good measure and, with the help of three putouts on the one play, wound up with nine in the game. It was a truly amazing day.

Meanwhile, blueprints for a new park on the site had been revealed on June 29. And when Cleveland's home schedule ended on Monday, September 6, some 10,000 fans filled the wooden park for one last time. On Tuesday, the dismantling of League Park began as "men swarmed the grand stand pavilion like an army of ants on a mountain of sugar," according to the *Plain Dealer*.[24] By Thursday, the concrete foundation was being poured to support steel girders. The plan of team secretary Ernest S. Barnard, who had joined the team as traveling secretary in 1903, was about to come to fruition. "Owners Kilfoyl and Somers are sparing no expense to give the fans in Cleveland the best that their money can buy," he said.[25]

Architect Frank Meade had been working on plans for the new park since just after Addie Joss's perfect game a year before. Osborn Engineering now was contracted to oversee the building of a new baseball edifice in the company's hometown. Construction was to be handled by the Hunkin Brothers Company and the Forest City Steel & Iron Company. League Park was about to become a member of the new era of ballparks!

2

Concrete and Steel

*Before the era when civic arenas were erected on spacious plots that
permitted parking areas as well as a stadium, the configuration of a
ball park was determined by the dimensions of the acreage on which it
was built.*—Lowell Reidenbaugh, *Take Me Out to the Ball Park*

A Model Home

Although owners Charlie Somers and Jack Kilfoyl considered calling it
Forest Field, they decided that continuity was best for the new League Park,
which was built around the same playing field as the original. It also would
retain its quirky dimensions and unusual placement of home plate in the
northwest corner of the property rather than the normal southwest corner
layout for home, leaving a notoriously tough sun field in left.

While the field orientation remained the same, the physical plant and
grandstand surrounding it made League Park one of the best facilities in the
country. Though smaller than its recently opened neighbors in Pennsylvania,
it boasted outstanding amenities for its time. Attendance had dropped by
almost 70,000 in 1909, but it was assumed that the new park was going to
rekindle the fans' interest.

Osborn Engineering created the new park with two decks, including box
and reserved seats in both sections. Quite a bit larger than Osborn's 11,000-
seat, single-deck effort in Toledo a year before, the new Cleveland plant's
projected capacity was 19,200. The three properties in the right-field corner
along Lexington Avenue were finally acquired, but the right field line was to
remain at 290 feet because the location of home plate needed to be pushed
out toward the outfield wall to accommodate the larger, double-decked grandstand. The lower deck featured 18 rows behind the plate, 26 down the first
base line and 24 down third. The upper deck consisted of 16 rows.

The exterior, a red brick façade supported by arches, was connected to
a new building constructed in the space formerly occupied the three recently
purchased parcels. It would serve as the team's offices as well as the park's
new main entrance and primary ticket sales area. This building became the

32

This artist's rendering of the exterior of League Park served as the first postcard of the site. It does a good job of showing the arches and brickwork on the ballpark from the perspective of behind home plate. The representation of the left-field bleachers, however, wound up being overstated. Those seats were not continuous from the left-field corner and did not extend all the way to the right-field wall. Room for the center-field scoreboard is completely left out (Cleveland Public Library).

park's signature mark, the subject of many postcards and photos. It remains standing to this day.

A total of nine ticket windows were built in order to cut down on the length of lines on game day. Different sources gave conflicting information about the new seating capacity. A review of those numbers resulted in the following breakdown: 600 box seats (260 were "front" boxes and 340 "rear" boxes), 10,100 in the remainder of the grandstand (2,400 reserved), 6,500 "pavilion" seats (located further down the baselines), and 2,000 bleacher seats in left field (apparently largely unchanged from the wooden park era) for an official seating capacity of 19,200. With standing room, available on the concourse behind the lower deck seats, another 2,000 could be accommodated without any fans having to stand on the field. Along the aisles, at the end of each row of chair back seats, a unique design in the side support arms featured a ball, bat and glove.

Ticket prices for the new park were set at $1.25 for front boxes, $1.00 for rear boxes and 75 cents for the remainder of the grandstand. Separate turnstiles would funnel patrons to their seating areas. Under the stands, concrete walkways featured electric lighting and powered refreshment stands.

The *Cleveland Press* reported that the distance from home plate to the grandstand was 76 feet. First base and the grandstand were separated by 78 feet, while the distance from third base to the grandstand was 70 feet.[1]

A 20-foot concrete wall was built from the right field foul pole to the

The main entrance and box office moved from behind home plate to the signature office building near the right-field corner of East 66th and Lexington when the park was rebuilt in 1910. Electric lines above the streets powered the trolleys that brought most of the fans to the ballpark. The building and part of the wall extending down 66th street still survive more than a century later (Cleveland Public Library/M.E. Peters/L. Baus).

scoreboard in center field to help neutralize the short distance to the right field fence. Some sources say that the height of this wall was 25 feet, but photographic evidence shows it to have been 20. The wall was topped by 24 vertical iron girders with chicken wire fencing attached to the back, raising the height an additional 20 feet and creating an uneven interior surface of girder and fence that would wreak havoc on baseballs and outfielders for decades to come.

At 40 total feet in height, this concrete and "screen monster" stood three feet higher than the now fabled "green monster" left field at Boston's Fenway Park, which was erected two years later. Line drives could hit the concrete portion and rebound hard toward the infield. Balls hitting higher could drop straight down off the chicken wire, get stuck in the wire and girders (a ground rule double) or rebound crazily off the girders onto the playing field. On high flies to right, the left and center fielders often hustled toward right field to help play the unpredictable caroms.

The screen was reportedly added in order to hinder Detroit's Sam Crawford, who regularly hit home runs to right during the park's wooden configuration. Upon seeing it on opening day of the park, Crawford said, "So that's Barney's dream ... I'll show him," referring to team Secretary/Treasurer Ernest S. Barnard, who had put together the plan and financing for the rebuilding of the stadium.[2] Upon its design, it was reported that hitting a home run over the new wall and screen in right "would be almost an impossible feat." While the wall did pose a challenge in the "dead ball" era of the teens, it was hardly an impossible feat and the live ball days, just a decade away, would dispel that myth for good.

The left field line was still nearly 100 feet longer than right, measuring 385 feet to the bleachers at the foul pole. The rectangular shape of the field made for plenty of room in the left-center field area, which measured 428 to left center and 460 to dead center.

Work had progressed rapidly and the park got rave reviews in various newspapers. In December, the *Elyria Evening Telegram* reported: "Already it shows signs that it will be the most complete baseball plant in the country." The article noted features such as visiting team dressing rooms, an umpires' room with showers, and parlors for women fans that were attended by maids. It also promised that seating areas would allow room to "actually stretch your legs!"[3]

The architects had looked at the new parks in Pittsburgh and Philadelphia, while also examining the renovations and construction done in Chicago, New York and St. Louis in preparing to rebuild League Park. The *Chicago Daily Tribune* stated, "While baseball fans of Chicago, Pittsburg, New York, Philadelphia and St. Louis are boasting of the remodeled or new parks, the residents of Cleveland are being promised for next season a plant which will surpass, from a spectators' standpoint, anything of its kind yet constructed."[4]

Even with support columns for the upper deck, the park still provided 12,000 seats with unobstructed views. Individual seats were several inches wider than in most ballparks. The walkway area behind the seats allowed standing-room patrons to station themselves there or in the areas that could still be roped off in left field and center field. A new drainage system was put beneath the playing surface and a large canvas tarp was added for use in the event of rain. There were five stairways connecting the upper deck to ground level. Twenty-six exits allowed for much easier departure than the original structure.

By mid–January, the concrete work on the ballpark had been completed and the steel work for the upper deck was being put in place. The one million bricks used would have been enough to stretch from Cleveland to Detroit if laid end to end. A total of 2,500 cubic yards of concrete and 500 barrels of cement were used. Lumber used in the structure totaled about a half million feet, with an additional 40,000 feet used for the seats. The park included 5,000 feet of sewers and 1,000 feet of conduit for telegraph and telephone wires. There was no netting to protect fans, even directly behind the plate. The ladies' restrooms, however, featured carpeted floors and easy chairs, similar to what was found in theaters of the day.

The Dunham School and the Andrews Storage Company, both located across Lexington Avenue from the right field wall, each provided "wildcat" seating, where brave climbers could get a limited view of the field for free. It is said that the proximity of these and other buildings would mean that the Cleveland club would pay for the replacement of some 20–40 broken windows a year from balls that left the park.

Amenities for the players were dramatically improved. Instead of wooden benches with backrests provided by the front wall of the seating area, fully covered dugouts now protected players from sun and wind. A clubhouse-style locker room with a trainer's area and plumbing facilities was connected straight to the dugout by way of a tunnel. There were even new-fangled gas driers for the laundry. The visitors' clubhouse was said to be a first in baseball, as visiting teams at the time normally arrived at the ballpark dressed for the game. Umpires also had their own rooms, also reached directly from the field via tunnel. And groundskeeper Frank Van Dellen was said to have had the grass field in "billiard table shape."

Final construction of the rebuilt park raced to completion right up until opening day of the 1910 season.

Re-Opening Day

Opening day in Cleveland for the 1910 season ushered in a new era of baseball on the shores of Lake Erie. The city had become the nation's sixth-largest in that year's census with a population of 560,000. The rebuilt League Park, which cost $300,000, had essentially doubled the seating capacity of its predecessor. The Naps, their fans and the ballpark staff were ready for the new facility. The open press box on the upper deck, destined to be known for being dangerously close home plate, was also ready.

Scheduled for Thursday, April 21, opening day was nearly a victim of bad weather. On April 18 it had snowed, but by game day the weather had turned mild. There was a threat of rain but as it turned out Mother Nature did not dampen the festivities. There were some union picketers outside the park, however, as some parts of the project had been built by non-union labor.

The fans had been caught up in the excitement. Two days before the first game, nearly 9,000 tickets had been sold, well exceeding any advance sale in Cleveland baseball history. Beginning the season on the road, Cleveland

Cy Young, best known for his career record of 511 pitching victories, also holds the distinction of having pitched the opening game in both the wooden version of League Park in 1891 as well as in the concrete-and-steel configuration in 1910 (National Baseball Hall of Fame Library, Cooperstown, N.Y.).

improved to 7–1 on April 20 as Addie Joss out-dueled Doc White in Chicago by throwing a no-hitter, while walking just two. The Naps arrived at their new home in first place, adding to the excitement of the day.

Gates opened at 12:30 for the scheduled 2:30 start. American League president Ban Johnson headlined the festivities, raising a white League Park flag and throwing out the first pitch. Johnson was chosen for the honor largely because of the union labor dispute, which caused local politicians to avoid doing anything that might antagonize those constituents. A band played "Hail the Conquering Heroes" before the game. On hand was Cleveland Police Chief Kohler along with 60 of Cleveland's finest, ten detectives and two patrol wagons.

Amazingly, the starting pitcher for Cleveland was the great Cy Young, the same man who pitched in the original League Park's first opening day in 1891. Now 43 years old, he had been reacquired by Cleveland in 1909 after eight seasons in Boston. He had posted a 19–15 record in old League Park's final year, bringing his career victory total to 497. The Detroit Tigers countered with Edgar Willett, who was starting his fifth year with the club and had won 21 games the previous year.

The first pitch thrown by Young was a ball, but eventually he got leadoff hitter Matty McIntyre to hit a ground ball back to the mound, which he threw to Nap Lajoie at first for the out. Young also retired the next two Tigers batters. Detroit got to Young for two runs in the third and three more in the seventh to provide plenty of support for Willett, who shut down the Naps hitters for a 5–0 win. Young did strike out six, including Ty Cobb twice.

Cleveland's Jay Clarke got the first-ever hit at the new park when he singled to center in the second inning. That was Cleveland's only hit over the first six innings. Detroit's Oscar Stanage scored the park's first run after doubling the following inning. Sam Crawford of the Tigers had the initial stolen base. The new wall did stop Crawford from homering in that opening series, as two of his hits ricocheted off it. He still collected seven hits in the three-game series, including a pair of triples.

The official capacity crowd count of 18,832 set a new opening day attendance mark in Cleveland, a huge number by previous standards. A banquet was held that night at the Hollenden House Hotel for all of the dignitaries who were in attendance.

After a 12–6 start, the Naps spent most of the season in fifth or sixth place, despite the efforts of Young, Joss and Lajoie. Crowds thinned as the season progressed and it would be a few years before the added capacity would pay off. One bizarre contest at League Park that first season came on August 15. Cy Falkenberg pitched a complete game for Cleveland in an 18–3 loss even though he allowed 14 runs over the final two innings and a total of 23 hits against Philadelphia. George Stovall went 5-for-5 for Cleveland in the same game.

A boycott of the games that season by union members, in response to the contributions of non-union personnel during construction, took a significant toll. Season attendance actually dropped from 354,527 in the final wooden park season to 293,456 in the new edifice. That year also saw co-owner Jack Kilfoyl retire, with Somers becoming sole owner of the club and Barnard being elevated to vice president.

Lajoie and Cobb

While 1910 was not a great season for the Cleveland team, its great second baseman, Nap Lajoie, captured the attention of all of baseball that year. The Rhode Island native had finished third in the American League batting race in 1909 with a .324 batting average. His average had rebounded from his career-low batting mark of 1908 after having given up his team's managerial duties that year in order to concentrate on his own play.

In 1910, Lajoie staged an amazing, controversial and highly publicized race with Detroit's Ty Cobb for the American League batting crown. Cobb had won his third consecutive AL batting title in 1909 with a .377 mark, more than 50 points higher than Lajoie. Driven to succeed, there was no question of Cobb's athletic ability, but his personality was another story. It was said, that even among some of his Detroit teammates, that Lajoie would have been the preferred batting champion.

Before the season began, it was announced that the Chalmers automobile company would present the batting champ with a new luxury car valued at $2,700. The prize was the talk of baseball and would certainly heighten interest if someone could challenge Cobb for the crown.

Lajoie and Cobb opened the season against one another in Detroit and met again a week later at League Park. By the time that Detroit returned to Cleveland in mid-season, the race was in full swing. Lajoie had two triples and a double in the series opener on July 1 while Cobb only pinch hit and was unsuccessful in an 8–3 Cleveland win.

After an 11–4 Nap win on Saturday, the teams headed to Detroit to evade the ban on Cleveland Sunday home games. That day's *Cleveland Plain Dealer* listed Lajoie leading the race, .393 to .380 for Cobb. After a 4–3 Detroit win and a boat ride back across Lake Erie, the teams were set for a split double-header at League Park on Monday, July 4. Lajoie went just 1-for-7 on the day while Cobb was 3-for-8. Over 14,000 attended each game as Detroit won the morning contest, 3–1, and Cleveland took the afternoon game, 6–3.

At the beginning of September, Cobb led Lajoie by a few percentage points, but by September 9, Lajoie had gone up, .372 to .364. The numbers were unofficial, as the league would make the final calculations after the season. On September 11, the *Plain Dealer* ran an ad saying "Lajoie and Cobb are running the greatest race for batting supremacy in the history of base ball for the Chalmers Car." On September 19, Lajoie retained his lead by rapping out three hits against first-place Philadelphia in a 5–4 Cleveland win at League Park.

On September 23, with Philadelphia still in first place, Detroit in second and Cleveland trudging along in fifth, Lajoie continued to hit, going 3-for-4 as the Naps beat New York. Despite the interest in the batting race, only 2,547 showed up for the game at League Park. The next day, rain cancelled the New York–Cleveland match-up while Cobb went 3-for-4 in a doubleheader in Boston.

When September 29 came, Lajoie was leading Cobb by a .374 to .370 margin. Lajoie did not play for Cleveland in the final regular season home game, nor in a charity game the next day at League Park. Next up for Lajoie and Cleveland was a trip to Chicago.

In the first game there, Lajoie went 3-for-4 as Cleveland won 8–5. Cobb, meanwhile, went 1-for-3 in a game at St. Louis. On Sunday, October 2, the White Sox stopped Lajoie, who went hitless in three trips to the plate. Against St. Louis, Cobb had four hits in five turns. The *Plain Dealer* listed Lajoie ahead .3754 to .3745 heading into the Monday day off.

The battle next went head-to-head as Cleveland traveled for a series in Detroit. Rain washed out the game on Tuesday but each player went 3-for-6 in a Wednesday doubleheader, keeping Lajoie in front by the tiny margin. By the end of the week, however, Cobb had taken the lead by four points.

It was at this point that things really began to get strange. The *Plain Dealer* reported that Cobb would not play anymore, implying that he was doing it to protect his lead in the race. He did play in the first two games of the Tigers' final series of the season at Chicago. The paper said that "he was not feeling well," but was going to Philadelphia to practice with an all-star team that was scheduled to play against the Athletics, who had clinched the pennant and were preparing for the World Series.[5] He departed via train after the game on Friday, October 7 and missed the final two games of the regular season in Chicago.

Meanwhile, on October 9, Cleveland played a season-ending doubleheader in St. Louis and a crowd of 10,000 watched a most unusual ending to the season. The last-place Browns were managed by Jack O'Connor, who had played for the Cleveland Spiders and who was no friend of Cobb. The first time up Lajoie hit a drive to center that may have been deliberately misjudged into a triple. The next seven times up Lajoie laid down bunts to third, where third baseman Red Corriden was playing extra deep. Six times Lajoie was able to get a hit, the other time resulted in a sacrifice. With the crowd cheering, Lajoie grounded to the shortstop Bobby Wallace in his final at-bat, but Wallace threw wildly to first and the official scorer generously gave Lajoie a hit.

The front page of the *Plain Dealer* the next day proclaimed "Lajoie wins auto in final stretch."[6] It did, however, note suggestions by St. Louis writers that the Browns had made it easy for him. American League president Ban Johnson looked into the affair and found out that St. Louis coach Harry Howell had gone to the press box during the game to influence the official scorer. Johnson held the players blameless but kicked O'Connor and Howell out of the league.

When the final, official statistics were released, Cobb was somehow listed as barely ahead of Lajoie. With all the extra publicity, no one came out a loser. Chalmers decided to award new cars to *both* players. In 1981, detailed research by *The Sporting News* indicated that Lajoie should have won the crown .3841 to .3833 but Commissioner Bowie Kuhn ruled that the official records would continue to list Cobb as having won the American League batting title in 1910.[7]

An All-Star Tribute

After four consecutive seasons in which he had won at least 20 games, Addie Joss slumped to a 13–14 mark in 1909. An arm injury was partially responsible, but he still finished the year with an outstanding 1.71 earned run average. In 1910, his early-season no-hitter in Chicago did not lead to another stellar season. Arm problems continued to plague Joss and he pitched in only 13 games, finishing with a 5–5 record.

During the winter of 1910–11, Joss reportedly was frequently ill, but he returned to spring training with a determination to regain the form that had made him one of the top pitchers in baseball. Before a spring training game in Chattanooga, Tennessee, Joss fainted. He was taken to the hospital and then sent to his home in Toledo. By the time Joss reached Cincinnati on the train trip home, he was complaining of chest pains. He was diagnosed with "lung congestion and a bad case of pleurisy."[8] In Toledo, he was examined by doctors who diagnosed his condition as tubercular meningitis. There was no cure. Over the next ten days he went in and out of consciousness. Early in the morning of April 14, 1911, Addie Joss died. His death came just two days after his 31st birthday.

The death of Joss was understandably devastating to his Cleveland teammates. Cy Young said that he had never met a man "fairer or squarer than

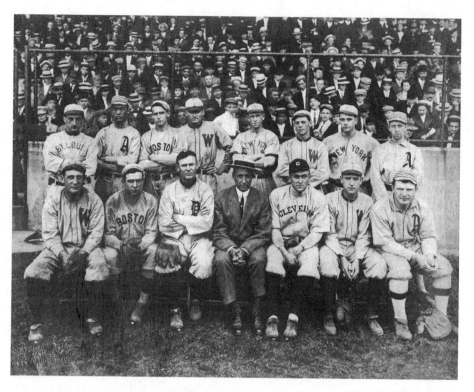

The Addie Joss benefit game, July 24, 1911, raised $13,000 for the late pitcher's family. It took place 22 years before the first American League vs. National League All-Star Game and featured the American League stars vs. the hometown Cleveland Naps. Detroit's Ty Cobb (front row, third from right) did not have his Tigers uniform and was forced to suit up in Cleveland attire. Ironically, the Naps had passed on a trade offer from Detroit in 1907 that would have brought Cobb to Cleveland. The All-Stars won, 5–3 (National Baseball Hall of Fame Library, Cooperstown, N.Y.).

Addie."[9] The funeral was held in Toledo on April 17. Cleveland's scheduled game in Detroit was postponed to allow the players to attend. Ban Johnson had originally objected to any postponement but finally relented when a threatened strike by the players forced his hand. A special train brought the Cleveland team to Toledo where the city witnessed a funeral the likes of which it had never known. Billy Sunday, a former major leaguer who had become a well-known evangelist, delivered the eulogy.

Joss's salary in 1911 was to be $5,500, enough for a very comfortable living at the time. In order to help provide for the welfare of Joss's family, owner Charles Somers and the Naps worked to organize a benefit all-star game. Monday, July 24 was selected because all the American League teams except Chicago and Boston had the day off.

Prior to the game, tickets were purchased for well above face value by civic leaders, businesses, baseball players and management. Ty Cobb sent a check for $100 but requested anonymity. Cleveland vice president Barnard, who was credited with the idea for the game, phoned Cobb and convinced him to allow his name to be used because it would lead to more donations. The *Cleveland News* reported: "Never before in the glorious history of baseball has such a galaxy of brilliants of baseball been assembled as that which will face the Naps at League Park Monday afternoon."[10] The paper's sports section featured a large photo of Joss's wife and their two children.

Washington manager Jimmy McAleer, a former Cleveland player, was picked to manage the all-stars. On game day, grandstand tickets were sold for $1. A huge crowd of 15,281 turned out on a cool and windy day. Flags were at half-mast, but there were no other displays of mourning.

Cy Young pitched the first three innings for Cleveland, giving up six hits. The first three batters he faced were Tris Speaker, Eddie Collins and Ty Cobb. All three got hits. Cobb was battling a bad cold but managed two hits in the game. He was also picked off first and caught stealing. In an odd twist, Cobb played the game in a Cleveland uniform after losing his Detroit uniform on the trip to Cleveland. The all-stars scored twice in the first and once in the second to take a 3–0 lead. Joe Wood pitched the first three innings against the Naps and gave up a single run in the second inning.

In the fourth inning, Frank Baker and Sam Crawford got hits and the all-stars tallied another run when Hal Chase hit a sacrifice fly. Walter Johnson, who had earlier said he would do anything for Joss's family, pitched the middle three innings and held Cleveland without a run. In the seventh inning, Collins singled in a run to give the all-stars a 5–1 lead. An eighth-inning rally off of Russell Ford produced two runs for the Naps, but the game ended with the all-stars winning, 5–3. Colorful Germany Schaefer, the former Detroit Tiger now playing for Washington, did the announcements during the game. Schaefer also entertained the crowd by serving as a base coach and imitating Hughie "Ee-Yah" Jennings, manager of the Tigers.

The employees of League Park had donated their services that day in the spirit of the event. The final tally of money raised totaled about $13,000. Addie Joss had only a nine-year major-league career, posting a record of 160–97 to go along with his 1.89 career ERA. He was not elected to the Baseball Hall of Fame until 1978, when the requirement of a minimum ten-year major league career was waived.[11]

Shoeless Joe in Cleveland

Toward the end of the 1910 season one of the most famous names in baseball history, "Shoeless" Joe Jackson, made his debut for the Cleveland

These two great players, Detroit's Ty Cobb and Cleveland's Shoeless Joe Jackson, met often at League Park during the first decade of the concrete-and-steel configuration. Both were known for their amazing hitting prowess and for attracting controversy (Library of Congress, Prints & Photographs Division, LC-USZ62–97880).

Naps. After appearing in just a few games for the Philadelphia Athletics the previous two years, Jackson had been acquired by Cleveland. He spent most of the 1910 season with the minor league team in New Orleans, playing in just 20 games for Cleveland. As a semi-literate Southerner, he had problems adjusting to the major leagues and his fellow players. His talent, however, was unquestioned. "He has a world of natural ability, hits and throws like a fiend, but will not be very valuable if he loses heart," the *Cleveland Press* reported upon his acquisition.[12]

His first game in a Cleveland uniform took place on September 16, 1910. The Naps defeated Washington, 6–5, at League Park as Jackson went 1-for-4 and stole two bases while playing center field. He batted .387 in his limited time with the Naps that year.[13]

Following the 1910 regular season, Cleveland played Cincinnati in a "Championship of Ohio" series. Back in July, a challenge had been made by Cincinnati manager Frank Bancroft which the Naps had accepted. The series opened in Cincinnati with Cleveland losing a 14–7 decision. Game two at League Park drew nearly 7,000 fans that saw the Naps win, 5–3. Cleveland won the next game, 7–1, in front of another good crowd at League Park. Cy Falkenberg pitched a gem for the home team. The series returned to Cincinnati where the Reds swept a doubleheader before Cleveland took game six at League Park, 9–5. Back in Cincinnati, the Reds won the deciding game, 8–5. Cleveland's players split nearly $3,500 for their efforts. Jackson played all seven games of the series, going 10-for-28 at the plate.

Opening day of the 1911 season in Cleveland was April 20 as the Naps were nipped by St. Louis, 4–3, in 11 innings with 14,379 in attendance. Jackson, wielding his thick-handled bat that he called "Black Betsy," had a triple, single and a walk as well as a stolen base. He also threw out a runner at the plate. Jackson starred again the following day before a crowd of 2,606 as Cleveland won, 6–5. He had a single, two walks and a two-run home run, the longest hit so far at the rebuilt park. It flew over the right-field wall, landing on the far side of Lexington Avenue.

That spring, the ban on Sunday baseball in Cleveland finally came to an end. In March, the Ohio House of Representatives had passed by a vote of 61 to 46 a bill repealing the laws preventing Sunday baseball. On May 15, the Naps hosted New York in League Park's first Sunday game. The well-behaved crowd had been given notices warning against "boisterous rooting" on the Sabbath.[14] The crowd of 15,585 included Cleveland's mayor and chief of police. Jackson went 2-for-5 with a triple and an infield single as Cleveland romped, 14–3. Sunday baseball was clearly a hit, as was the case again the following week as Cleveland defeated Washington before 13,618 League Park fans. Somewhere, Frank DeHass Robison likely was thinking, "I told you so."

Jackson's torrid hitting continued throughout the season. He had a 28-game hitting streak from mid–July to mid–August. A doubleheader split with Detroit closed the regular season at League Park as the Naps finished in third place with Jackson batting .408 and earning respect throughout baseball. "There is no denying that he is a better ball player his first year in the big leagues than anyone who ever was," observed Ty Cobb.[15] Attendance jumped more than 110,000 from the previous year to 406,296.

Once again in 1911, a series was played with Cincinnati for the "Ohio Championship." Cleveland lost the opening game at Cincinnati, 4–0, in front of a crowd of just 580. Game two was October 13 at League Park and Cincinnati won again, 10–2, before 2,314. The series concluded with doubleheader splits the next two days at League Park, giving the championship to Cincinnati, four games to two. The Saturday doubleheader drew 4,400 while the Sunday crowd was 8,797.

The Cleveland team fell below .500 in the 1912 season and attendance dropped accordingly, but Jackson continued to exhibit his individual prowess. He led the league with 26 triples and his batting average of .395 was second only to Cobb's .409. Cleveland's other star, Napoleon Lajoie, was honored with a "Lajoie Day" at League Park on June 4, 1912. The popular infielder had now been a member of the Cleveland baseball team for more than a decade.

The 1912 season also saw an independent minor league team, the Cleveland Forest Citys of the United States League, open up the season at the baseball diamond located at the Luna Park amusement park, charging 25, 35 or 50 cents per admission. This site was also on Cleveland's East Side, less than three miles southeast of League Park at Woodhill Road and Woodland Avenue. The experiment was short-lived as the team ceased operations after its game on June 1.

Opening day at League Park in 1913 took place on April 11, having been postponed a day because of rain. The 14,000 in attendance saw the Naps win 3–1 over Chicago. Jackson doubled off the right-field wall, tripled off the screen to the right of the scoreboard in center field and doubled to left, picking right up where he had left off the previous year. Vean Gregg, on his way to his third consecutive 20-win season for Cleveland, allowed just seven hits.

That season, manager Joe Birmingham and the Naps were accused by Washington of locating a signal in the scoreboard to communicate stolen signs to Cleveland hitters. Their only evidence was the success of some of weaker Nap hitters against better Washington pitchers.

Also that year, another minor league team, this one from the Federal League, tested the Cleveland market by using the Luna Park field. On Saturday, May 3, the team debuted before a crowd of 1,200 as Cleveland and Covington, Kentucky, played to a 6–6 tie in 11 innings. Again, tickets were priced at 25,

35 and 50 cents. Known as the Cleveland Green Sox and with now-retired Cy Young serving as manager, the team placed second with a 64–65 mark. The league had intentions on an all-out challenge to the AL and NL as a third major league the following year.

Two days after the Green Sox' opener, the Pittsburgh Pirates came to Cleveland for an exhibition game against the Naps. An aging Honus Wagner had a double for Pittsburgh as the Pirates won, 6–5. Jackson had four hits and stole three bases. The crowd of 9,385 was second only to the Joss benefit game of two years earlier for an exhibition at League Park.

On May 11, the second-place Naps hosted New York before a Sunday afternoon crowd of 18,626, to that point the third-largest in Cleveland baseball history. The Naps won, 7–2, as Jackson went 4-for-4 with an inside-the-park grand slam.

A week later, the Naps played first-place Philadelphia in front of 23,617, by far a new Cleveland record. Over 3,000 fans stood, including many behind ropes in the outfield, to witness the contest. Chief Bender pitched the Athletics to a 4–2 win. The *Cleveland Plain Dealer* praised League Park's design, noting how quickly the overflow crowd was able to leave the park, many of them exiting across the outfield and through a gate in the wall in right center field.[16]

It was an exciting month as Cleveland bounced between first and second place. Another highlight came on May 22 when the Naps beat Washington and Walter Johnson, at the peak of his career, by a 5–0 score to start a 10-game winning streak. The team got 13 hits, including three by Jack Graney.

The Naps stayed in the pennant race for most of the 1913 season, finishing in third place. Attendance likewise ranked third in the loop with a club record 541,000 passing through the League Park turnstiles. Jackson batted .373 and led the league in hits, doubles and slugging percentage. In June, he became the first player to hit a home run over the new roof at the Polo Grounds in New York, a feat that would not be matched for six years. Lajoie continued his fine hitting with a .335 mark. Cy Falkenberg wound up 23–10 on the mound after a 10–0 start while Gregg went 20–14, his third straight 20-win season. Cleveland baseball interest had reached an all-time high.

Blocking Out the Feds

Financial woes and declining attendance marked the following season, 1914. The problems came as a result of the formation of the Federal League, even though it opted not to place a team in Cleveland. The former United States League had declared itself a major league and was outbidding its AL and NL counterparts for many players. The FL began operations as an eight-team circuit, competing head-to-head with AL and NL clubs in Brooklyn, Chicago, Pittsburgh and St. Louis while rounding out the league with teams in Baltimore, Buffalo, Indianapolis and Kansas City.

In Cleveland, owner Charley Somers decided to move his minor league Toledo team of the American Association to League Park in order to fill the dates when the Naps were on the road. This way, no potential Federal League team would be able to play in Cleveland without another pro team already scheduled in the recently rebuilt League Park.

Somers wound up operating two struggling teams that did not generate much interest or income. New shortstop Ray Chapman set a dubious record by committing 4 errors in the fifth inning of a 7–1 loss to New York on June 20 at League Park. Lajoie did provide a memorable moment at League Park on September 27, late in what would become his final Cleveland campaign, by becoming just the third player (joining Honus Wagner and Cap Anson) to reach 3,000 career hits. He reached the milestone with a double in the sixth inning of the first game of a doubleheader against New York. The Naps wound up last in the American League, 51–102 and 48½ games out of first place. They drew just 185,997 fans, last in the league and the fewest since the club's debut season in the American League in 1901. That mark did surpass half of the National League teams and all but one from the fledgling Federal League, however. Pitching was the team's biggest weakness as Falkenberg had jumped to the FL team in Indianapolis and Gregg had been traded to the Boston Red Sox by midseason.

As for the minor league team, its season began with a prolonged 24-game road trip that included visits to every other league site. League Park finally hosted its American Association tenant on May 14, more than three weeks after the AL home opener. The minor leaguers, already struggling on the field, drew just 500 fans to their first home game, a 7–5 loss to Minneapolis. Tickets were as cheap as 25 cents for seats in the left field pavilion, but the team had fallen to last place by mid–May, a distinction it shared with the faltering Naps. An eight-game winning streak did change things and on May 24 a crowd of 8,000 saw the team split a doubleheader with St. Paul.

Oddly, each of the Cleveland newspapers used a different nickname for this team. Realizing the absurdity, the sports editors got together and came up with a single name, Bearcats. The *Cleveland News* reported, "From now on there will be no Warriors, Shecks, Spiders, Scouts or Associations."[17] As the summer continued, the Bearcats hovered around the middle of the standings while the Naps were compiling the franchise's worst-ever winning percentage, just .333. The minor leaguers fared better, finishing in fifth place in the eight-team league with an 82–81 record. They also finished fifth place in the American Association in attendance, drawing 99,732 fans.

Call Them Indians

In January 1915, Lajoie was sold to the Philadelphia Athletics, where his career ended after the 1916 season. The lone star to return for Cleveland in 1915 was Joe Jackson. So it was that the Naps would be renamed. The new moniker came from a suggestion that the club honor the former Native American player, Louis Sockalexis, who had made a brief splash with the old Cleveland Spiders just before the turn of the century, and now the team became known as the Indians.

Despite the new nickname, the 1915 Cleveland squad improved by just six wins to a 57–95 mark. On May 16, Guy Morton had a no-hitter against visiting Boston through eight innings but ended up losing 3–0 in 14 innings. A few days later, Joe Birmingham was relieved as manager and succeeded by Lee Fohl. A crowd of 15,000, the largest since 1913, came to League Park on May 23 to see Walter Johnson pitch for Washington. He threw a five-hitter, winning 4–1, and also hit what was described as "the longest home run ever on the grounds."[18] The blast came in the fifth inning and sailed over the left field scoreboard. The *Cleveland News* listed it at 415 feet, quite a feat for the era. Later that game, Johnson hit a ball to deep center field but was thrown out at home while trying for an inside-the-park home run.

The minor league American Association team returned in 1915, now using the familiar Spiders nickname. This helped to stave off the potential of a Federal League team relocating to Cleveland. That league had abandoned its head-to-head battle in Brooklyn, as that team instead moved across the Hudson River to Newark, New Jersey, for the 1915 season.

Poor attendance was continuing to cause financial problems for owner Charley Somers. Somers had been the subject of mounting criticism in recent years, beginning with his removal of popular manager George Stovall in 1911 and continuing with everything from game times to scorecard sales. American League attendance in Cleveland fell to 159,285 in 1915 while the minor leaguers drew only 86,977 fans.

Joe Jackson was traded to the Chicago White Sox in August for two players and $20,000 cash in order to help make ends meet. By July, there was talk that the Federal League would try to take advantage of the team's struggles by expanding or relocating into Cleveland in 1916. On July 19, the fortunes of the last-place Indians hit a new low when the team was defeated by Washington, 11–4, in front of just 700 fans at League Park. The Senators stole *eight* bases in the first inning alone. A doubleheader with Detroit on August 16 drew only 1,500 as the Indians lost both games. The pitching of Guy Morton continued to be a bright spot, however. On August 22, he tossed a one-hitter over New York for his sixth shutout of the season.

One of the great ironies of the small crowds watching the Indians and Spiders at League Park was the tremendous fan support for sandlot baseball in Cleveland that year, which must have fueled the Federal League rumors. On June 20, while the Indians dropped a doubleheader to the White Sox in front of 8,000 fans, a crowd of 10,000 saw amateur teams representing department stores Baileys and May Company play at Edgewater Park, with Baileys winning, 11–1. On the following Sunday, 8,675 saw Detroit defeat Cleveland, 12–2, at League Park while 10,000 watched White Auto beat Tellings-Strollers, 3–1, at Brookside Park.

On August 8, a doubleheader was played at League Park, the Spiders meeting Minneapolis in one game and Baileys facing Preisels in the other. The attendance was 20,479, described as "60 times as many as normally sees the Spiders."[19] A White Auto game on September 12 drew a crowd estimated at 75,000 in the natural bowl field at Brookside Park! White Auto then played a game at League Park on September 16 and drew 28,000 — the largest crowd there yet, eclipsing the record of the Naps-Athletics game of 1913. Then, on October 10 at Brookside Park, a crowd estimated at 115,000, believed to be the largest crowd ever to see a baseball game, saw White Auto defeat a team from Omaha.

Following the 1915 season, the Federal League ceased operations, ending the rumors as well as the need for the minor league team playing at League Park. The American Association club returned to Toledo for the 1916 season. The fortunes of League Park and the Indians also were about to change. They were about to be sold by Somers to a syndicate headed by James Dunn.

James Dunn and the Grey Eagle

"Tris Speaker Comes to Cleveland" shouted the headline of the *Cleveland Plain Dealer*'s sports section just prior to the opening of the 1916 season.[20] With railroad contractor James Dunn having purchased the Cleveland franchise from financially strapped Charles Somers, things were looking up. "I'm going to give Cleveland a pennant," promised the new owner. Landing Speaker was a big step toward that goal.

Known as the "Grey Eagle" due to his prematurely grey hair, Speaker had been embroiled in a salary dispute with the Boston Red Sox. He was peddled to the Indians in return for two players and $55,000, the largest sum ever paid for a ballplayer at the time. Speaker himself got a $2,500 signing bonus and a two-year contract for a reported $15,000 per year. Dunn had made the biggest deal in the history of the game, replacing Joe Jackson in center field at League Park with another superstar and setting the stage for a drive to fulfill his promise of an American League flag for the city.

Having played for Boston since 1907, "Spoke" was recognized as one of the top hitters in the game as well as its best defensive outfielder, where he was known for his habit of picking and chewing blades of grass. His speed and shallow center field play allowed him to make an amazing four unassisted double plays in his career, each time making shoestring catches and beating stunned runners who had strayed too far from second base back to the bag. The year before coming to Cleveland, Speaker had amazed League Park fans with a throw to the plate in the eighth inning of a tie game to nail Joe Jackson, who was trying to score from second on a single. He set records for the most career putouts, assists and double plays by an outfielder; two of these still stand. At times, he even covered second base and turned an infield double play.[21]

Opening day at League Park in 1916 took place on April 12, a Wednesday afternoon. Dunn priced 6,500 of the seats at League Park at 75 cents. Festivities included a band, singers and colorful bunting. Ten thousand Indian head-dresses were given out as souvenirs. Despite inclement weather, a crowd of 18,351 filled the grandstands, as interest in the team had been rekindled by the new owner and the debut of his new star player. But the fans went home disappointed as Speaker walked three times and was put out once as the Tribe was defeated by the St. Louis Browns, 6–1.

On June 26, at the suggestion of club vice president Bob McRoy, Dunn experimented with numbers on the sleeves of the Indians players which corresponded to numbers in the scorecard sold that day for the game against Chicago. It was another first for League Park, but it didn't last. The New York Yankees permanently adopted uniform numbers in 1929, and the practice became standard throughout baseball in 1932.

With Speaker leading the way, the improved Indians actually held first place for part of the summer before finishing with a 77–77 record. Speaker enjoyed the cozy confines of League Park, upping his batting average to .386 to take the batting title away from Ty Cobb. Another milestone occurred at the park on September 23, when Martin Kavanagh hit the first pinch-hit grand slam in American League history, leading Cleveland over Boston, 5–3. The fans responded, as Cleveland drew 492,106, more than triple that of 1915 and the second best total in franchise history.

The next year, 1917, Cleveland finished in third place as Speaker hit .352 to finish third in the batting race behind Ty Cobb and George Sisler. Several notable games took place during the year at League Park. A new home opening day attendance mark of 20,729 saw the Indians beat Detroit, 8–7, on April 19. On May 16, it was "Speaker Day" at the home grounds, drawing a crowd of 6,500 on a cloudy Wednesday afternoon. Speaker was given an arrangement of flowers by the club but went hitless as Boston won, 5–1. On Sunday, July

The mayor's box on opening day 1916 with Mayor Harry Davis seated in the front, right seat. Traction commissioner Fielder Sanders is seated next to the mayor and has topped his fedora with one of the souvenir headdresses which were handed out to the crowd that day by new team owner James Dunn (Cleveland State University, Cleveland Press Collection).

22 Cleveland defeated Philadelphia, 20–6. Leading 3–0 after five innings, Cleveland scored 17 runs over the next three frames. Ray Chapman paced the Indians' 17-hit attack with three hits, including a home run. On August 12, first-place Chicago defeated Cleveland 4–3 in 13 innings in front of a Sunday crowd of 20,000. Two days later, Speaker was knocked unconscious by a fast-ball to the head, a frightening incident that would be recalled with grim significance three years and two days hence. Attendance dropped slightly to 477,298, but only the pennant-winning White Sox drew more fans.

    The 1918 season was shortened by America's involvement in World War I. A doubleheader sweep of the Yankees at League Park on the 4th of July put the Indians in first place. Cleveland wound up finishing with just two fewer wins than Babe Ruth and the pennant-winning Red Sox. Though his batting average fell to .318, Speaker led the league with 33 doubles. Stan Coveleski led the pitching staff with 22 wins. As a result of the shortened season, Cleveland attendance fell to 295,515, but the total enabled Cleveland to lead the league for the first time ever. The onset of war had damaged attendance throughout the majors.

Opening day in Cleveland in 1919 was not until May 1. Detroit got the better of the home team by the score of 8–1. By July, Cleveland was in third place and playing host to Boston in a key series during which Ruth blasted a grand slam over the screen in right with two outs in the ninth inning to give Boston an 8–7 victory. There had been dissatisfaction with Lee Fohl's managing, and with the pressure building, Fohl resigned following the game. Speaker reluctantly took over as player-manager.

On August 24, veteran Ray Caldwell pitched his first game for the Indians after being released by Boston. With two outs in the ninth inning, a tremendous lightning strike literally knocked Caldwell off the mound. After a few tense moments, he rose unassisted and finished the game, getting Joe Dugan of Philadelphia to ground out and preserving a 3–2 Cleveland win.

Just a few days later, a huge series took place at League Park between Cleveland and Chicago as the Indians tried to catch the league-leading White Sox. The first game, on Friday, August 28, saw Eddie Cicotte and the White Sox down Ray Caldwell and the Indians, 3–2. The *Cleveland Plain Dealer* noted the unusually high number of women at the game for the era, stating that it was played "before 20,000 baseball maniacs, close to 4,000 of them of the sex that rooted in the soprano tone."[22]

The second game of the series saw Elmer Myers throw a five-hit shutout as the Indians won, 4–0, in front of 21,000. The Sunday game was also a Cleveland victory, as they chased Claude Williams from the mound in the first inning on the way to a 6–1 win. Stan Coveleski threw a six-hitter to pick up the win. The game was played in front of a new franchise record attendance at League Park, 26,925, with the crowd filling all standing areas and spilling onto the outfield.

Cleveland stood six games back of the White Sox and faced a 22-game road trip to all seven AL cities over the next 25 days. Amazingly, the Indians went 15–5 to start the trip but had only picked up two games on the Sox. They lost a pair of games at Detroit and closed the season by splitting two games with St. Louis at League Park on September 27 and 28, finishing 3½ games back. Although they hadn't reached first place, Speaker's leadership helped guide the team to a 40–21 mark down the stretch. The team finished in second place, behind those infamous 1919 Chicago White Sox, who would later be scrutinized for fixing that year's World Series, a surprising loss to the Cincinnati Reds. With the war over, Cleveland's attendance increased to 538,135 in 1919. Now ten years into the ballpark's concrete and steel configuration, the stage was set for League Park's most monumental year.

3

1920 and the World Series

It was a simple park. It had human scale and blended in with the local area. It was made of brick and had those arches that people felt comfortable with. — Dale Swearingen, Osborn Engineering

Most Significant

From the time that Frank Robison chose the Northeast corner of East 66th and Lexington in Cleveland as the location for his baseball park in 1890, the site had racked up an impressive list of significant events and happenings. No year, however, would ever match 1920 for the sheer number of legendary occurrences tied to League Park. And it all took place as the biggest upheaval in the game's history was beginning to unfold with the story of the tainted "Black Sox" World Series of 1919. The timing of the resulting investigation directly influenced League Park history and the consequences of that incident helped Cleveland clinch its only American League pennant during the Indians' League Park era.

So as the city of Cleveland peaked in population rank at fifth in the nation, so too its baseball team reached a new peak in popularity and success. Further, that success led to many key upgrades to the grounds during that year. Unfortunately, after these upgrades were completed, the ballpark was destined to begin its long spiral downward that continued into the next century.

An Upgraded Park and Team

With superstar player-manager Tris Speaker leading the way from his center field position, the Indians were considered a formidable challenger to the defending champion Chicago White Sox entering the 1920 campaign. Cleveland led the race for most of that spring and summer, with both the New York Yankees, boasting the recently acquired Babe Ruth, and the defending league champion Chicago White Sox in pursuit.

Cleveland topped St. Louis on April 14, opening day at League Park, by a 5–0 score as Stan Coveleski tossed a five-hitter while 19,784 watched. Despite very cold temperatures, that attendance was within a thousand of the city's opening day record from 1917.

Fan support continued as the team won six of seven and 10 of 13 to begin the year. The team took over first place on May 9 and then spent only four days out of the top spot over the next three months. Through mid–August, the Indians had never fallen more than a game out of first place.

It was during this time that team management had decided to add some 3,000 seats to the left field corner, connecting the bleacher seats with the "pavilion" section and the main grandstand. Photographs show that the left field bleachers appear to have been rebuilt and upgraded at this time as well. The front of the new bleacher wall was configured at three feet high, with a seven-foot fence atop that. Meanwhile, in right field, Dunn had raised the "screen monster" from 20 to 28 feet atop the concrete wall, bringing the total height to 48 feet.

These changes further enclosed and added intimacy to an already very intimate setting as left center field was shortened to 382 feet with the expanded bleachers. Center field came in from 460 to 420 feet. Another unusual feature that appeared after this upgrade was a unique two-flagpole design, with the stars and stripes now flying both in left center field and atop the scoreboard in center.

There was also some additional construction of new lower field box seats just beyond the dugouts that jutted out into foul territory. From those seats, fans were able to look back into the dugout! These seats were so close that fans not only could hear the players curse but, it has been said, even feel the spray of their tobacco juice. Foul territory was reduced so much that these seats became perhaps the closest ever to a major league infield. Another unusual arrangement created by these seats was that fair balls beyond them into the now even tighter bullpen areas remained in play, so outfielders could throw a live ball over these seats and back toward the infield. Joe Sewell, destined to play a key role in the 1920 season, years later referred to the proximity of these seats when he said of the park, "It was so damn small fans practically fell on the field."[1]

A very somber moment occurred on May 28 when ace pitcher Stan Coveleski reported to League Park to pitch the series opener against Chicago. The spitball pitcher was one of 23 in the majors "grandfathered" in by being allowed to continue to throw the pitch although it had been outlawed beginning with this season. On this day, he was called to the team offices, where a telegram had arrived. Coveleski's wife, ill but not thought to be in critical condition, had died at their home in Shamokin, Pennsylvania. Coveleski left for home and League Park flags flew at half mast.

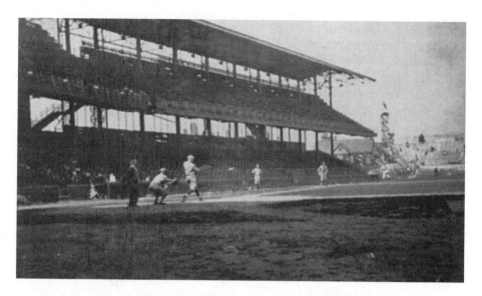

Significant improvements were made to League Park during the 1920 season. This photograph from the spring of that year shows action from a high school game involving then-neighboring University School at League Park. The significance of this photograph is that it shows the construction of the seating in the left field corner in progress. Workers and the support structure are evident as the enlarged left-field seats were added to and curved to meet the main grandstand down the left field line (University School Archives).

Overall success continued, however. In June, with the expanded seating available, a League Park record crowd of 29,266 filled all the seats and spilled onto the playing field for a game against New York. After a win over Philadelphia on August 8, the Indians held their biggest lead, 4½ games over New York and five over Chicago with the Yankees coming to town for a four-game series. Baseball writers dubbed it the "Little World Series" due to its importance. Ticket demand was so high that Jim Dunn added temporary wooden plank "circus seat" bleachers beyond the new field box seats and down the foul lines to the bullpens. During the Yankees' previous visit, Dunn had allowed fans to stand behind ropes in the outfield for extra ticket sales, but several ground-rule doubles were hit into those fans which could have been caught by the Indian outfielders. He didn't want to hurt his team's chances, but of course he still wanted the extra income!

Cleveland lost the series opener, 6–3, on Monday, August 9, with 70 old-time players in attendance for Dunn's "Golden Year of Baseball" day, honoring the fifty years since professional baseball had come to Cleveland. League Park was also symbolically in the midst of the sport's transition out of the dead ball era that day. Babe Ruth had come to town with an amazing total of 41 home runs and was honored by the Cleveland fans before the game. He was presented with a 12-foot floral bat, and the presenter said that he hoped Ruth would hit 100 home runs, but "none of them against Cleveland."[2]

The next day, 21,000 fans turned out in threatening weather, but a second-inning downpour caused a postponement. Some 27,000 jammed in on Wednesday, the largest weekday crowd ever at the park. Carl Mays, winner of 10 of his last 11 decisions, was set to pitch for the Yanks. Ruth batted in the first but injured his knee while sliding into second base. With Ruth out of the game, Elmer Smith of Cleveland sent the crowd into a frenzy with a third-inning grand slam. Straw hats littered the League Park field. But New York battled back to tie and won 7–4 in ten innings as Tribe hurler Jim Bagby lost to the Yanks for the first time that year after three victories.

On Thursday, Coveleski dropped a 5–1 decision and New York had closed to within a game-and-a-half in the standings. Chicago was in second, just a game back. New York finished the sweep on Friday as Carl Mays, who pitched all ten innings two days earlier, relieved in the eighth inning to end a Cleveland rally. He also shut down the Indians in the ninth as the Yankees won, 4–3. A once-commanding lead had all but evaporated in just five days as both New York and Chicago were now just a half-game behind Cleveland in the American League standings.

The Indians then split a pair of home games with St. Louis before getting a chance for revenge against the Yankees in New York. Cleveland opened the series at the Polo Grounds in a virtual tie for first place with Chicago, while New York was just a half game back.

The News That Shook League Park

With every game crucial, the Indians and New York began the three-game Polo Grounds series on August 16. Pitcher Carl Mays, who had closed out the series in Cleveland on Friday, again took the mound for the Yanks. Known for his submarine pitching style, Mays had been the subject of a *Cleveland Press* story on the day before the season opener that year, April 13, which was headlined "In Defense of Carl Mays." The piece stated that Mays had been accused of experimenting with the "bean ball," a pitch at the head. Red Sox manager Ed Barrow came to the Yankees pitcher's defense: "Mays is a good fellow and I don't believe he would try to hit a batsman any more than would Walter Johnson. Nobody ever questions Johnson's fast ball, although sometimes it speeds so close to the batsman's head that it looks intentional. Mays is a great pitcher and doesn't have to resort to intimidation."[3]

On this Monday afternoon, Mays threw the first pitch of the 5th inning

THE RAY CHAPMAN STORY

THE TABLET BELOW HONORS THE MEMORY OF INDIANS
SHORTSTOP RAY CHAPMAN WHO WAS KILLED BY A PITCHED
BALL ON AUGUST 17, 1920. FOLLOWING CHAPMAN'S DEATH
MORE THAN 50 DESIGNS WERE SUBMITTED BY ARTISTS AND
BRONZE MANUFACTURERS THROUGHOUT THE COUNTRY. A
COMMITTEE WAS FORMED, AND THE DESIGN BELOW-
A COMBINATION OF TWO SUBMISSIONS-WAS APPROVED.

IN 1921, THE TABLET WAS PLACED JUST INSIDE THE
LEXINGTON AVENUE ENTRANCE OF LEAGUE PARK. IT WAS
MOVED TO CLEVELAND STADIUM WHEN THE INDIANS
CHANGED HOMES ON A PERMANENT BASIS IN 1946. THOUGHT
TO BE LOST, THE TABLET WAS THANKFULLY FOUND AND
PLACED HERE AT HERITAGE PARK IN 2007.

RAYMOND JOHNSON CHAPMAN
1891   1920

SHORTSTOP OF
THE CLEVELAND
BASEBALL CLUB FROM
SEPTEMBER SEVENTEENTH
NINETEEN HUNDRED AND
TWELVE, UNTIL HIS DEATH
ON AUGUST SEVENTEENTH
NINETEEN HUNDRED AND TWENTY.

THIS TABLET IS
ERECTED BY LOVERS
OF CLEAN SPORT AS
AN AFFECTIONATE TRI-
BUTE TO HIS INSPIRING
ENTHUSIASM, CHEER-
FULNESS AND UNFAILING
LOYALTY TO HIS CLUB.

"HE LIVES IN THE HEARTS OF ALL WHO KNEW HIM"

high and tight to Indians shortstop Ray Chapman. It was said that Mays pitched to that spot in defense of an anticipated bunt toward first base by the speedy Chapman. Chapman froze and the ball cracked his left temple (these were the days before batting helmets), making a sound heard throughout the park. Mays, thinking that the ball had bounded off the bat, fielded it and threw to first base. First baseman Wally Pipp caught the ball and looked to home, where Chapman had stood motionless for moment, but was now collapsing to the ground.

Coach Jack McCallister, fearing the worst immediately, rushed in first from the coach's box. Umpire Tom Connolly shouted to the crowd for a doctor. Speaker, who remembered having been knocked out by a pitch three years earlier, was on deck. He hurried to his teammate while players from both teams followed, converging at the plate. Unable to speak, Chapman nonetheless was helped to his feet and was led to the clubhouse in center field, still bleeding from the ear.

On the field, the Indians took advantage of the leadoff base runner, increasing their lead to 4–0, then holding on for a 4–3 decision. But in the clubhouse, doctors had determined that emergency surgery was needed to relieve pressure on Chapman's brain. An ambulance rushed him to the hospital, where he lapsed into unconsciousness. Surgery that night relieved the pressure, but showed extensive damage. Chapman's wife Kathleen took a train from Cleveland to New York but by the time she arrived at 10 A.M. it was too late. "Chappie" had died at 4:40 A.M. on Tuesday, August 17, at age 29, still the only casualty in major league history.

The members of the Cleveland team were distraught. The afternoon editions of the Cleveland papers that day announced the sad news, plunging the entire city into grief. Mayor W.S. Fitzgerald wrote a letter to the citizens that ran on the first page of the *Plain Dealer*. That day's game was cancelled, and by 6:30 P.M., Chapman's body was aboard the Lake Shore Limited, heading back to Cleveland.[4]

Among the tributes was a huge floral basket containing 2,063 flowers from 20,023 persons who had contributed ten cents each. The remainder of that money went to create a bronze tablet in Chapman's honor to be placed at League Park. That memorial eventually made its way to Cleveland Stadium, and was later taken off display in the early 1970s. When the team moved to Jacobs Field in 1994, it was moved in a box with other items and was not rediscovered until February 2007. The team had it restored and it now hangs

Opposite page: The bronze tablet that was installed at League Park to honor Ray Chapman is now on display at the Indians' historical tribute area known as Heritage Park, which is located in the center-field area of Progressive Field.

Ticket buyers line up at the booths located at the main building on Lexington Avenue, just east of East 66th Street in 1922. Note the trolley tracks embedded in the street, as well as the all-male, well-dressed crowd, all wearing caps or fedoras (Cleveland State University, Cleveland Press Collection).

in the renamed Progressive Field's Heritage Park, which pays tribute to the team's history.

Pennant Chase

Following the postponement, the Tribe managed to split the final two games at New York. With a one-game lead, the team now returned home for Chapman's funeral on Friday, August 20. The Red Sox postponed the scheduled game with Cleveland and Saturday became a doubleheader.

With the combination of the extra train travel and grief, the Indians dropped four of five in Boston and two straight in Philadelphia to fall 3½ games out of first place on August 26. They regrouped to win the series finale in Philly and then took three out of four games in Washington. On Friday, September 3, Cleveland returned to League Park for the first time since Chapman's death, ahead by a half game in the AL standings.

A crowd of 15,000 watched as a lone bugler stood at shortstop to play taps. In the clubhouse, Chapman's home uniform and locker remained untouched in memoriam. As if the fans' hearts weren't already broken, the team lost by a 1–0 score to Detroit on that Ray Chapman Memorial Day. Harry Lunte, Chapman's replacement at shortstop, had received a huge ovation when the lineups were announced.

By September 6, however, with Lunte batting just .197, the Indians purchased Joey Sewell, just 21 years old, from New Orleans to take over at short. The team retained first place with a September 9th win over the Yankees in Cleveland, but New York won the next two games and Cleveland dropped to second place. But then the Indians won nine of their next ten, all at home over Philadelphia, Washington and Boston, to regain first place on September 17.

Meanwhile, New York lost three straight games to the White Sox on September 17, 18 and 19 while Chicago was on a streak of 10 wins in 11 games, dealing a severe blow to the Yankee hopes. The White Sox came to Cleveland on September 23 to close out the Tribe's 21-game homestand with a three-game set.

Mail Call

Chicago won the opener, 10–3, but Cleveland evened the series the next day, September 24, with a 2–0 victory behind the pitching of lefty Walter "Duster" Mails, who had been acquired less than a month earlier from Sacramento. In the fifth inning, Mails struck out Swede Risberg to start the inning but walked the bases full. He then whiffed Buck Weaver and Eddie Collins, stranding Joe Jackson on deck as well as the runners on every bag.

Mails had been making an amazing late-season contribution to the team's pennant hopes. Cleveland had outbid several teams for his purchase from Sacramento after he had been recommended to Speaker by Frank Chance, the former manager of the Yankees and Cubs. His minor league manager, Bill Rodgers, said that Mails "has speed, curves and control ... he'll knock the catcher over."[5] He wound up knocking the socks off Cleveland's opponents, going 7–0 with a 1.85 ERA for Cleveland down the stretch. Although he only played in the major leagues during seven seasons, he appeared in three World Series with three different teams.

Black Sox Impact

The Cleveland–Chicago series concluded on Saturday, September 25. Some 33,000 fans packed League Park for the series finale as Chicago again drew to within a half-game with a 5–1 win.

Club President James Dunn announced on Monday, September 27, that he planned to add temporary bleacher seating, which he hoped would accommodate as many as 6,000 additional fans if the team hosted the World Series.

With the pennant not yet clinched, he admitted that "It is a gamble ... but inasmuch as the stand can not be completed in less than seven days, I could not afford to wait until the winner of the flag is decided, as it would be too late."[6] He then traveled to Chicago for a September 28th meeting, where he planned to ask the National Baseball Commission to delay the World Series opener until October 7. He wanted to allow time for the seats to be added. Some 2,000 were to be inside the right field wall, built upon the usual deep outfield area with more above and beyond the wall, actually outside the park and built above the sidewalk along Lexington Avenue.

With Dunn in Chicago, his team was working on a four-game sweep at St. Louis to pull a game and a half ahead of the White Sox. That day, September 28, eight 1919 White Sox players (seven still on the roster) were indicted by a Cook County grand jury for conspiracy to fix the previous World Series and were immediately suspended for the final three games of the season. Now severely shorthanded, the Sox still managed to win one of those final three games while the Indians, with six games still left, completed the sweep of St. Louis and split a four-game series at Detroit, winning the pennant by two games over the White Sox. Cleveland had clinched the pennant with Bagby's 31st win of the year on the second-to-last day of the season with a 10–1 victory at Detroit on October 2. Speaker hit .388 for the year, second in the league to the .407 mark posted by St. Louis's George Sisler. Sewell, who had taken over at shortstop, batted .329 in 22 games down the stretch.

League Park turnstiles spun like never before in 1920. Only the Polo Grounds in New York attracted more fans than Cleveland. The Yankees, with the dual attractions of Babe Ruth and tight pennant race, drew an all-time record of 1,289,422, nearly double the previous record by any team in a season. The Giants totaled 929,609 for their schedule in the same park. The Indians' final tally was 912,832 fans for 73 home dates, an average of 12,505. Those three teams, along with Brooklyn and the White Sox, all drew higher season totals than any team had done previously in baseball history. To put the Indians' 1920 figures in perspective, Cleveland, with one team, outdrew the combined attendances for the two-team cities of Philadelphia (A's 287,888 and Phillies 330,998), Boston (Red Sox 402,445 and Braves 162,483) and St. Louis (Browns 326,836 and Cardinals 419,311).

As the World Series approached, mail orders for the tickets streamed into the team's office building at the corner of 66th and Lexington, at $5.50 for box seats and $4.00 for reserved. A limit of two tickets per game and a total of eight tickets (with the four potential home games) was imposed with only one order per person allowed. E.S. Barnard, who had been demoted from vice president to director of park operations in favor of newcomer Bob McRoy when Dunn bought the club in 1916, was meticulous in examining the mail orders. Having been elevated to the general manager position earlier in 1920, Barnard personally weeded out many duplicate applications from would-be ticket scalpers.

Best-of-Nine

The cloud on baseball due to the still-breaking Black Sox scandal did not affect enthusiasm in Cleveland for the 1920 World Series. Some naysayers said that Cleveland's pennant was tainted by the Chicago suspensions. In reality, if Chicago had won all of its remaining games after the suspensions, they still would have only tied Cleveland for the flag. Moreover, the Indians undoubtedly would have approached the final game in Detroit, a 6–5 loss, differently had they not already clinched.

The Indians were favorites over the National League champion Brooklyn Robins, not only due to statistically superior hitting and pitching, but also because Brooklyn sportingly agreed to allow shortstop Joe Sewell to be eligible for the World Series even though he had joined Cleveland after the September 1st deadline. Experts also believed that the presence and experience of superstar player-manager Tris Speaker leaned in Cleveland's favor.

Originally scheduled to open at League Park, the series schedule was reversed in order to allow owner James Dunn time to complete the additional seats for the games in Cleveland. This was a compromise selected as a result of Dunn's request to push back the entire series schedule. Rumors circulated that any series would go the full nine games (a best-of-nine format had been re-instituted a year earlier) in order to maximize the gate receipts. Such were the suspicious times in the wake of the Black Sox scandal.

The added seats included a few rows at field level behind the plate, shortening the distance to the backstop. The majority were added to the outfield adjacent to and below the scoreboard and into right-center field in front of the famous wall. A few more were built atop the wall, which extended above the sidewalk along Lexington Avenue. It was said that this idea was later copied in Detroit's Navin Field (later known as Tiger Stadium), where the permanent addition of a second deck behind right field not only protruded beyond the back wall of the lower deck but also hung out farther over the playing field than the first row of lower deck seats.

As the seats were being added, the Indians were on a train from Detroit to New York to begin the World Series at Ebbets Field in Brooklyn.

In Brooklyn

Stan Coveleski took the mound on Tuesday, October 5, for Cleveland's first world championship series since the Spiders played for the Temple Cup

An aerial view of League Park as it appeared during the 1920 World Series. Seating capacity was expanded early in the season with the addition of stands in the left-field corner and field boxes. It was further enlarged for post-season play with seating atop and in front of the wall in right-center field as well as with left-field bleachers and standing room extending all the way to the scoreboard in center field (Cleveland Public Library/Stanley L. McMichael).

in 1896. He allowed five hits, the same as Brooklyn's Rube Marquard did to Cleveland, but sufficiently spread them out while walking just one to post a 3–1 victory.

The Indians got all the runs they needed in the second inning when George Burns led off with a single and moved to second on a walk by Smoky Joe Wood. Sewell singled home Burns and Steve O'Neill doubled home Wood for the 2–0 lead. In the fourth, a one-out double by Wood and another two-bagger by O'Neill made it 3–0. Coveleski's shutout bid went by the board in the seventh when Zach Wheat, who had doubled, scored on an Ed Konetchy groundout. "Covey" set Brooklyn down in order in five of the nine innings and threw just 85 pitches for the win with 23,573 (not a sellout) looking on in the New York borough.

Burleigh Grimes shut out Cleveland 3–0 on seven hits the next day to even the series before 24,559. Jim Bagby took the loss for the Indians, allowing single runs in the first, third and fifth innings.

Brooklyn took the series lead with a 2–1 win on Thursday. Ray "Slim" Caldwell gave up back-to-back RBI singles to Wheat and Hi Myers in the bottom of the first for Brooklyn's only scores of the day. Caldwell had been named the starter when Duster Mails told coach Jack McAllister that he had a sore arm just before game time.

Nevertheless, it was Mails who warmed up in the bullpen when Caldwell got in trouble early. And it was Mails who came in after Myers' hit, to Speaker's evident frustration. Mails settled in and shut down Brooklyn through the eighth and reliever George Uhle, a native Clevelander, did likewise in the final frame. But Cleveland could manage only a single run in the fourth when Speaker doubled and came all the way around to score on Wheat's error in left field.

On the special train back to Cleveland that night, Dunn, already concerned about whether or not the extra seats in League Park were ready to go, now also had to worry about his team's two-game-to-one deficit. But Speaker got the owner to promise him a new suit if Cleveland could win four straight at League Park and avoid the trip back east. "Sunny Jim" agreed and Speaker was certain that his club would make it happen.

Game Four

The World Series was coming to Cleveland on Saturday and the fans couldn't wait. Years of hope and anticipation were being fulfilled and hundreds of fans lined up along Linwood Avenue on the night before the first game. They were waiting to buy $1.10 unreserved bleacher tickets so that they could be first in and get prime spots. It was reported that those nearest the bleacher gate were offered as much as $20 to sell their spot in line. Similarly, $2.20 unreserved grandstand general admission tickets were also sold on the day of the game. One fan who had snuck into the park on Thursday or Friday was discovered hidden beneath the right field stands, complete with a stock of food.

As game time approached, fans who couldn't get in tried to find any spot they could in a tree or on a building with a glimpse of the playing field. The streets around the park were filled with people milling around, hoping to be a part of the action and perhaps find a way inside. In 1920 radio broadcasts of baseball were still a year away. There was a wireless Morse Code–type transmission of the play-by-play, however, which was provided by The *Cleveland Press* that could be received over a 750-mile radius.

With the off day on Friday, Coveleski took the League Park mound for Game Four with a full three days of rest. Brooklyn manager Wilbert Robinson countered with Leon Cadore, who had gained notoriety earlier in the season when Brooklyn had played the Boston Braves to a 1–1 tie in the longest game in major league history. Cadore had thrown all 26 innings!

Cleveland scored two runs in the first, two more in the third and added an insurance run in the sixth as Coveleski again held Brooklyn to five hits and one run, the same as in the opener. His pitch count again was low, report-

During the 1920 World Series, the streets surrounding League Park were filled with activity. This view, which has been mistakenly published in "reversed" fashion on occasion, shows Linwood Avenue along the north side of the ballpark. The error in some printings of this view is known because Linwood ends at the intersection with 70th Street at the upper-right-hand corner of the picture. The third-base and left-field grandstand ran along the sidewalk on the right (Cleveland State University, Cleveland Press Collection).

edly needing only 86 pitches to nail down the win. Sewell made a trio of outstanding defensive plays at shortstop before 25,734.

The series was now even at two games apiece.

Game Five

What was destined to become League Park's most chronicled day was at hand. In fact, it was one of the most memorable days that any ballpark would ever see.

Cleveland won 8–1, clearly not a score that signifies much drama or excitement. But it was how the Indians got to that final count that left 26,684 fans, and all of baseball, abuzz.

After Brooklyn had stranded a runner at third in the top of the first against pitcher Jim Bagby, Cleveland built a threat of its own in the bottom

Following Game Five of the 1920 World Series, when Bill Wambsganss turned the unassisted triple play, "Wamby" posed with the three Brooklyn victims of the play, Pete Kilduff, Clarence Mitchell and Otto Miller. Notice that this photograph was taken in front of the temporary seating area, which was built in front of the regular grandstand in order to increase capacity while encroaching on the field (National Baseball Hall of Fame Library, Cooperstown, N.Y.).

half of the inning. Charlie Jamieson and Bill Wambsganss led off with a pair of singles. Speaker beat out a bunt to load the bases. Next, on a two-strike pitch, clean-up hitter Elmer Smith drove the ball over the temporary seats atop the right field wall for the first grand slam in World Series history! It took some time for the game to resume as the field had been littered with papers and seat cushions, thrown in celebration.

Bagby was not particularly sharp, surrendering 13 hits and striking out only three. But he did not allow a walk and held the visitors scoreless until the ninth when three singles accounted for the lone Brooklyn tally.

It was at the plate, however, where Bagby truly made his mark that day. In the bottom of the fourth, with Doc Johnston on third and Steve O'Neill on first, Bagby looped a fly ball into the temporary seats that had been added in right center field. Cleveland led 7–0. It was the first ever homer by a pitcher in World Series play.

Cleveland turned double plays in the second, third and eighth innings to help keep Brooklyn at bay, but it was what happened in the fifth that clinched the game. Pete Kilduff and Otto Miller were on first and second with nobody out after back-to-back singles as the visitors tried to rally. Clarence Mitchell followed with a line shot toward right center field and the runners took off on what looked like a sure hit. But Wambsganss leaped high at second base and caught it. He then ran to tag second, doubling off Kilduff. He then turned to throw to Johnston at first but Miller had stopped dead in his tracks and "Wamby" tagged him out — an unassisted triple play!

Only Neal Ball, who had accomplished the feat on the same field for Cleveland in 1909, had previously turned the trick. More than ninety years later, it has only happened 15 times, and never since in the World Series.

Cleveland led the series three games to two.

Game Six

Duster Mails started game six on Monday with no sore arm and no problems. An even larger crowd of 27,124 was on hand after Sunday's events. Mails was masterful, allowing only singles in the second and fourth innings along with a double in the eighth. He walked just two while striking out four.

It was scoreless in the sixth when Speaker singled to left with two out. Burns followed with a double to the same field and Speaker scored. The run held up. The Indians won, 1–0, and led the series, 4–2. Brooklyn's Sherry Smith was the hard-luck losing pitcher. Leadoff hitter Joe Evans of the Indians had three hits on the day.

Now Cleveland needed just one more win to take the series and the team could do so at League Park the next day. Tris Speaker was a game away from getting a new suit from team owner James Dunn.

Game Seven

Speaker chose to bring back Coveleski on two days' rest to try and wrap up the series on Tuesday, October 12 in Cleveland. Brooklyn could have come back with its game one starter, Cleveland–native Marquard, but team management was furious with him for getting caught reselling series tickets in front of the team's downtown hotel. Newspaper accounts had stated that the $5.50 tickets to the games in Cleveland were being sold by scalpers for as much as $40. So Brooklyn sent out Grimes, who had pitched all nine innings while winning game two, but who had been knocked out in the fourth inning on Sunday. A crowd of 27,525 hoped to see the Indians win the series at League Park and avoid a trip back to Brooklyn.

The 1920 world champion Indians posed for their team photograph after the death of shortstop Ray Chapman in August, so his picture was inset in the upper-left-hand corner. Also, notice the black arm bands that the team wore in honor of Chapman (Cleveland Public Library).

Coveleski was on his game again. He had allowed three singles and no walks through the first four innings, and Cleveland plated its first run in the bottom of the fourth. With two out and Larry Gardner on third and Doc Johnston on first, Johnston took off for second and stopped short of the bag. Grimes threw wildly to the outfield and Gardner scored.

Speaker made it 2–0 in the fifth, tripling home Jamieson on a drive to the base of the wall in the right field corner. In the seventh, O'Neill doubled but was out on a rundown as Coveleski tried to bunt him to third. Jamieson followed with another double and Coveleski scored. It was 3–0 in favor of Cleveland.

In the ninth, Brooklyn managed its fifth hit of the game, but with two out and the clock reading 3:57 P.M., Coveleski induced Konetchy to hit a ground ball to Sewell at short. His throw to Wambsganss at second ended the game, and the series. It was another five-hitter for Coveleski, this one with no walks and a shutout on 90 pitches. Covey had pitched three complete-game victories in the World Series, while allowing just 15 hits and two bases on balls.[7]

League Park and the city exploded with joy. Fans filled the field to celebrate four straight wins at the home grounds and the championship of baseball. Player–manager Tris Speaker hugged his mother in the box seats near the Indians dugout. An estimated 50,000 turned out for a celebration at Wade Park the next day.

Meanwhile the *Plain Dealer* editorial page, like the city, basked in the thrill of the series victory and boasted that "Sunday's wonderful game, which made Smith and Wambsganss immortal, will be remembered as long as baseball is played."[8] The paper was absolutely right, as this was certainly the most remembered day, and series, in the history of League Park.

4

Call It Dunn Field

Funny thing about stadiums — you're out in the fresh air, but you're really inside a building. You enter the park via a gate, walk through a tunnel, go up a ramp until you reach the top — and then you're outside again. — Ira Rosen, *Blue Skies, Green Fields*

World Champions

By the time the Indians took the field in 1921, League Park had been rechristened as Dunn Field. The owner agreed to change it to his name, telling the *Cleveland Press*, "And now that the Indians are World Champions I have consented to let the name of the ballpark be something else besides simply League Park, as it has been called since I became identified with the club."[1] Over the years, many sources have incorrectly listed the name change as having occurred when Dunn purchased the team in 1916.

He had promised the city a pennant under his guidance when he bought the club and the ballpark, but had decreed that no name change would occur until the promise had been fulfilled. It was a common practice of the day for parks to have the owners' name on them. Examples from the era include Robison Field in St. Louis, Comiskey and Weeghman parks in Chicago, Crosley Field in Cincinnati, Griffith Stadium in Washington and Ebbets Field in Brooklyn, where Cleveland had just played in the World Series. In fact, League Park had even been referred to on occasion as Somers Park before Dunn purchased it and the team from Charles Somers.

As the defending champions of major league baseball, the Indians' jerseys proudly proclaimed "World Champions" across their chests, instead of "Cleveland." Ticket prices were raised a quarter in most areas, and now stood at $1.50 for upper and lower deck box seats, $1.25 for some box seats and all reserved seats, $1.00 for general admission, 75 cents for pavilion seats and 50 cents for the bleachers. More rows were now designated as reserved seats than in the past. Tickets were color-coded in order to assist patrons and the ushers who guided them to their seats.

Opening day for the champs came on Thursday, April 21, against the St.

Louis Browns. Jim Bagby pitched for Cleveland and threw a five-hitter as Cleveland won, 4–3, before 20,000 fans.

During the 1921 season, the Indians donned these somewhat pretentious uniforms in recognition of the 1920 World Series victory. Here pitcher Jim Bagby shows off the outfit (Library of Congress, Prints & Photographs Division, LC-DIG-ppmsca-18474).

Carl Mays made his first Cleveland appearance since the beaning of Ray Chapman on May 16 when New York came to town. With 10,000 in attendance, a large crowd for a Monday, silence greeted Mays as he took the mound. When he came to bat in the second inning, the reaction was also muted. Mays pitched the Yankees to a 6–3 win, and after the final out Cleveland police rushed out to ensure his safety, but there was no incident. The *Cleveland News* said that the "Cleveland baseball fans have again proven that they are the fairest and squarest among the fair and square fans in the country."[2]

For most of the season, the Indians battled the Yankees for the league lead. A July 4th doubleheader at Dunn Field saw first-place Cleveland sweep the White Sox, 11–10 and 6–4. Guy Morton picked up relief wins in both games. He also helped his cause at the plate, garnering three hits, including a double.

On July 20, New York visited to start a big series, taking over first place with a 7–1 win in the opener. The following day, Cleveland reclaimed the league lead, shellacking the Yankees, 17–8, while pounding out 22 hits. The third game was a 3–0 Cleveland win as Allen Sothoron pitched a three-hitter. The final game of the series was on Sunday, July 24. After leading 2–1 in the seventh inning, the Indians fell 7–3 before a packed house of 27,000.

The following Friday, July 29, with the Indians in Boston, Dunn Field was the scene of an Old-Timers game to celebrate the 125th anniversary of the founding of the city of Cleveland. Fifty-five-year-old Cy Young pitched in the game, and the lineup included Napoleon Lajoie, Chief Zimmer, Elmer Flick and Bill Bradley. The Old-Timers defeated a local sandlot team by a score of 11–6 in front of a crowd of 7,500.

August 17 marked the one-year anniversary of Ray Chapman's death and the day was designated as Chapman Day at Dunn Field. The bronze tablet commemorating his career was draped in mourning and young ladies from the YWCA handed out rosebuds to fans. Chapman's widow, Kathleen, declined an invitation from Jim Dunn to attend. In fact, she would never return to the park. Her father, M.B. Daly (the president of the East Ohio Gas Company), attended in her place and sat with Dunn in the owner's box.

With another tight pennant race raging, the Indians defeated last-place Philadelphia 15–8 as Charlie Jamieson, George Burns and Elmer Smith each collected three hits for Cleveland, which held on to first place by a half-game. Eerily, Philadelphia first baseman Johnny Walker was struck in the head and knocked unconscious while diving for a hard shot off the bat of Charlie Jamieson in the first inning. He was rushed to Lakeside Hospital, where the diagnosis was a severe concussion, not a fractured skull, to everyone's relief.

Meanwhile, at Dunn Field, another touching tribute was paid to Chapman in the fifth inning. With Wambsganss at the plate leading off the bottom of the frame, Rollie Naylor delivered ball one. It was at this point in the game a year earlier that the fatal pitch had been delivered. Umpire Billy Evans called time. Wamby and his teammates, now on the top step of their dugout, removed their caps and bowed their heads. A minute later, Evans bade the game go on.

The following week, New York returned to Cleveland for a three-game series. On August 23, the Yankees won the opening game, 6–1, as Babe Ruth blasted a pair of home runs. The next day the Yanks won a controversial decision. With the score tied at two in the top of the ninth, Elmer Miller was on second base for New York. Roger Peckinpaugh bunted, but then stood in front of the plate instead of running to first. Cleveland catcher Steve O'Neill had to shove him out of the way to field the ball and throw to third. Miller was barely safe, but no interference was called and Miller scored the go-ahead run on a sacrifice fly by Wally Pipp as the Yankees won, 3–2. The Indians, now a half-game back of the Yanks, filed a protest but to no avail.

The final game of the series the next day saw Cleveland trounce the Yankees, 15–1. Speaker had two doubles and two singles to pace the Indians and regain first place while closing out the series, which had drawn over 60,000 fans despite being played on a Tuesday, Wednesday and Thursday.

After leading the league for most of the year, Cleveland fell to second place by the end of August and remained there until September 16, when the seventh win of an eight-game winning streak put the Tribe back on top. The streak came at the outset of a 21-game road trip to end the season. The rigors of that trip and a nagging knee injury to Speaker in the final month cost Cleveland its chance to repeat as champions. The Indians went 4–8 in their final 12 games and finished two behind the Yankees. Stan Coveleski won 23 games for Cleveland, which finished with a record of 94–60. The team again ranked second to the Yankees in league attendance at 748,705.

Another old-timers' game was staged late that season at League Park. Featuring former American and National League players, it took place on September 28.

Changing Fortunes

The Indians opened the home schedule in 1922 at Dunn Field on April 12 as Guy Morton pitched a 7–4 win over Detroit. Stuffy McInnis, newly acquired from the Boston Red Sox, played first base and had a single, double and triple for Cleveland. Cold weather kept the crowd down to 14,527 in the first game at the park to be worked by one of the newly instituted three-man umpiring crews.

Another change occurred that year, which was reflected on the League Park scoreboard. Instead of listing the lineups on the board by last name, numbers representing the players were used, although the uniforms remained without numerals. The scoreboard's numbers did match up to numbers and names printed in the five-cent scorecards sold at the ballpark, so this was a ploy to increase scorecard sales.

Just four days later, on a Sunday afternoon, the crowd was 26,000 as Cleveland defeated St. Louis, 3–0, behind the pitching of Walter Mails. After his 7–0 mark down the stretch in 1920 and a 14–8 campaign in 1921, Mails was now known as "The Great" in addition to his original nickname of "Duster." But Mails would go on to win only four games that year, his last in Cleveland.

On June 9, owner Sunny Jim Dunn died of influenza after an extended illness at age 57. His six years as owner had produced the 1920 championship and three second-place finishes. Ownership of the club passed to his wife Edith. Ernest Barnard, who initially had been demoted by Dunn, was now elevated to president of the operation under the guidelines of Dunn's will. Barnard was to hold the title for as long as Dunn's wife retained ownership the team.

The 1922 season ended up being a disappointing one for the Indians as well. A fourth-place finish left them 16 games out of first place with a 78–76 record. Attendance also tumbled to fifth at 528,145. Tris Speaker did have an

While playing at League Park, the Indians were the first team to experiment with uniform numbers that matched roster names in scorecards in 1916. In 1922, the team began listing players by number on the scoreboard that corresponded to the program roster in order to enhance scorecard sales. It was not until the early 1930s that uniform numbers were adopted. Scorecards were both printed and bound within the League Park plant, as seen in this 1940 image showing the binding process taking place (Cleveland State University, Cleveland Press Collection).

outstanding year, batting .378 and leading the league in doubles. George Uhle picked up 23 wins to lead the pitching staff.

The team tried caps with longer bills in 1923 to help out on sunny days and the Indians improved to 82–71, but still finished 16½ games out of first. Attendance was fourth in the league at 558,886. Speaker batted .380 and led the loop in doubles for the fourth straight year. Jamieson hit .345. Cleveland topped the league in team batting average and runs scored, making for some very high-scoring affairs at Dunn Field that year.

In June and July, Cleveland had an extended 32-game homestand at Dunn Field. Offense was in style. On July 3, the Indians led Detroit 8–0 after 6 innings but lost, 12–8. The teams then split a July 4th doubleheader as Cleveland won game one, 10–7, but dropped the nightcap, 15–3. The Tigers pounded out 35 hits on the day. The following Saturday, the Indians opened a doubleheader with Boston by getting 24 hits in a 27–3 win. Scoring in every inning (just the second time an AL team had done so), the Tribe set a league scoring mark for runs in a game that would stand until 1950. The Indians also took game two, 8–5. The next day, 8,600 watched the locals win by a 15–10 margin.

A week later, the Yankees invaded Dunn Field. In the second game of a Saturday doubleheader on July 14, Babe Ruth walked four times and added a single and a long homer over the right field screen. The final game of that series saw Uhle throw a four-hitter as Cleveland won, 12–0. Carl Mays still went the distance for New York, giving up 20 hits as Commissioner Kenesaw Mountain Landis looked on.

The marathon homestand finally ended with a series against Washington and yet another League Park milestone. Walter Johnson, pitching for the second time in the series on Sunday, July 22, 1923, defeated the Indians 3–1. He struck out five, including what was chronicled as the 3,000 of his fabled career, becoming the first pitcher ever to attain that mark. He had taken over as the career strikeout leader two years earlier and would finish with 3508, a mark that stood until Nolan Ryan passed him on April 27, 1983. Johnson was destined to have further influence on League Park history, as he would become the Indians' manager in 1933. Cleveland had won 17 and lost 15 during the home stretch, which had begun on June 23 and ended on July 22. All seven American League foes visited Dunn Field during the homestand.

The Indians outfield that year featured Speaker, who hit .380, Jamieson at .345 and newcomer Homer Summa at .328. Summa went on to gain a reputation as the most proficient outfielder at playing balls off League Park's legendary right field wall and screen.

Cleveland opened the 1924 season at Dunn Field on April 23 with a game against Detroit. A new record opening day attendance 23,815 saw Cleveland score twice in the ninth inning to tie the score at four apiece. George Burns singled in two runs in the tenth to give the Indians a 6–5 victory.

On July 24, the National League New York Giants came to Dunn Field for an exhibition game. Their opponent wasn't the Indians, however. A game had been arranged against the Rosenblums, considered one of the top semi-pro teams in the country. The Giants had concluded a series in Cincinnati the day before and had an off day before resuming their regular season in New York. With a crowd of nearly 10,000 on hand, the Giants won handily, racking up 20 hits in a 19–1 win.

The Indians slumped badly in 1924, finishing the season with a record of 67–86 and in sixth place in the American League. Attendance fell to seventh place at 481,905. One of the great individual hitting performances in park

On opening day in 1924, Cleveland city manager William Hopkins stands in the front row of the upper deck, just to the first-base side of home plate. By looking closely, you can see the tables in the front two rows of the area to the right, which is the open press box area behind home plate. Cleveland's airport is named in honor of Hopkins, who would shortly become involved with plans for the gigantic downtown Cleveland Municipal Stadium (Cleveland State University, Cleveland Press Collection).

history, however, took place that year. On August 2, Joe Hauser of the last-place Philadelphia Athletics hit three home runs over the right field wall and added a double in the visitors' 12–6 win.

Amateur Day in 1924 saw a doubleheader to benefit medical services for sandlot umpires. An old-timers' team faced an amateur team in the opener. The old-timers' lineup included Nap Lajoie, Elmer Flick, Nick Altrock, 57-year-old Cy Young and 63-year-old Chief Zimmer. The old-timers defeated the amateur team, 11–3. In the second game, the Rosenblums returned to Dunn Field and beat White Motors in front of 20,000 fans, who paid 50 cents for grandstand seats and 25 cents for the bleachers.

The 1925 Dunn Field opener had the St. Louis Browns defeating Cleveland, 3–2, in 10 innings. The Indians loaded the bases with one out in the bottom of the ninth inning but were unable to push across the winning run. Attendance was 22,616.

On May 17 that year, Tris Speaker went 3-for-4 and became only the fifth player in baseball history to reach 3,000 career hits. He joined Nap Lajoie as both the second to do it in a Cleveland uniform and the second to reach the milestone at League Park. A Sunday afternoon crowd of 20,000 at Dunn Field saw the Indians lose a 2–1 decision to Washington that day.

Three days later, Cleveland scored a dramatic 10–9 victory over the Yankees by scoring six runs in the bottom of the ninth inning. Speaker scored the winning run all the way from first base on a bases-loaded single by Joe Shaute.

Honus Wagner made a return to League Park in a semi-pro game on Sunday, May 31. The former Pittsburgh star, now 52 years old, was playing for his hometown Carnegie Elks. Wagner played first base for the Elks as they were defeated by the Tellings Cream Tops, 6–5, before 3,000 fans.

On June 19 Goose Goslin led Washington to a 7–5 win at League Park with three homers and a shoestring catch. By that stage of the season, it was clear that Cleveland would not be a factor in the 1925 pennant race, as the team had dropped to the second division, some 14 games out of first place. But one Indian did achieve a noteworthy feat that season. Shortstop Joe Sewell set an amazing record by striking out just four times the entire season. The mark would be bettered, again by Sewell, with just three whiffs in 1930.

As Cleveland's 1925 season wound down toward a second straight sixth-place finish (though fifth in attendance), another old-timers' game turned out to be a late-season highlight. Originally scheduled for September 13, the game was postponed for a week because of rain. Former Cleveland players Jack Graney, Napoleon Lajoie, Terry Turner and Earl Moore were among those who faced a Chicago old-timers' team. Mordecai Brown played for Chicago, as did 72-year-old Jimmy Forest. Intermittent rain held the crowd down to 8000 as the teams played to a 6–6 tie, called after eight innings. A second game featured Collinwood Shale Bricks versus Spencer Diamonds. The gate proceeds were used for the National Baseball Federation tournament.

Seven-year-old Phillip Appelbaum slipped under a turnstile at the home opener in 1926 and wandered right onto the field just beyond Detroit's third-base dugout. That's where a *Cleveland Press* photographer caught him curled up inside the infield tarp during the pre-game ceremonies. The child wound up back in the grandstand for the game, reunited with his older brothers and some 25,000 other fans as the Indians won, 12–2. That win was part of a 15–10 start that had the team tied for first on May 10 but Cleveland fell all the way to sixth by the end of the month. Then the Indians again caught fire and reached second place on July 21. The Tribe stayed in that spot in pursuit of the Yankees through mid–September when New York, with a 5½ game lead, came to Dunn Field for a crucial six-game series.

George Uhle, who had beaten New York five straight times, got the start. In addition, Uhle had held Babe Ruth to just five singles all year, having struck him out seven times, three with the bases loaded. But the Yankees beat Uhle this time, 6–4, before a crowd of 22,000 on Wednesday, September 15. Cleveland came back with four wins in a row, sweeping a doubleheader 2–1 and 5–0 the next day as Ruth was walked five times by Indians pitchers Emil Levsen and Garland Buckeye. The Indians won 5–1 on Friday behind the pitching of Joe Shaute and 3–1 on Saturday with George Uhle again on the mound for his 25th victory of the year. A crowd

Tris Speaker emerges from the dugout, bat in hand. Speaker was player-manager of Cleveland's 1920 world championship team and was an original inductee to the Baseball Hall of Fame in 1936. His name is among the top four from the League Park era of Cleveland baseball, along with Cy Young, Nap Lajoie and Bob Feller (Cleveland Public Library).

of 27,000 saw the Saturday game as pennant fever gripped the city and Cleveland moved to within 2½ games of first.

The final game of the series, on Sunday, saw more than 10,000 fans turned away at the gates as a new record crowd of 30,805 jammed inside Dunn Field. Mounted police were on hand to maintain order. But home runs by Babe Ruth and Lou Gehrig keyed the Yankees to an 8–3 win.

The Indians still were only two games back heading into the final weekend series at Philadelphia, but the Tribe lost three of four and settled for second place with a record of 88–66. Uhle finished with a record of 27–11 to lead the pitching staff. First baseman George Burns, from nearby Niles, Ohio, batted .358 and set a new major league record with 64 doubles. A right-handed hitter, Burns peppered League Park's right field wall and deep gap in left center to set a mark that has since been bettered only once in major league history. He was named the American League's Most Valuable Player for 1926. The late-season pennant run helped improve team attendance to 627,426, inferior only to the 1920 and 1921 crowd counts. When the Indians opened the 1927 season, long-time hero Tris Speaker was gone. In November 1926, Ty Cobb had resigned as manager of Detroit and Speaker did likewise a few weeks later. The pair had been implicated in a betting scandal by former Tigers pitcher Dutch Leonard. The allegation was that Speaker and Cobb had fixed the outcome of a game in 1919 in order to guarantee third-place money for the Tigers. The issue reached the desk of Commissioner Landis, who exonerated both Speaker and Cobb, partly because Leonard refused to appear for hearings on the matter. Speaker moved on to Washington while Cobb wound up with the Philadelphia Athletics. To this day, Speaker remains baseball's career doubles leader with 792. A total of 386 of those two-baggers came during his 11 seasons in Cleveland and, of course, many at League Park. His 3514 career hits still rank fifth all-time.

April 12 was opening day in 1927, with Jack McAllister the new Cleveland manager and the Chicago White Sox the opponents. Bernie Neis was filling the shoes of Speaker in center field. George Uhle pitched a six-hitter and went 3-for-3 at the plate as Cleveland won, 3–2, before 21,902.

Speaker made his return to Cleveland on May 14 and another "Speaker Day" was declared. Numerous city officials were on hand, including representatives of the police and fire departments. The 70-member Martins Ferry High School marching band provided the music. Speaker was presented with a floral arrangement and a life-sized painting of himself, though he went hitless in four at bats and the Indians won, 5–2. Six days later, a game against the Yankees was held up midstream for the playing of "The Star Spangled Banner," as word had reached Dunn Field that Charles Lindbergh had successfully completed his trans–Atlantic flight.

That season was dominated by what many consider the greatest baseball team of all time, the 1927 New York Yankees. At Dunn Field, however, the Yanks were swept in a series for the only time that year. Mired in sixth place and 34 games behind the vaunted "Murderers' Row" squad, Cleveland opened the series on Saturday, August 20 with a 14–8 win in front of 11,000. Babe Ruth homered but the Indians had 19 base hits to take the game. The next day, with Willis Hudlin pitching, Cleveland won 7–4 in front of 20,000 fans. The Indians concluded the sweep with 19 more hits on Monday to register a 9–4 win. New York still had a 12½ game lead over second-place Philadelphia. Cleveland attendance wound up falling to seventh in the league for the year at 373,138 as the team finished at a disappointing 66–87.

Ballpark Memories

Nineteen twenty-seven was also the year that Wes Ferrell, a 19-year-old prospect from North Carolina received a tryout with the Cleveland team.

Years later, after a career in which he was a 20-game winner six times, Ferrell related the story of his tryout.

> So here I go, still a little old country boy with a drawl thick as molasses, getting on the train and heading out to Cleveland. When I got off the train I asked somebody how to get to League Park. They put me on a streetcar and I told the conductor where I wanted to get off. It was quite a long ride and finally he looked at me and said, "This is it."
>
> I get off the streetcar and I'm looking for a ballpark. Now the only ballparks I'd ever seen were back home and what those were, were playing fields with wooden fences around them. So I'm looking around and I don't see a ballpark. Some kids were playing in the street and I asked them where League Park was. They pointed and said "That's it."
>
> Well, I turned around and looked up. And there's this great stone structure. Biggest thing I ever saw in my life. They call this a ballpark? I couldn't believe it. Then I heard a little noise in the back of my mind: *major leagues.* The sound of those two words was an instant education.
>
> So I took a tighter hold of my suitcase and walked through the gates of that thing, staring up and around at everything like I was walking through a palace. I went past all those great stone pillars and got up onto a concrete runway and looked way down and there at the end was a beautiful green ball field and guys playing ball on it. There was a game going on. And all of a sudden the notion of baseball got as big as all get-out in my mind. Seeing it played down there in that setting was just beautiful."[3]

It was beautiful to the fans of that era as well. Kids would fight for baseballs hit onto Lexington Avenue during batting practice and turn them in for free admission. From their stomachs, they would plead through the space at the bottom of the exit gates for the players to throw one over the wall. They would drill holes wherever possible for a peek at the action, and drill them again when management covered them up. Schoolchildren would clamor for and trade the free tickets that the club distributed through the school system for games during the summer. Some kids were lucky enough to get jobs selling scorecards or concessions. Kids throughout the city also played "wall," throwing and fielding balls as they bounced off neighborhood walls just like their heroes at League Park.

Ladies' Day, a popular promotion throughout baseball over the years, was also staged at League Park. The ladies sat for free in the upper deck while the ticket-buying gentlemen sat below. Purportedly, some of the ladies brought their knitting and used the yarn to dangle notes down to the men in the lower deck. Sometimes they even tried to "talk" to the players in this way.

The neighborhood thrived off the games and local residents charged a quarter each for cars to park on their lawns. Along East 66th Street, across from the back of the first base grandstand, were a number of businesses that took advantage of the ballpark's proximity. These included the Ma and Pa Sandwich Bar, Gensert's Drug Store and soda fountain, a saloon known as

Hilliard's Wind-Up Cafe, and a bowling alley and billiard parlor called the Ball Park Recreation Co., all frequented by fans and players alike. Roblin's blacksmith shop and Gus Nickel's barber shop were also fixtures along the street.

Sometime in this era a leather-lunged character known as "Baltimore" first made his mark with the persistent comments that he bellowed from the left field pavilion seats. It was said that Baltimore earned the nickname because his voice boomed like a foghorn on the ships in the Chesapeake at that city's port. Legend also has it that Baltimore's voice and comments invoked the ire and response of various players over the years, including White Sox pitcher Milt Gaston, who supposedly responded to some remarks by engaging in fisticuffs with Baltimore one day beneath the stands. His presence remained synonymous with the ballpark for many years.

It was also around this time that Joe Bertman, who had founded his Bertman Foods company in a garage not far from the Indians' home in 1925, convinced the team to serve his spicy brown mustard for hot dogs at the park's concession stands. The product is still made on Cleveland's East Side, less than a ten-minute drive from the League Park site, and it is still served at Cleveland Indians games today.

While the mustard became a Cleveland tradition, change was in the offing for the ballclub after the 1927 season. Cleveland's 66 wins were only enough for a sixth-place finish for the third time in four years, this time 43½ games behind the Yankee juggernaut. Dunn's widow, now remarried to a man named George Pross, sold the team and the ballpark that her late husband had purchased for $500,000 in 1916. She was paid $1 million by a syndicate headed by local real estate businessman Alva Bradley. It also marked the end of a run for longtime club executive Ernest S. "Barney" Barnard, who had overseen the park's transformation to concrete and steel nearly two decades earlier. Barnard was named president of the American League. In his place, former umpire Billy Evans became the new general manager of the Indians, and former Cleveland player Roger Peckinpaugh, born in Wooster, Ohio, and a product of the Cleveland sandlots, was hired as field manager.

The Public Be Pleased

Although the Dunn Field name was still often used, fans had never really let go of the League Park moniker. The original name became even more common as Jim Dunn's legacy became more distant following the sale of the club by his widow. Meanwhile, the new ownership promoted a renewed commitment to fan satisfaction. "The Public Be Pleased" was the slogan that General

Manager Evans adopted for the 1928 season. The promise was to improve the team on the field while placing a premium on customer service at League Park. The team even paid tribute to its longtime ticket office overseer, Miss Edna Jameson, and her "faithful and efficient" service to the Cleveland fans. Edna had begun with the Naps in 1913 and eventually worked for the team for over 40 years.

One thing that the renewed approach couldn't change that year was the Yankees' dominance in the American League. But the New Yorkers did provide for some of the memorable games at League Park again that year. On June 6, New York opened a series with Cleveland by pounding out 16 hits in an 8–3 win. The next

Radio broadcasts of Indians games from League Park did not begin until the 1928 season. Here is an early "portable" radio being used in the stands. This view also gives a good look at the ballpark's seats, as well as a glimpse at the ornate armrests at the end of each row, visible just to the left and above the man's hand and knee (National Baseball Hall of Fame Library, Cooperstown, N.Y.).

day, Cleveland led 1–0 in the seventh inning before Tony Lazzeri, Babe Ruth and Lou Gehrig all homered over the right-field fence and the Yankees won, 8–2. Following a rainout on June 8, the Indians turned a triple play in the second inning the next day, but the Yankees won 7–3 with Gehrig homering again. New York already led second-place Philadelphia by 10½ games at that point with a record of 39–8.

Philadelphia came to town the following week, and Lefty Grove pitched the visitors to a 12–5 win on June 15. Ty Cobb, in his final season, doubled and wound up stealing home plate for the record 54th and final time of his career.

A brass band plays "The Star-Spangled Banner" during pre-game ceremonies as dignitaries honor the flag on opening day in 1928. This view from field level gives a good view of the separation and difference in construction between the main grandstand and the pavilion seats beyond third base (Cleveland State University, Cleveland Press Collection).

On July 25 and 26, Cleveland swept visiting Boston in back-to-back doubleheaders, 10–2 and 15–5 the first day, and 4–2 and 4–3 the next. Obviously thin in pitching at that point, Cleveland's scheduled single game on July 27 versus New York was rained out, although the "official announcement that the game was off was made at a time when the sun was shining brightly," according to the *Plain Dealer*.[4] The following day became a doubleheader, which New York and Cleveland split, as the Indians rapped out 19 hits to win the second game, 9–4. But that was just a prelude to what would happen the next day, July 29, when Indians batters totaled 27 hits in a 24–6 win over the Yankees, including a major league record 24 singles. A crowd of 25,000 was on hand for the contest, which saw the Tribe score eight times in the first inning and add nine more runs in the second. Johnny Hodapp became the first American Leaguer to record two hits in an inning twice in the same game, getting a pair of singles in both the second and sixth innings. Cleveland's 24 runs that day still stands as the most ever allowed by the Yanks in a game.

Cleveland finished the 1928 season ranked seventh in both the league standings and attendance, compiling a season record of 62–92 before 375,907 home fans. That season marked the first for baseball on the radio from League Park as chronicled in the book *The Golden Voices of Baseball*. Baseball had debuted on the radio on Pittsburgh's KDKA in 1921, but many owners were hesitant to "give" the games away to the fans and potentially hurt ticket sales. This apparently had been the thinking under the previous Cleveland ownership, but on June 26 GM Billy Evans placed games on WTAM with Tom "Red" Manning at the microphone. Manning had done the announcing at League Park over a megaphone since the 1920 world championship season.

The event with the greatest potential to affect League Park and its future came in the off-season. In the November 1928 election, Cleveland voters approved financing for the construction of a huge $2.5 million downtown multipurpose stadium on the lakefront. The new ballpark had been supported by former team president Barnard, so the assumption was that this new park would replace League Park as the Indians' home when finished. But a publicly financed stadium was still a new and controversial concept and legal delays held off groundbreaking until 1930. So for the time being at least, it remained business as usual for League Park in its role as the home for big league baseball in the city of Cleveland.

Ruth's 500th

After the poor showing during the 1928 season, the 1929 Cleveland team had a number of new names. Leading the way was hard-hitting outfielder Earl Averill, who was acquired from San Francisco of the Pacific Coast League. Averill had so impressed during spring training that he was put in the number three spot in the batting order for his major league debut on opening day, April 16 at League Park. Detroit pitcher Earl Whitehill's first pitch was on the fists of the left-handed-hitting rookie. Averill powered it over the right field wall and the Indians went on to win, 5–4 in 11 innings. Averill had become the first-ever American Leaguer to homer in his first big league at-bat. He went on to become a fan favorite and a Hall of Famer.

Later that season, a doubleheader sweep of St. Louis in front of 22,000 on Labor Day at League Park lifted Cleveland into third place. And that's where the team finished, with a record of 81–71, a marked improvement over the previous year, but still 24 games out of first place. Home attendance did increase by more than 150,000 to 536,210, good enough for fourth in the AL.

On August 11, with construction of the new ballyard still looming, League Park once again showed its propensity for hosting memorable events. One of the great milestones in baseball history was reached that day when Babe Ruth blasted the 500th home run of his career.

Ruth had had quite a bit of success against Cleveland over the years, especially at League Park, with its inviting right-field wall for left-handed hitters like the Babe. Even during his first full big league season as a pitcher in 1915, Ruth had success at League Park, twice taking the mound as a starter and winning both games. In 1916, he tossed a pair of shutouts against the Indians in Cleveland.

It was Ruth's home runs, however, that brought fans to League Park and ballparks across the country. And it wasn't just the quantity, though the numbers were staggering. It was that he also hit the ball farther than anybody else ever had. On June 5, 1918, while still splitting time as a pitcher and hitter for Boston, he hit his seventh home run of the season at League Park, "crushing the ball so hard that it went past a house on the other side of the street."[5]

. After slugging the amazing total of 54 homers in 1920, his first year in New York, Ruth came to Cleveland on May 14, 1921. With a crowd of 20,000 on hand, Ruth hit the first home run ever into the center field bleachers at League Park, just to the left of the scoreboard. Reportedly, center fielder Tris Speaker never even moved, simply turning to watch.[6]

During Ruth's record-setting 60 home run season in 1927, three of his circuit clouts came at League Park. The first, on May 22, was a towering fly ball that went as high as it did far before dropping over the fence. In August he added homers 39 and 40 while in Cleveland.

When the Yankees came to Cleveland in August of 1929, Ruth was on fire, having homered in five of his last six games. He didn't homer in the series opener against Cleveland on Saturday, so the Sunday crowd of 25,000 hoped to see history. Before the game, Ruth said to H. Clay Folger, the head of security at League Park, "Listen, I'm going to hit number 500 today, and I tell you what I'd wish you'd do. I wish you'd find the kid who gets the ball and bring him to me. I'd kinda like to save that one."[7]

Right-hander Willis Hudlin was pitching for the Indians that day. Ruth, the first batter he faced in the second inning, drove the first pitch over the screen in right and onto Lexington Avenue. The ball was retrieved by 12-year old Jake Geiser of New Philadelphia, Ohio, who was outside the park along Lexington Avenue when the blow was struck. He was brought to the Yankees dugout where Ruth traded two new autographed baseballs and $20 for the milestone ball. Lou Gehrig also homered for the New York that day but Cleveland won the game, 6–5.

Big Brother Looms

Following the stock market crash of 1929 and the onset of the depression, the 1930 census showed that the city population dropped slightly below 900,000. But the region had continued to grow and the 25,000 seats at League

The first-base grandstand and right-field-line seats as they appeared in 1930, likely with the park set up for opening day with the bunting hanging off the front of the upper deck. Notice the field box seats on both sides of the dugout, which were added in the 1920 expansion. The section of seats furthest down the right-field line at that time were still of the temporary, "circus-style" variety. The 1920 field box additions afforded those fans with one of the most unique views in the history of baseball, where fans could look over their shoulder and back into the dugout. Also, note the open press box area of tables directly behind home plate in the front of the upper deck. Finally, the girders allowed for a roof to cover many of the ballpark's seats and allowed the upper deck to overhang dramatically out toward the field for outstanding views (Cleveland State University, Cleveland Press Collection).

Park now seemed inadequate, even in tough times, when the top contenders came to town.

Despite those tough times, a fresh coat of green paint covered League Park on opening day 1930. In the sixth inning, a 16-year-old came onto the playing field and prevented Charlie Jamieson from making a catch, costing Cleveland a run in a 4–3 loss to Chicago. In its coverage the next day, the *Plain Dealer* stated that "This will be the last full season (at League Park) if the city gets the new lake front stadium done on schedule."[8]

On Sunday, May 11, the Indians hosted Philadelphia and the limited seat-

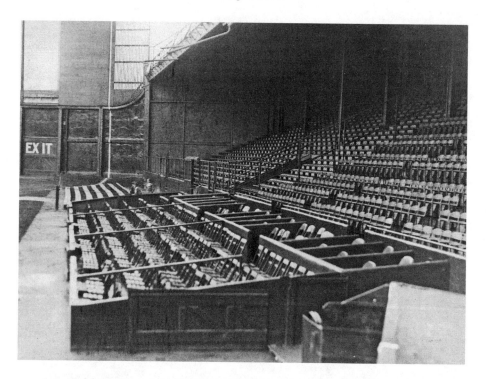

A ground-level view of the field box seating area that was added in 1920 shows the detail and scope of the project in this 1930 photograph. The "wildcat" bleachers, beyond the field boxes, would be replaced with a permanent seating area when the team returned to League Park in 1934 after its season-and-a-half shift of games to gigantic Cleveland Municipal Stadium (Cleveland State University, Cleveland Press Collection).

ing was again at issue. The expected crowd caused the *Plain Dealer* to report that "There are about 25,000 men, women and children who are keenly disappointed over the inability to purchase seats for this game — folks who would surely go if they could gain admittance."

Those who couldn't fit into League Park that day missed quite a game. Those who did, 28,332 of them, saw the Indians destroy Philadelphia by a score of 25–7. Cleveland had 25 hits, including a 5-for-5 day by Bibb Falk. In the seventh inning, Indians pitcher Sal Gliatta committed balks on two consecutive pitches, most certainly a rarity.

Later in that month, on May 26, Indians third baseman Joe Sewell was struck out twice by Chicago's Pat Caraway at League Park. Amazingly Sewell, the greatest contact hitter in baseball history, struck out just one other time in 414 plate appearances that season.

The next day, May 27, Dave Harris of Chicago hit a ball onto Lexington

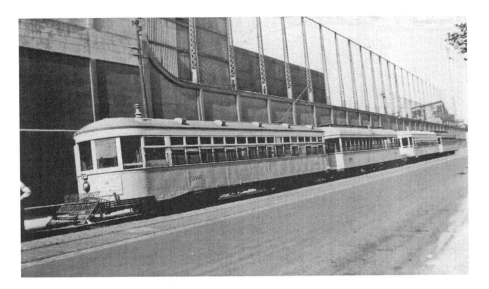

Perhaps the two most important features of League Park are pictured together here in the 1930s or 1940s. Trolley lines served the location throughout its history, and the line that passed by the location in 1891 was also owned by Cleveland Spiders owner Frank DeHass Robison, leading him to select the location for his new ballpark. The park's famed right-field wall looms behind the cars, with an excellent view of the 25-foot-high "screen monster" atop the 20-foot concrete wall. The center-field scoreboard is also visible at the far right (Cleveland State University, Brookins Collection).

Avenue, homering on a ball "that would have been no more than a two-base hit a couple of days ago," according to the *Plain Dealer.*[9] He was the first player to take advantage of an adjustment to the screen above the wall in right center field, part of which had been removed from above the exit gate in that area. Pitcher Mel Harder still tossed a complete game, 3–2 win for the Indians that day.

New York made its first visit of the season to League Park in mid–June. For a decade the Yankees had been baseball's biggest draw and when they came to town on Saturday, June 14, the Indians were tied for first with Philadelphia, with Washington a half-game back and New York two behind. The Yanks swept the three-game series in Cleveland, but the Sunday game was historic. Not because of the 17–10 defeat suffered by the Indians, but for the fact that somehow 33,628 fans attended, League Park's greatest throng ever. Thousands stood in deep left field behind ropes and in front of the bleachers for a total that would never be topped.

When the Yankees returned for a series in July, Cleveland was in fourth place, but the fans were provided with some of the most exciting baseball of the year. The first game, on July 20, had New York ahead 8–7 in the ninth inning. Ruth and Gehrig had already homered for the visitors, Gehrig twice. But Eddie Morgan smacked a game-ending, two-run homer to give Cleveland a 9–8 victory.

The next day, the Yankees won, 7–3, as Ruth and Gehrig again homered. The following day a doubleheader was scheduled. With 18,000 in the stands, the Indians came from behind to win the first game, 6–5. In the second game, Earl Averill hit two home runs to help Cleveland sweep with a 10–8 win. The series finale saw Wes Ferrell win his 15th game of the year for Cleveland, 10–6. Morgan set a new club record with his 19th home run of the season.

Philadelphia solidified its hold on first place in the next series at League Park, beating Cleveland 8–6 in the opener. Jimmy Foxx and Al Simmons homered for Philadelphia while Morgan launched one for the Indians that landed on a rooftop across Lexington Avenue. The A's got three more homers in each of the next two games, winning 14–1 and 10–9 before Ferrell salvaged the final game for Cleveland, 7–4.

In the 14–1 Philadelphia win on July 25, the Athletics pulled off not one, but two, *triple* steals, yet another remarkable League Park achievement. Al Simmons scored the run on the first triple swipe as part of a three-run first inning with Pete Jablonowski on the mound for Cleveland. Mickey Cochrane came home on the second three-bag theft during the seven-run fourth with Pinkey Shoffner pitching.

The longest game in innings yet played in League Park occurred on August 14 as Philadelphia beat Cleveland 5–3 in 17 innings. Lefty Grove pitched the entire game for Philadelphia, giving up 20 hits and raising his season record to 18–2.

Earl Averill had a huge day at League Park on September 17. He homered three times (one a grand slam) and had eight runs batted in during a 13–3 win in the opener of a doubleheader with second-place Washington. He homered again in game two and just missed a fifth, barely foul, in the eighth inning. Only Stan Musial and Nate Colbert have bettered the feat in major league history, with five homers in a day.

The season concluded on September 28 as the Indians met St. Louis in a doubleheader at League Park. Cleveland had 34 hits for the day, losing the first game, 11–5, and winning the second, 15–5, to put the team's record at 81–73, good for fourth place in the final standings. Attendance just about held even from the year before at 528,483.

On June 24, 1930, the first bulldozer had arrived to begin construction on the mammoth stadium by Lake Erie. On July 1, 1931, barely a year later, the new park and its 78,189 seats would be ready, but would the Indians?

5

Surviving the Stadium

The most beautiful thing in the world is a ballpark filled with people —
Bill Veeck, team owner

Uncertain Times

As construction on the new lakefront stadium quickly progressed, the Indians opened the 1931 season at their Lexington Avenue home on April 14 against the White Sox. A public address system had been installed at League Park to replace the megaphone announcements and another new opening day record crowd of 25,162 saw Wes Ferrell pitch and hit the Indians to a 5–4 win. He scattered eight hits while scoring twice and driving in two runs to help his cause.

Flags were at half-mast for the opener in respect for former team president, and sitting American League president, E. S. "Barney" Barnard, who had died of a heart attack on March 30 at the age of 56. Instrumental in the 1910 conversion of League Park to concrete and steel, Barnard had worked for the team from 1903 to 1927. Ironically, among his many innovations was the introduction of megaphone announcers to the League Park grounds during the time of its wooden configuration.

Another Cleveland tradition that remains to this day was already in place. When the Indians were home and the game was on, a special flag flew atop the recently completed Terminal Tower on Cleveland's Public Square for all to see. The Terminal Tower, completed just a few years earlier, remained the tallest building in the United States outside of New York City until 1967.

Rookie Joe Vosmik, a native Clevelander, had opened many eyes by starting the 1931 season 12-for-18 at the plate, with 22 total bases. During that stretch, he hit his first career home run on Sunday, April 19, before a capacity crowd at League Park off Detroit's Earl Whitehill, the same pitcher who had allowed Earl Averill a homer on his first career at bat two years earlier. Whitehill and the Tigers did win the game, however, 7–2.

Two weeks into the campaign, on August 29, Ferrell threw a no-hitter

91

Inside League Park on an opening day in the early or mid–1930s, with virtually every available space was occupied. Vendors, because of their white coats, are easily identifiable throughout the crowd (Cleveland Public Library).

against St. Louis at League Park, picking up his fourth win of the young season. With his brother Rick at bat for St. Louis in the eighth, the Indians hurler allowed a grounder to deep shortstop, where Bill Hunnefield was charged with an error when his throw to first pulled Lew Fonseca off the bag, keeping the no-hitter intact. But it was Wes's hitting that day that truly made the performance special. The pitcher thrilled the Wednesday afternoon crowd of 4000 with a home run, a double and four RBI in the 9–0 win. The feat of homering while throwing a no-hitter was another major league first at League Park and has only been accomplished three times since. Ferrell's hitting that day was not a fluke as he wound up posting 36 career homers, the big league record for a pitcher.

Ferrell's feat turned out to be the fourth and final no-hitter at the League Park grounds (all by Cleveland hurlers) and the only one in the park's steel-and-concrete configuration. It was the first since the famous Addie Joss perfect game of 1908. The others had been tossed by Cy Young in 1897 and by Bob Rhoads, whose no-hitter occurred exactly two weeks before Joss's gem. There is no doubt that throwing a no-hitter with the looming right field wall in League Park was quite a feat.

One legendary story from League Park history is also credited to the 1931 season, but this one is just that ... only a legend. It has been chronicled that Chicago right fielder Smead Jolley made three errors on one play on September 9 that year. It is true that Jolley was known for his sub-par fielding prowess and that League Park's right field wall could be especially tough to judge. But there is no evidence to support the story that Jolley let a ball go through his legs to the wall for one error, that it rebounded past him for a second, and that he recovered the ball and threw wildly to the infield for a third.

In fact, Jolley was charged with an error that day on a double by Vosmik that did get to the wall. He was charged with that single error when his wild throw to the infield allowed Ed Morgan to score. And it is likely that the ball had initially skipped past him to the wall. He may have even had a difficult time with the rebound. But the three-error tale is clearly an exaggeration, as research later showed that he was never charged with even two errors in any one game. The tale was later credited to other ballparks and dates, likely perpetrated by story-tellers who wanted to emphasize Jolley's reputation as a poor fielder.

Jolley had, in fact, turned an outstanding defensive play at League Park the season before, on May 27, 1930. In the fourth inning of the second game of a doubleheader, he charged in and caught a short fly off the bat of pitcher Pete Jablonowski and beat baserunner Carl Lind back to the bag at second for an unassisted double play. This was the same play that legendary Cleveland defender Tris Speaker had become noted for during his career. Jolley also went 4-for-4 at the plate in that game (and 6-for-9 on the day), including a home run in both ends of the doubleheader, again proving that League Park magic (both offensively and defensively in this case) could work for visiting players too.

Meanwhile, on July 1, 1931, Cleveland Stadium had officially opened with a ceremony before a crowd of more than 8000. Two days later, Max Schmeling retained his heavyweight boxing title in the new venue's first sporting event before 37,396, fewer than anticipated by the promoters, but still more than League Park had ever held for an event. Two weeks later, the first baseball game was played there, but it did not feature the Indians. As part of the Shriners' national convention that was in town, the Koran Shrine defeated Al Sirat Grotto, 6–1, before 26,000 conventioneers.

Despite the playing of that showcase event, and likely to the consternation of city officials, owner Alva Bradley made no public expression of a desire to leave League Park. After all, he owned that facility and had no rent to pay. Ultimately, that fact would allow him to hold out for the best possible deal from the city, although the *Plain Dealer* did report in July that Bradley was offering to sell League Park for $300,000 (the same amount as its construction price in 1910) if the team did move to the new stadium. Additionally, despite excellent seasons by Morgan and Averill, as well as the emergence of Vosmik, League Park's capacity had only been pressed only on opening day, as the team posted a mediocre fourth-place finish and 78–76 record as 483,027 watched that year.

Negotiations continued and League Park's days appeared more and more to be numbered, but the 1932 season began as usual at League Park. After both teams paraded to the center-field flagpole for "The Star Spangled Banner" (not yet an everyday occurrence at American sporting events) and mayor Ray T. Miller threw out the first ball, Cleveland lost 2–1 to Detroit in the home debut on that Wednesday, April 20. The game drew 22,995, but general manager Billy Evans ominously stated, "If the opener has [sic] been played at the Stadium, we would have had a crowd of more than 40,000."[1] Evans cited that advance requests far exceeded the number of reserved seats available and added that the club "turned back in the mails ... more than $15,000."

One other precedent-setting change for 1932 took place in League Park's broadcast area. Jack Graney, the former player who had recently served as the ballpark's megaphone announcer, took over as play-by-play man as the game broadcasts switched to WHK. It was another League Park first, as Graney became the first of many former athletes to make the transition to the broadcast booth.

Holding On

Though the Park's days were seemingly dwindling, its propensity for the spotlight did go away. One of the ballpark's most disturbing events took place after a Memorial Day doubleheader on May 30. Umpire George Moriarty was attacked and severely beaten by a group of Chicago players after the Indians completed a doubleheader sweep of the White Sox. A former Detroit Tiger, the now 47-year-old umpire had ejected Chicago coach Johnny Butler in the second game. Former Indian Lew Fonseca, now managing the Sox, claimed that Moriarty had been abusive to his team throughout the game. Chicago's frustrations mounted as Cleveland won game one and then scored four runs in the bottom of the ninth of game two to pull out a 12–11 decision. Tempers had flared over a disputed ball-strike call on Averill during the rally.

After the game, Chicago's Charlie Berry challenged Moriarty to a fight and Moriarty accepted the challenge in the runway to the clubhouse. Moriarty was getting the best of the fight when four other White Sox players joined in, including Milt Gaston, who had also once engaged in a fight with the loud

Members of the grounds crew lay sod in foul territory just beyond first base in 1932. Negotiations for the use of Cleveland's new Municipal Stadium were going on at the time and the Indians would eventually abandon club-owned League Park in August, only to return in 1934 (Cleveland State University, Cleveland Press Collection).

League Park fan known as "Baltimore." Cleveland players finally interceded to stop the beating. Indians president Alva Bradley took the injured umpire to the Cleveland Clinic for treatment. American League president Will Harridge investigated and wound up suspending three Chicago players and Fonseca, while doling out fines of $1350 to them, along with a reprimand to Moriarty.

Then, on July 10, things turned downright bizarre when the Philadelphia Athletics came to Cleveland for a single contest. Philadelphia was still fighting its city "blue laws" against Sunday baseball that Cleveland had finally overcome some 20 years before. So the A's were scheduled to play the Indians in a single game that day at League Park before the teams continued the series in Philadelphia on Monday. Philadelphia was coming off of consecutive doubleheaders on Thursday, Friday and Saturday at Shibe Park in Philly. The A's had won four of those six games and stood in second place behind New York.

Cleveland, meanwhile, was in Washington, with twinbills on Thursday and Saturday and "just" one game on Friday. So both teams took overnight trains into Cleveland on Saturday night. It was a recipe for disaster.

Some 10,000 fans showed up at League Park to watch the exhausted players. A's manager Connie Mack left starting catcher Mickey Cochrane home to give him a day off and brought just two pitchers, rookie Lew Krausse and 34-year-old knuckleballing reliever Ed Rommel. After all, there would be another train ride back to Philadelphia after the Sunday game and there was another doubleheader looming on Monday, followed by single games on Tuesday and Wednesday.

Philadelphia got two runs in the top of the first but Krausse gave up three in the bottom of the frame on a blast over the screen in right by Earl Averill. Krausse struggled to get out of the inning as Cleveland again loaded the bases on a pair of singles and a walk. A double play ended it, but Mack had seen enough. He sent Rommel to the mound in the second. Jimmie Foxx, on fire at the plate, tied the game with a homer to the bleachers in left, his 31st of the season.

Then things really began to unravel. The A's scored twice in the fourth and Cleveland responded with three runs of its own. The Indians made it 7–5 in the fifth and each team added another run in the sixth, making it 8–6 in favor of the Tribe. But Philadelphia rallied for a seven-run seventh, including another long homer to left by Foxx. The boos from the faithful at League Park turned again to cheers in the last of the seventh as the Tribe answered with six runs, making it 14–13 Cleveland.

That score held through the eighth inning, but Foxx hit a two-run double in the ninth and Philly led 15–14. Willie Kamm scored on a hit by Johnny Burnett for Cleveland in the ninth to tie matters again. But Mule Haas made a diving catch of a Joe Vosmik drive down the right field line with two out to send the game to extra innings.

Rommel continued to toil through the extra frames for Philadelphia. And Wes Farrell, who had entered in the seventh, was now racking up innings for Cleveland. Neither team could score during the first six extra frames. Finally, in the 16th, Foxx struck again with his third round-tripper of the day, scoring Al Simmons in front of him and making it 17–15 Philadelphia.

Empty streetcars waited outside the Lexington Avenue gates as afternoon turned to early evening and Cleveland came to bat. Dick Porter doubled to center and Johnny Burnett followed with his *ninth* hit of the game, still a major league record, sending Porter to third. Both wound up scoring, Burnett tallying the tying run on a single by Ed Morgan. With two on and two out, Bill Cissell's drive to the wall in right was tracked down by Haas with a leaping grab. The score now stood at 17–17.

After a scoreless 17th inning, Foxx got his sixth hit of the day with two out in the 18th. Eric McNair followed with a hit to left that bounced past Vosmik and Foxx scored the lead run. So Rommel came out for the bottom of the 18th and struck out Averill, got Vosmik to ground out and whiffed Morgan to end the game. Rommel threw an amazing 17 innings of relief to get the win, the 171st and last of his career, giving up 29 of Cleveland's 33 hits in the 18–17 decision. The 18-inning contest broke the record set by the same two teams just three years earlier for the longest game in innings in League Park history. When the teams got back to Shibe Park the next day, however, Cleveland proceeded to knock off the A's four straight times, pushing Philadelphia 9½ games behind New York.

Meanwhile, a stadium rental agreement between Bradley and city had finally been worked out, so the final days of League Park were winding down. The team had been wavering between second and fifth place over the course of the spring and summer. They stood in second place at 7½ games back, having taken three of four at home from the Yankees, when third-place Philadelphia came back to town to begin a series on Saturday, July 30. It was scheduled to be the last game at League Park. When Eddie Morgan struck out with the bases loaded in the ninth inning, sealing the 7–2 loss, it was expected that the Indians would never again play at the corner of East 66th and Lexington. Only 5000 showed up for the game, as the fans were clearly waiting for the team's Stadium debut the next day. Immediately after the game, the grounds crew began removing anything that could be used at the new Cleveland Municipal Stadium field.

The new ballpark became known commonly as Cleveland Stadium, Municipal Stadium, Lakefront Stadium, or simply, The Stadium. It was certainly big enough to warrant a host of monikers. And its impact on sports, and stadium evolution, would certainly turn out to be just as big.

An unbelievable crowd of 80,184 (76,979 paid) saw the next day's game at the lakefront ballpark, as Mel Harder dropped a 1–0 decision to Lefty Grove and the A's. Cleveland fans weren't used to such low-scoring games or the distance from the seats to the field. Nevertheless, the team remained at the giant ballpark for the rest of the year. The outfield in the horseshoe-shaped park was a reasonable 320 feet down the foul lines, but that quickly jutted out to 435 in the gaps and some 460 feet to the bleachers in dead center field. The huge outfield affected the Indians' team batting average, which was .316 for games at League Park that year compared to just .269 in games at the Stadium. Although the pitching statistics correspondingly improved at the Stadium, gone were the homers and excitement brought on by League Park's quirky dimensions. The team did post an improved record of 19–12–1 in games at the new park that year after going 24–21 at the old grounds. And

Cleveland finished the year in fourth place with an 87–65 record but home attendance actually dropped slightly from the 1931 full season at League Park to 468,953 for the split ballpark year of 1932.

This lease for use of the new stadium marked the first-ever agreement for a major league team to play its games in a public facility. It is likely that no one realized it then, but it was a move that would forever change the landscape of baseball and all sports.

You Can Go Home Again

The Indians played all their home games at Cleveland Stadium in 1933, drawing season-best crowds of 48,000 and 46,000, but general manager Billy Evans called it "bad business." He explained that "Outside of those three crowds [those two and the first game there the year before] there wasn't a game during the 1932 and 1933 seasons that we couldn't have accommodated at League Park."[2]

Cleveland players called it the "Municipal Morgue" despite the fact that they posted a 45–32 record there in 1933. Babe Ruth, who would never homer there, said that you needed a horse to cover the vast outfield. Team president Alva Bradley admitted, "The Stadium is worth more than we paid for (using) it, but we just cannot afford to pay even what we have been paying."[3] Reportedly the team had paid $37,000 in rent to the city. But the club still owned League Park, where taxes came to about only $8000 per year while the club had paid an additional $100,000 in taxes during its year and a half at Municipal Stadium.

Worse, in 1933 the team drew only 387,936 fans, down some 80,000 from 1932 and nearly 100,000 less than the final full season at League Park in 1931. Surprisingly, the depression was not blamed; rather, the lack of offense and home runs at the huge stadium was considered the problem. Adding to the team's woes with the team batting average at .260 (second lowest in the league), the 1933 Indians posted their worst overall record in five years, 75–76.

So Bradley moved the Indians back to League Park for 1934. New concrete stands near the right and left field pavilions (where the wooden "circus" seats had been placed during the 1920 pennant run) added 1,000 more seats. The scoreboard had been remodeled. New seats were installed in the lower boxes. And fresh paint included new markings on the outfield wall. A return to League Park also meant a revival of games on the radio. Bradley had scuttled the broadcasts in 1933, hoping to improve attendance at Municipal Stadium.

On the Sunday prior to opening day, the Indians hosted the New York Giants in an exhibition game to reopen League Park. A Saturday game had been scheduled as well, but it was cancelled because of bad weather. The exhibition game drew 8500 and the Indians won 5–4 as Hal Trosky drove in Ray Spencer in the bottom of the ninth with a drive off the screen. It was reported that the fans were happy to return to the cozy atmosphere at League Park. And the neighborhood, once again alive, had people climbing on roofs to catch a glimpse of the games.

Mayor Davis threw out the first ball at the regular season opener on April 17 against St. Louis. The Indians came away with a 5–2 victory with 21,000 fans on hand. Earl Averill drove in three runs with a home run and a double. The homer was a thrilling inside-the-parker to center field. Oral Hildebrand started on the mound and picked up the win for Cleveland.

Manager Walter Johnson, who had taken over in mid-season of 1933, saw his Cleveland team beat the visiting Yankees before 27,000 on Sunday, May 20, as another 5000 to 10,000 were turned away at the gates. The premium on tickets at the smaller park may have actually increased demand. That win sent the club on a run of eight wins in nine games, and eventually into first place on May 29 after a 5–0 victory over the White Sox. The next day, a Wednesday, another 27,000 fans turned out as the Chicago series continued with a doubleheader. The Indians dropped the opener, 8–7 in 12 innings, but Cleveland won game two, 5–4, as Hal Trosky slammed three home runs, the last smashing a car windshield in a parking lot across Lexington Avenue. The League Park magic was back ... and high scoring baseball had returned.

Despite a slump that had dropped the Indians to fourth place, 25,000 saw the team sweep a pair of 10–8 decisions from Washington on Sunday, July 15. New York followed with a series in Cleveland and offense again prevailed. After dropping a 5–4 game in the series opener, the Indians rebounded with 17 hits to win 13–5 on Tuesday and 18 more hits on Wednesday in a 15–14 victory. In that final game of the set, Cleveland led 12–9 after eight innings. New York scored five runs in the ninth to go up 14–12 before the Indians scored three times in the bottom to get the win. The crowd of 12,500 thrilled to the League Park–style of ball.

Babe Ruth made what would be his final playing appearance in Cleveland that year, pinch-hitting against Mel Harder on Sunday, September 16. Two weeks later, the season closed with a doubleheader against Chicago. Between games, a two-inning old-timers' game was staged. Lajoie, Flick, Wambsganss and many more returned once again to 66th and Lexington. Cy Young, now 67 years of age, pitched to two batters.

Cleveland finished the season in third place with an 85–69 mark. Mel Harder was the ace of the pitching staff, posting a record of 20–12. Attendance was up slightly over the 1933 season at the stadium, with ticket prices now at $1.65 for box seats, $1.50 for reserved, $1.10 for general admission and 55

cents in the bleachers. Those prices, plus the improved financial situation outlined by Bradley and Evans most certainly meant a better bottom line for operations at League Park.

Once again in 1935 the Indians completely avoided Municipal Stadium, playing all 62 home dates at League Park. There was still one major league game at the stadium that year, however, as Cleveland played host to the third annual All-Star Game on July 8. A crowd of 69,831 witnessed the American League's 4–1 win over the National League. Cleveland's Joe Vosmik hit leadoff, going 1-for-4 in right field, and Mel Harder pitched the final three innings, allowing one hit and no runs for the save. It was the perfect event for the cavernous ballpark: a special event sure to draw a huge crowd.

The 1935 home regular season had opened with a thrilling win over St. Louis before 21,500 at League Park when Cleveland scored twice in the bottom of the ninth for a 7–6 win. Boxer Max Baer, who had a bout scheduled downtown at Public Hall that night, was among the crowd. Though the Indians had a respectable final record of 82–71 and finished in third place, they never really were in the pennant race, trailing by 10 games or more for most of the time after mid–July.

This was also the year that Emil Bossard took over as League Park's head groundskeeper. He became the most legendary person in baseball history in that role, largely for his ability to manicure the field in the home team's favor, but also because his family has remained in the business ever since.

Bossard had to prepare the League Park field for 14 doubleheaders that year. Cost-conscious fans during the depression wanted the most for their dollar and doubleheaders made financial sense for the club too. During a home stand from August 17–28, the Tribe hosted five doubleheaders and just six single games. Only when the vaunted Yankees visited did management avoid doubleheaders, instead spreading out the revenue for baseball's best draw over as many dates as possible.

On August 24, a pitchers' duel took place at League Park with Philadelphia in town. With the combination of the wall in right and the live ball era,

Opposite page, top: Manager Walter Johnson, the all-time great pitcher for the Washington Senators, addresses his Cleveland team in the clubhouse after taking over as manager of the club during the 1933 season, while it was playing exclusively at Cleveland Stadium. The team returned to League Park on a full-time basis the following year (Cleveland Public Library). *Bottom:* Outside the ticket building in 1935 there was plenty of business as the Indians had returned from their year-and-a-half foray into Cleveland Stadium. This was the last year in which the team played exclusively at League Park, although the team continued to use the site for more than a decade. This picture also shows a good view of the famed left-field wall from outside the park, looking down Lexington Avenue (Cleveland State University, Cleveland Press Collection).

a game like this was a rarity at League Park. Willis Hudlin of Cleveland matched up with George Turbeville in a scoreless contest that extended into extra innings. Finally, in the bottom of the fifteenth, Earl Averill hit a game-ending, two-run homer. Both pitchers went the distance. Hudlin was excellent, allowing just eight hits and one walk in 15 innings.

Above: The left-field bleachers, which were the outfield seats extending from the end of the wrap-around grandstand in left field toward the scoreboard in center, as they looked in 1935. Overflow crowds were accommodated in this space throughout League Park's history and restrained only by a simple rope, as seen here. The depth of left field, 385 feet to the foul pole and even deeper toward center field, meant that allowing fans on the playing field in this area would rarely affect the game (Cleveland State University, Cleveland Press Collection).

Opposite page, top: Here is a wintertime interior view of the famous right-field wall, near the right-field corner, dated 1934. One of two exit gates for fans in the wall is visible here. The other was located near center field. They allowed the stands to clear much more quickly after games as fans could walk right across the playing field and exit onto Lexington Avenue and waiting trolleys (Cleveland State University, Cleveland Press Collection). *Bottom:* A group of boys on the south side of Lexington Avenue, just west of League Park's signature building, which is visible in the upper, right hand corner of the photo, with a portion of the back of the upper deck also in view. Gensert's Drug Store, with the Coca-Cola sign on its facing, is at the northwest corner of 66th and Lexington (Cleveland State University, Cleveland Press Collection).

Although Cleveland didn't figure in the pennant race, Vosmik's run for the AL batting title did stir interest. He had led the league for most of the year and held a narrow advantage as St. Louis visited League Park for a pair of doubleheaders on the last weekend of the season. But Vosmik went just 2-for-11 in those final four games while Washington's Buddy Myer went 4-for-5 on the final day to edge out Vosmik for the crown, .349 to .348.

Total attendance edged up only about 6000 over 1934, but the average jumped nearly 600 per home date, from 5755 to 6311, because of the added doubleheaders. The organization was learning how to maximize profits through careful scheduling. That thinking would take on an added dimension in 1936.

Back Downtown ... Sometimes

Taking what he had learned from the All-Star Game "event" the year before, Alva Bradley took a single home game away from League Park to Municipal Stadium in 1936. The game was promoted as part of the Great Lakes Exposition, a sort of World's Fair that was being held in the summers of 1936 and 1937 in the area adjacent to the stadium. Baseball ticket holders were allowed admission to the fair as well that day. The experiment worked, as the team and city wisely chose baseball's best attendance day, Sunday, and its strongest draw, the Yankees. It was quite a show, including pre-game contests between Indians and Yankees players. Even the Marx Brothers, in town while performing at the Palace Theater on Playhouse Square, made a zany appearance on the field before the game along with a dozen "chorus beauties."

So that Sunday, August 2, the Indians met New York in a spectacle at Cleveland Stadium. It also didn't hurt that the Tribe had climbed to second place and within 7½ games of first when the series opened at League Park on Friday. A crowd of 21,000 turned out for the Friday game and another 15,000 on Saturday, both Yankees wins. On Sunday, 65,000 wound up paying their way into the lakefront ballpark and they got their money's worth. The teams battled through 16 innings and had to settle for a 4–4 tie as darkness finally forced plate umpire George Moriarty to stop the contest. On the field, the Indians did not win, but they certainly did at the box office and management was poised to expand on the idea.

Rapid Robert

Overall, the 1936 season had brought success at the gate as attendance topped a half million for the first time since 1930, an increase of more than

Top: Action takes place at first base during opening day, 1936, versus Detroit. This photograph gives an excellent view of how closely League Park's famed right-field wall loomed behind the infielders as well as a good look at the wall itself. The exit sign indicates where fans could leave the park to Lexington Avenue after a game by walking across the outfield, expediting the clearing of the grandstands (The Western Reserve Historical Society, Cleveland, Ohio). *Bottom:* Fans line up for bleacher tickets in 1936. This special entrance was deep in the left field corner, along Linwood Avenue. Note the homes along Linwood, just beyond the perimeter of the ballpark (Cleveland State University, Cleveland Press Collection).

100,000 from 1935. And this came with the team having fallen to fifth place, 22½ games out of first. Cleveland featured Hal Trosky, who had the best year of his career, setting team records with 42 home runs and 162 RBIs while batting .343. Earl Averill continued his fine hitting with a .378 average. Pitcher Johnny Allen, in his first year with Cleveland after spending four years with the Yankees, was a 20-game winner.

The *Plain Dealer* did report that year that the team had purchased 20,000 square feet of land east of League Park beyond the left field bleachers in order to potentially expand League Park. The plan was to spend $250,000 to add more seating.[4] Osborn Engineering was consulted about a plan to double deck the seating areas in the left field corner and the outfield seats in left. Additionally, it was said that new bleachers would be constructed in center field. Perhaps the plan was genuine. Perhaps ownership was using this as a negotiation tool in talks for future use of Cleveland Stadium.

The home season had again begun with a pair of exhibition games against the New York Giants on Saturday, April 11 and Easter Sunday, April 12. When Detroit came for the regular season opener on Tuesday, 18,000 showed up in a drizzling rain as Cleveland lost, 3–0.

But another reason for an attendance spike was on the horizon. It was the addition of a 17-year-old pitcher who joined the team in midseason: Bob Feller, the greatest pitcher in Cleveland Indians history.

Coming from Van Meter, Iowa, Feller had learned to pitch on his family farm. The high school phenom with a blazing fastball was signed by Cy Slapnicka, a highly respected scout who had taken over as Cleveland's general manager in 1935. Feller became a member of the Indians after his junior year in high school, but came to Cleveland with a sore arm. Once he was again ready to throw, Slapnicka arranged for him to pitch a game for the local amateur Rosenblums team. "Rapid Robert," as he became known, beat a semipro team from Akron in extra innings at Cleveland's Woodland Hills Park.

Feller debuted for Cleveland at League Park on Monday, July 6, in an exhibition game against the defending the world champion St. Louis Cardinals, known as the "Gas House Gang." The practice of in-season exhibitions was still in vogue as teams looked for extra income when travel and open dates allowed. And this day was the first of the All-Star break as the Indians had come home from Chicago before resuming the regular season later that week in New York. The Cardinals had played a weekend series in Cincinnati and would play next on Thursday in St. Louis.

The crowd of 3500 that afternoon was described as consisting of 1500 people who came to see the National League's leading team and 2000 who wanted to see the debut of Feller. In the fourth inning, Feller entered the game in relief with it tied, 1–1. Cardinals catcher Brusie Ogrodowski was the

Bob Feller, perhaps the greatest right-handed pitcher ever, in a posed warm-up position with the left-field wall bleachers visible in the background. The left field corner seats, which connected to the main grandstand, were fenced off from the bleacher patrons (Cleveland Public Library).

first batter he faced. Ogrodowski laid down a bunt but was thrown out at first. Feller pitched three innings, giving up just one run. The next eight outs he recorded were by strikeout! Cleveland won the game, 7–6.

Feller pitched one more time for the Rosenblums at Brookside Park before his first regular season appearance on July 17 in the final inning of a game at Washington's Griffith Stadium. Feller got the final three outs that day, but walked two. He threw hard and wild, but clearly showed signs of greatness. His next outing was his first official appearance at League Park. He threw the final two innings of a 16–3 win over Philadelphia on July 24. Feller appeared in relief four more times before getting his first start on Sunday, August 23, at League Park against St. Louis. And what a start it was!

A crowd of 9000 saw Feller record the first eight outs via strikeout en route to 15 whiffs on the day, just one shy of Rube Waddell's American League record for strikeouts in a game. He allowed only six hits in a 4–1, complete-game win over the Browns. He lost starts at Boston and New York during the ensuing 13-game road trip, but when the team returned to League Park on September 7, Feller again faced St. Louis, this time winning 7–1 with ten strikeouts.

The following Sunday, September 13, Feller tied Dizzy Dean's major league record with 17 strikeouts in the opener of a doubleheader against Philadelphia, again at League Park. William Feller, Bob's father, attended the game and was seated in a field box near the Indians' dugout. Feller gave up only two hits but walked nine and hit one batter in the 5–2 win, throwing to a raw rookie catcher named Greek George. The 17 strikeouts broke Waddell's AL record of 16, which had stood since 1908. Philadelphia manager Connie Mack said he "Never saw the likes of Feller's fastball before."[5] Denny Galehouse pitched the second game for Cleveland and won, 5–4. Threatening weather held the crowd down to 6,500.

On September 23, Feller took the mound again at League Park, this time facing the Chicago White Sox. Aided by 19 hits and 11 runs in the seventh inning, Feller coasted to a 17–2 win while striking out ten. All this took place while controversy surrounded Feller's contract with Cleveland. The minor league team in Des Moines claimed territorial rights to Feller under rules of the day, and Commissioner Landis reviewed the case with speculation by the press that Feller could be made a free agent.

Feller pitched one more time at League Park before the season ended. Facing Detroit on September 27, he struck out six in a 9–1 victory that was shortened to six innings because of rain. For the year, he ended up with a 5–3 record, striking out 76 batters in 62 innings pitched. On December 10, Landis fined Cleveland $7500 but allowed Feller to stay with the Indians, where he remained for his entire Hall of Fame career.

Weekday Home

Beginning on Memorial Day weekend in the 1937 season, Alva Bradley started taking all of the Sunday and holiday games for his team away from

League Park and playing them at Cleveland Stadium. Opening day games also moved to the larger facility, so the 1937 home opener was the last to take place at League Park. On April 23, against the St. Louis Browns, Johnny Allen pitched Cleveland to a 9–2 win in front of 20,752. A photographer's balcony had been added under the boxes in the upper deck of right field. One year earlier, 13 photographers had circulated about the field during opening day.

The prudent use of Cleveland Stadium was not the only factor that helped attendance. The 1937 Indians also had individual stars who had considerable fan appeal, including Johnny Allen who was a stellar 15–1 on the mound, and Mel Harder, who also came through with 15 victories. Hal Trosky led the team's hitters with 32 home runs and 128 runs batted in. The result was a total attendance of 564,849 between the two parks, the most since 1926, as the team finished in fourth place. While the use of two regular home fields for the same team was very unusual, things went smoothly and ticket prices were the same at both parks.

On Ladies' Day, free admission was provided in the upper-deck pavilion seats. This view, from 1937, shows the seating along the first-base foul line, overlooking right field (Cleveland State University, Cleveland Press Collection).

After the opening of Cleveland Stadium, the Indians were the only team in Major League Baseball history to share two home ballparks on a regular basis, doing so from 1936 to 1946. The sign on the ticket/office building indicates that this day's game was being played at the downtown stadium. (Cleveland Public Library).

In 1938, the home opener and all Sunday and holiday games were again shifted to the Stadium. A couple of weekday doubleheaders and Friday and Saturday games versus New York were also shifted. And attendance rose nearly another 100,000 to 652,006, third best in team history behind 1920 and 1921.

The Indians continued their recent practice of hosting the New York Giants in exhibition games at League Park prior to the regular season opener. A huge crowd of 31,600 attended the regular season opener at the Stadium on Tuesday, April 19 against St. Louis, but then only 4500 showed up at League Park the following day. However, League Park stole the show as Cleveland lost at the Stadium, 6–2, but came back with a 9–0 win on Wednesday at the old park as Bob Feller threw a one-hitter.

Cleveland led the league for much of the way until mid–July, when the Yankees took over first place. On September 9, a rookie named Lou Boudreau

The open-style lockers in the Indians' clubhouse beneath the first-base grandstand. Player names were written on narrow chalkboards above the stalls. These were the spaces occupied by Frank Pytlak and Johnny Allen during the 1939 season (Cleveland State University, Cleveland Press Collection).

made his major league debut at League Park. Boudreau went on to be named player-manager of the team at age 24 prior to the 1942 season and led the team to a World Series title in 1948.

The 1938 Cleveland team once again wound up with a respectable third-place finish and a record of 86–66. Hal Trosky batted .334 with 19 home runs and outfielder Jeff Heath had a great year, batting .343 with 21 homers and 112 RBIs. Pitchers Harder and Feller, who broke his own strikeout mark with 18 in a game at the stadium, each won 17 games.

Away at Night Too

Night baseball had begun in the major leagues at Cincinnati's Crosley Field in 1935. The league had imposed a maximum of seven night games per team in those early years of nocturnal baseball, however. The installation of lights at Cleveland Stadium in 1939 meant that more dates would be moved away from League Park, beginning on Tuesday, June 27.

Bob Feller, who had set a new major league single-game strikeout record with 18 a year earlier at Detroit, got the start in this historic game against the Tigers. He responded with a one-hitter in the 5–0 win. League Park, meanwhile, never had lights installed, sealing its fate.

Fans had already been responding to games at the Stadium. A few weeks earlier, for example, Cleveland had hosted St. Louis in a Tuesday doubleheader at the stadium, attracting 26,504. The New York Yankees followed St. Louis into town for a three-game series at League Park on Thursday, Friday and Saturday to begin the month of June. Crowds of only 3500, 8000, and 6000 turned out for the Yankees' sweep as Cleveland fell to fourth place.

Despite hosting fewer games, League Park against showed its tendency for memorable moments later that year. On August 25, Cleveland destroyed Philadelphia in a doubleheader by 10–2 and 17–2 scores. Trosky knocked out two homers in the first game.

On August 27, Jeff Heath was ejected from a game for throwing his bat in frustration after striking out. Johnny Broaca tried to calm Heath in the Cleveland dugout but Heath would have none of it. Heath told Broaca to mind his own business or he'd let him have it. Broaca, a former collegiate boxer at Yale, went at it with Heath in the dugout. Manager Oscar Vitt separated them with a threat of fines.

The next day, Heath popped out on a 3–0 count in the ninth inning. A reportedly drunken fan near the Indians dugout yelled, "Why don't you throw your bat in the stands again?" Heath walked over and delivered a punch to the man's chest. Neither the umpire nor Vitt saw it, so Heath got away with the act as police and ushers quickly intervened. Heath explained, "The fellow had been hurling abuse at the Indian players throughout the game."[6] Ted Williams hit a three-run homer and Boston beat Cleveland, 6–5, that day.

The Indians finished the 1939 season in third place with a record of 87–67. The team's attendance fell by nearly 90,000 to 563,926.

Neighborhood boys sneak a peek at the action inside League Park sometime in the 1930s or 1940s. During the park's original configuration, views through the then-wooden fence were plentiful. With the concrete wall put up in 1910, sneak peeks were much more limited. These holes were in the gate near center field where fans could exit onto Lexington Avenue by walking across the playing field (Cleveland State University, Cleveland Press Collection).

Cry Babies

Beginning with Bob Feller's opening day no-hitter at Chicago, it was evident that the 1940 season would be a notable one for Cleveland baseball. In the first game at League Park that year, April 25, Feller again beat the White Sox, 3–1, giving up eight hits and striking out eight. Jeff Heath had a home run onto the roof of a building across Lexington Avenue that day. A game account described a new scoreboard sign designating a hit or error as an improvement to the park. It was a telling sign that substantial investments in the old park could no longer be expected.

On May 17, the Indians crushed Washington, 18–1, after a ten-run first inning at League Park. Cold weather kept the crowd down to 3000, but Indian bats were hot with 15 hits. Heath had two home runs. The team alternated between first and second place all season long, dropping to third on just one day, June 15. It was about that time when a group of players went to owner Bradley to complain about Vitt's critical style of managing. The owner backed his manager.

Cleveland and Detroit were tied for first place when the Tigers came to League Park for two key games beginning on Monday, August 12. The Monday game drew 23,720 as Feller picked up his 21st victory in an 8–5 Cleveland win. The next day 16,128 saw Cleveland prevail, 6–5. The game ended with quite a spectacle, as a "tremendous shower of straw hats floated on the playing field."[7] Cleveland fans, with their team now up by two games were acting like it was 1920 all over again. With interest peaking, all of the September games were moved to Municipal Stadium. The final game at League Park for the year had been held on August 17. Feller's magnificent 27–11 record was not enough, however. The controversy that had emerged from the player complaints had created friction in the Cleveland clubhouse after the press had learned of the attempted mutiny. The team was labeled the Cry Babies and Detroit clinched the pennant at the stadium on the first game of a season-ending weekend series. A total of 902,576 watched the Indians at home that year, second only to the 1920 championship season, as the team finished second at 89–65. Due to the late-season shift, only 33 of 77 home games were played at League Park in 1940. The final shift of the year came in the clubhouse as Vitt was fired as manager after the season ended.

Controversy

Playing at two home sites did not come without controversy. Opposing teams had begun accusing the Indians of using their two vastly different homes to gain a competitive advantage and it's likely they did.

Fans eagerly wait to buy tickets to see the Cleveland Indians in 1940. The team spent most of the season in first place before winding up in second to the Detroit Tigers. In fact, home games for the final month-and-a-half that season were all moved to larger Cleveland Stadium to accommodate pennant-race crowds. This summertime shot shows the more casual dress of fans of the era (Cleveland State University, Cleveland Press Collection).

This especially became an issue during the 1940 pennant race, when Cleveland switched the sites of games mid-season. Indians brass was accused of putting weaker-hitting foes in League Park, so the home team could take advantage of the short porch in right while their opponents, especially those heavy on right-handed hitters, suffered. Likewise, the Tribe was accused of putting games against the better-hitting teams in the spacious grounds of the stadium. The league office eventually ruled that the Indians had to declare the sites of all games before the beginning of the season and stick to those commitments.

The League Park wall continued to be a topic for commentary, with many players offering their observations. Tribe slugger Hal Trosky told *The Sporting News*, "Hitters, especially lefthanders who go for distance, are confused in Cleveland. They open at League Park, which has the shortest right field fence

Joe DiMaggio, seen here in a posed action shot at League Park, hit safely in the final game of his all-time record 56-game hitting streak at the site on July 16, 1941. The streak ended the following night at Cleveland Stadium before he returned to League Park the next day to begin a new 16-game streak (Cleveland Public Library).

in the league, and it's a picnic. Then they'd move over to the Stadium, which has the biggest playing expanse in the majors. What might be a home run in League Park is an easy out at the Stadium. It discourages you. And then you get on the road and your timing is all off for those normal-sized parks."[8]

Yankee pitcher Lefty Gomez wrote, "There are a lot of hazards in baseball. The worst of these mental and physical hazards is in the little League Park in Cleveland, with that short right field fence. The hitters aim at the fence and the pitchers aim to keep the hitters from walloping the wall, and so the game is a battle of wits which most often winds up being very tough on the wall. When we come to Cleveland, I always spend the day before I pitch in a small room. The morning I am going to work, I spend in a telephone booth. Then, by contrast, the ball park seems so much bigger."[9]

DiMaggio's Streak

It had started innocently enough on May 15, 1941. One of the greatest hitters of all time, Joe DiMaggio, got a hit to begin a consecutive game hitting streak that would set a record that may never be broken. Fifty-six has become a number that will forever be linked with the name DiMaggio. And in a game as dominated by statistics as baseball is—along with Cy Young's 511 pitching wins—DiMaggio's 56-game hitting streak is perhaps the most untouchable number in the sport's history.

So it was fitting that DiMaggio's streak climaxed at the site where Cy Young had earned so many victories. Games 17 and 18 of the streak had come at Cleveland Stadium while game 19 had been at League Park on Monday, June 2. After passing Wee Willie Keeler's record of 44 from 1897, the pressure and attention grew. (Keeler's streak, by the way, included game numbers 28 and 29 at League Park on May 27 and 29 of that year.)

When the Yankees returned, the team was as hot as DiMaggio himself, on a 14-game winning streak. And Joltin' Joe had hit in 55 in a row when New York opened a series at League Park on Wednesday, July 16. A crowd of 15,000 came out to see if the streak would continue. Pitching for the home team was lefthander Al Milnar, a native Clevelander.

DiMaggio settled the matter early as he swung on the first offering in his first inning at-bat. The hit was a sharp single to center and the streak reached 56. He singled again in the third inning, once again to center field. DiMaggio came to bat three more times in the game. A walk and a groundout were followed by a double off relief pitcher Joe Krakauskas. The Yankees easily won the game, 15–3.

The streak ended the following night at Cleveland Stadium. A throng of 67,468 witnessed history as DiMaggio garnered a walk but was put out in three other plate appearances to finish the record streak. Shortstop Lou Boudreau and third baseman Ken Keltner were credited with solid defensive plays to help end DiMaggio's run. The Yankees did win the game to extend their win streak to 16 in a row.

The next day, the teams returned to League Park for a Ladies' Day game.

With 18,000 watching, Bob Feller ended the team's streak by a 2–1 score with his 19th victory of the season. The Yankees had only six hits, two by DiMaggio, as he began another 16-game hitting streak.[10]

Boston's Ted Williams had his own special year in 1941, hitting .406 as the last big leaguer to top the .400 mark. He went 5-for-11 (.455) in four games at League Park that season (he did not play in games there on July 14 and 15). His only extra-base hit at the site was a home run on June 5. Cleveland pitchers also walked Williams nine times in those four games.

Cleveland's drop from contention that year was accompanied by a drop in the standings. The team's record fell to 75–79, still good enough for a fourth-place finish, but attendance fell more than 150,000 to 745,948, which was still second best in the league. It was the last year in which League Park would host more games than the stadium, 45 to 32.

War Years

After again opening the home season in 1942 at Cleveland Municipal Stadium, the Indians played their first regular season game of the year at League Park on April 20 under "boy manager" Lou Boudreau. The home dugout had been moved ten feet forward and closer to the first base line in order to provide privacy from some of those seats that extended close to the foul line beyond the dugouts. Permanent benches replaced stools in the clubhouse, but these were small tweaks for the aging and less frequently used ballpark. Missing from that dugout and clubhouse was Bob Feller, who had signed up for the military after the bombing of Pearl Harbor in December, joining Hank Greenberg and several other big leaguers who had enlisted during the 1941 season.

The season's initial game at League Park had Al Smith on the mound for Cleveland and former Indian Denny Galehouse pitching for St. Louis. Keltner blasted a home run into the left-field bleachers as the Indians won, 4–3. An announcement was made before each game that year that balls hit into the stands should be returned for distribution to the armed forces for use in military recreation baseball. It was another small reminder that the country was at war.

One unusual game played at League Park in 1942 came on July 29, as the Indians picked up an 11-inning 7–6 win over Boston. An amazing 21 walks were issued in the game before Roy Weatherly's line drive to the right-field wall drove in the winning run.

Jim Bagby closed the season at League Park with a six-hitter and an 8–0 win over Detroit on September 27. The Indians finished the year in fourth place with a 75–79 record, identical to their standing and record of a year earlier, but the war contributed to attendance dipping dramatically to 459,447. The drop also came despite the fact that the seven-game limit on night contests had been lifted and Cleveland had played 16 times after dark at the stadium.

With World War II raging in 1943, less than 14,000 attended the season opener at the stadium on April 21 against Detroit. The next day's game, the League Park opener, attracted just 2500 as the Tigers held the host team to just four hits, shutting out Mel Harder and the Indians, 4–0. Cleveland did improve to third place and a mark of 82–71, as rosters began to change dramatically

An excellent view of the League Park scoreboard as it appeared mid-game on May 13, 1943. Note the 460-foot marker just to the right of dead center field, the deepest part of the park. Cleveland went on to lose the game that day to Washington, 3–2 in 12 innings (Cleveland State University, Cleveland Press Collection).

with more and more wartime enlistments. Attendance slid even further, as 438,894 saw the Indians play their home games that year.

With an expected small crowd on August 7, the Saturday game with St. Louis was allowed to be shifted from the stadium to League Park. The *Plain Dealer* noted that the move affected the game's outcome.[11] The Indians lost 2–0 and the newspaper pointed out that the two doubles that accounted for the St. Louis runs would have been outs at the stadium. Its account also claimed that a line drive out to left field by Cleveland's Ray Mack would have been a home run downtown. On August 18 in a doubleheader against New York, the largest League Park crowd of the year, 15,000, saw Jeff Heath have quite a day. He drove in seven runs with a homer in each game as Cleveland won twice, 9–8 and 7–5.

Bob Feller is shown here warming up with the famous right-field wall looming behind. This picture is reported to be from 1945, after Feller returned from his service in World War II. Notice the Mobile Gas sign atop the concrete portion of the wall at that time, adding yet another surface for a ball to bounce off of in addition to the concrete, wire and girders (Cleveland State University, Cleveland Press Collection).

The 1944 season saw Lou Boudreau lead the league in batting with a .327 average, but the Indians fell to fifth place with a 72–82 record. Overall attendance did increase slightly over 1943 to 475,272, but with the wartime factories whirring, daytime baseball on weekdays at League Park suffered. Two late-season League Park games that year against Boston on September 20 and 21

The ornate brickwork and arches are easily visible on League Park, including the remaining portions today, but this close-up look at the ticket windows from 1945 shows the similarly elaborate light fixtures that were included on the building's façade (Cleveland State University, Cleveland Press Collection).

drew 500 and 650, respectively. The game on the 20th did turn out to be a League Park thriller, as Cleveland won 11–10 in 13 innings.

Even with excitement like that and the Yankees coming to town next, the crowds were still uninspired. New York only managed to attract 4196 on Friday night, September 22, to the stadium, and 2500 on Saturday afternoon back at League Park.

Add in the fact that the Cleveland team was a second-division club for virtually the entire season, and the drop in interest was certainly understandable. The Indians finished in fifth place with a record of 72–82.

Change was in the offing in 1945 as the Tribe again finished fifth, though with an improved mark of 74–71. It may have been even better had not Boudreau suffered a broken ankle. Crowds began to pick up, as the War in Europe ended in the spring. On August 15, the Allied forces announced the surrender of Japan and the end of the World War II — V-J Day. League Park was where 12,000 Clevelanders heard the news on that famous day, as the Indians were in the midst of an 8–3 win over Philadelphia. After the announcement was made, players hugged one another and the crowd cheered and celebrated for 15 minutes.

Detroit managed to hold on and win the pennant by a game and a half over Washington despite having dropped both games of a crucial series late in September at League Park. Bob Feller, back from the service, pitched a one-hitter as the Indians beat the Tigers, 2–0, on September 19. Jeff Heath hit a long homer over the center field wall. On the 20th, Allie Reynolds tossed a five-hitter and Cleveland won 6–1.

Season attendance had rebounded to 558,182.

Veeck and the End

The 1946 season followed a familiar pattern. The New York Giants came to town for their traditional exhibition games at League Park on April 13 and 14. The home opener was held at the stadium and the League Park opener, an April 25 loss to Chicago, followed with little fanfare. There were again minor upgrades to League Park as the look of the scoreboard was tweaked and the board operator now used a walkie-talkie to communicate with the press box. But League Park was once again relegated to hosting mostly secondary games.

On May 15, a pair of Tribe pitchers pulled off a tough feat at high-scoring League Park. Mel Harder and Steve Gromek each hurled complete game shutouts as Cleveland swept a doubleheader from Philadelphia, 3–0 and 5–0.

Dramatic change came to Cleveland in June when the Indians were purchased by a syndicate headed by 32-year-old Bill Veeck, an experienced baseball operator who was about to become a big league owner for the first time. Veeck had become convinced that the possibilities for baseball in Cleveland were huge and he loved the income potential that the vast number of seats at Cleveland Stadium represented. So he purchased the shares of several mem-

Opposite page, top: A view of the packed grandstand extending down the first-base line to the famous wall in right field during the Cleveland Indians' final season at League Park in 1946. The extended field box seats became permanent when the team returned to League Park following a full season at Cleveland Stadium in 1934, creating the tight, pie-shaped bullpen space against the right-field wall (Cleveland State University, Cleveland Press Collection). *Bottom:* After purchasing the Indians in June 1946, new owner Bill Veeck installed an Indian teepee deep in center field at League Park. Fans are shown here being entertained there after a 4–1 win over Boston on July 31. A close look at the right side of the photograph shows a rare view of fans actually exiting the park through one of the gates in the right-field wall (Cleveland State University, Cleveland Press Collection).

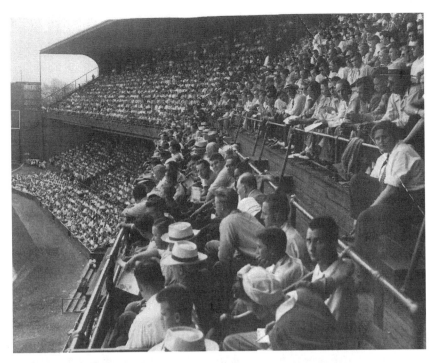

bers of Alva Bradley's ownership group in order to take over the club. It became official on June 21 when transfer of the team was executed for $1.6 million.

On Saturday, June 22, the Boston Red Sox took on the Indians at League Park. The energetic and personable Veeck circulated throughout the stands and introduced himself to many of the patrons as his team was taking care of Boston, 4–3. He soon added his legendary pizzazz to the grounds, bringing in an orchestra and constructing a teepee in deepest center field, near the scoreboard. But this was just the beginning. His eyes were on bigger and better things downtown.

No formal announcement was made about the future of League Park, but as it had in 1932, the old concrete-and-steel edifice seemed to make a last gasp in order to prove its worth. Feller registered his 20th win of the year on July 31 at the old ballyard, beating the Red Sox 4–1 with a one-hitter. He struck out nine and was well on his way to a team record 348 for the season. It would turn out to be his greatest season with a record of 26–15, 36 complete games and 371 innings pitched in 48 appearances.

Although the Indians did not hoist a pennant at League Park that year, a visiting team did so on September 13, 1946, in a game that was out of character for the ballpark. Cleveland's Red Embree allowed Boston only two hits that Friday afternoon before 3295 fans. One of those two hits, however, was a first inning inside-the-park home run by the Red Sox' Ted Williams, the only inside-the-parker out of the 521 homers in his fabulous career, and it clinched first place for Boston. Even in its waning days, the venerable Cleveland field seemed to be a magnet for the unusual. Boston hurler Tex Hughson had outdueled Embree, blanking the Tribe 1–0 with a three-hitter.

Attendance numbers were soaring around the country as the troops returned home and sought out the enjoyment of baseball. Cleveland drew a new record of 1,057,289 spectators that year. New owner Bill Veeck was firmly in charge by the time League Park was set for its final game on September 21. Perhaps Veeck hadn't made up his mind to vacate League Park yet. Or maybe he wanted to use it as a potential negotiating tool before he got a lease with the city, as previous team operators appear to have done. Or it might just not have occurred to him that a final game at an old ballpark was something that could be promoted. Whatever the reason, there was no celebration and only 2772 fans were there for League Park's final major league game that Saturday afternoon.[12]

Cleveland was mired in sixth place and, although visiting Detroit was in second, the game had no pennant implications since Boston had clinched the pennant in Cleveland eight days earlier. In addition, Detroit had trounced the Indians 15–1 at League Park on the previous day, hardly an outcome to encourage a large turnout. There was an ad in the *Plain Dealer* that morning promoting ticket sales for the day, but it was of the usual size and style and made no mention of that day being the final game at League Park.

It was cloudy and warm for the 1:30 game. Bob Kuzava was Cleveland's starting pitcher while Detroit sent Dizzy Trout to the box. Detroit scored single runs in the second and third innings, the latter on Hank Greenberg's 118th RBI of the season. The Tigers added another run in the fifth, and Cleveland finally broke through with two in the sixth. Cleveland tied it with a run in the eighth. Tom Jordan, who had singled and stole second, scored on a hit by Heinz Becker, who was pinch-hitting for Kuzava.

Neither team scored in the ninth or tenth innings. It seemed as though League Park was unwilling for the game to end. In the eleventh, Hoot Evers finally broke the deadlock with a single to right that scored Eddie Lake. Dick Wakefield then singled home George Kell to make it 5–3 in favor of Detroit. Trout set down the Indians in the bottom of the eleventh inning and Detroit won 5–3. Tribe shortstop Jack Conway made the final out, in the last major league at-bat in League Park.

As Detroit and Cleveland played the next day at the Stadium, the corner of East 66th Street and Lexington Avenue was quiet. But this time it was different as the Indians would not return. Fifty-five years of big league baseball at League Park had come to an end.

6

Negro League Park

The loss of old ballparks, in many ways, is baseball's loss. Ballparks hatch nostalgia in gushes, and baseball is a game of memories.—Bill Shannon and George Kalinsky, *The Ballparks*

Black Baseball in Cleveland

While the major leagues, and even amateur baseball, garnered great attention in Cleveland during the League Park era, the city had experienced a checkered history in the Negro Leagues. Nevertheless, black baseball in Cleveland had a fairly continuous presence beginning after World War I and even continuing for a time after the integration of the major leagues in 1947. Much of that history took place at League Park, culminating with the Cleveland Buckeyes from 1943 to 1948 and 1950. As a result, Negro League baseball not only co-existed with the Indians at 66th and Lexington, but actually outlasted the ballpark's owner, the Indians.

While the era of black baseball in Cleveland peaked with a Negro League World Series championship in 1945 and with another appearance in that event in 1947, the city had first been represented in the Negro Leagues in 1922. In that year, the Cleveland Tate Stars, organized at Tate Field on Cleveland's south side in 1918, joined the Negro National League. The Tate Stars lasted only that year and part of 1923. In 1924, a team called the Browns took up residence at the same location, now renamed Hooper Field, followed by the Elites in 1926 and the Hornets in 1927.

Yet another Negro National League team was fielded in 1931, the Cubs. Playing at Kinsman Hardware Field, located at the corner of Kinsman Road and East 79th Street, the small park also has been referred to as Cubs Stadium. The Cubs won a game by forfeit on June 2, 1931, when the St. Louis Stars walked off the Hardware Field diamond in protest of the umpire's decision to eject their catcher for using profanity. Just over two weeks later, on June 17, the Cleveland team turned a triple play at the site during a 7–5 win over Louisville.

The following season, 1932, a Negro East-West League team called the

Stars also set up shop at Hardware Field. The next year, the Negro National League returned, this time to Luna Park, which had been configured into an expanded football stadium since the Cleveland Green Sox last played baseball there in 1913. That 1933 entry was the Cleveland Giants, a team that had begun the year as the Columbus Blue Birds before moving to Cleveland to finish out the season.

League Park was first used as the home field for Negro League baseball when the Cleveland Red Sox began playing there in 1934. Some sources also cite Luna Park as the venue for some Red Sox home games; however, the local black newspaper, the *Call and Post*, confirms that League Park was indeed the team's home.[1]

Like many black teams of the era, the Red Sox provided part-time jobs for the players and games were concentrated on Sundays when potential attendance would be at its best. The team opened the season on June 3 against Nashville, but problems plagued its entire season. The *Call and Post* noted that the team was lax in reporting roster and player information, game scores and other information that would help the paper cover the team.[2] After a series of disagreements with the league administration, the team left the Negro National League and played out its season as an independent team.

On August 12, the Red Sox had one of their best days of the season, sweeping a doubleheader from the Birmingham Barons by scores of 5–0 and 7–2 at League Park. Pitchers Dick Byrd and Lefty Reese held the visitors to a combined total of just seven hits on the day. But the team folded following the season and Cleveland was without a Negro League representative in 1935.

Exhibitions and Neutral Site Games

During the years that no team represented Cleveland in the Negro Leagues, and even in some years when Cleveland did have a team, League Park was a frequent stop for regular season games between other Negro League teams and postseason exhibition contests.

One such game, on July 27, 1931, brought something never before seen at League Park, night baseball. The white House of David team, bringing its own portable lighting system by truck, met the famous Homestead Grays in Cleveland that night. Another fabled Negro League team, the Kansas City Monarchs, had first used such a system in 1930.

On this Monday night, it was expected that the meeting in Cleveland would be one of the greatest baseball games of the season, according to the *Chicago Defender*.[3] Pitching for the Homestead Grays was Willie Foster, probably the best left-handed pitcher in the Negro Leagues. The House of David, known for its bearded players, featured one clean-shaven player, former major league great Grover Cleveland Alexander. Foster and the Grays won, 10–0, with over 4000 people in the League Park stands, who paid from fifty cents up to $1.25 for a ticket. Alexander pitched only two innings, giving up five runs in the first.

On July 23, 1933, some of the greatest players in Negro League history played a doubleheader at League Park as the Chicago Giants faced the Pittsburgh Crawfords. Chicago, winners of the first-half title, featured Foster and Larry Brown. Pittsburgh boasted Oscar Chamberlin, Cool Papa Bell and Josh Gibson. Pittsburgh swept the doubleheader, 8–1, and 13–12 in 12 innings. Gibson pleased the crowd with a home run in the second game.

The Crawfords returned to League Park later that year, sweeping a doubleheader from the Nashville Elite Giants on October 1. Those wins clinched the Negro National League's second-half title. Cool Papa Bell's inside-the-park home run to left center field won the first game in extra innings.

On Sunday, October 21, 1934, one of the most memorable days at League Park came in an exhibition game between the Crawfords and a team that included brothers Dizzy and Paul Dean of the recently crowned World Series champion St. Louis Cardinals. The Deans played for the Cleveland amateur champion Rosenblums team and ticket prices ranged from 30 cents to $1.20. A week earlier, American League president Will Harridge had called for an end to barnstorming as a result of a career-threatening injury sustained by Philadelphia Athletics star Jimmy Foxx. The game went on anyway and attracted a crowd of 12,000, the largest at that point to have seen a black team play in Cleveland.

The Deans were scheduled to pitch against the legendary Satchel Paige. Dizzy Dean pitched three innings, giving up four hits and one run, with Paige collecting one of the hits. Dizzy also played three innings in right field and spent one inning in the coaching box. The Deans signed many autographs after coming out of the game in the eighth inning, but it was Paige who was the star of the game. He struck out the first six batters he faced and whiffed 13 in six innings as the Crawfords won. After the game, Paige was cheered by the crowd and surrounded by autograph seekers.

In 1935, the Crawfords again appeared at League Park, hosting a doubleheader against Chicago on July 21. With no Cleveland team in the Negro Leagues that year, some 8000 fans turned out to see a Pittsburgh hitting display that racked up wins of 17–2 and 12–8.

That success led the Crawfords to return to League Park for several dates in 1936. On June 14, a crowd of 10,000 watched a doubleheader split with the Newark Eagles. Satchel Paige pitched the opener for Pittsburgh and threw a five-hitter in a 6–0 shutout victory. Newark took the nightcap, 8–4. The Crawfords returned on July 5, playing host to the Homestead Grays. It was another split as Pittsburgh lost the first game, 2–1, but came back to win the second behind Paige once again, 3–0.

A four-team doubleheader was staged on August 30, as the Crawfords beat the Philadelphia Stars, 9–3, in game one while the Nashville Giants defeated the New York Black Yankees in game two, 6–4. Each game was just five innings.

The Crawfords and Grays returned on September 6 for another twin-bill, with Homestead winning 6–4 in the opener. Game two was canceled due to wet grounds and rain.

The next year, 1937, promoter Lem Williams tried to organize a Cleveland team for the Negro National League but fell short of his goal. Instead, he pro-moted several Sunday doubleheaders at League Park over the course of the season. The first of those was notable as Negro League legend Josh Gibson blasted a pair of home runs over the famous right-field wall for the Homestead Grays in a 20–7 win over the New York Black Yankees. New York did bounce back to win the second game, 6–3.

A number of games in 1938 were promoted at Cleveland Stadium. League Park did stay in the mix, however, and on July 17 the Grays and Black Yankees split a doubleheader. Also that year, a doubleheader including four north-eastern Ohio black teams took place at League Park. The Cleveland White Sox, who normally used a site called General Electric Field (presumably at the company's huge Nela Park plant in East Cleveland), defeated the Warren Game Cocks 6–3, followed by the Cleveland Ramblers beating the Miles Heights Cardinals by the same score. In game one, White Sox pitcher Alonzo Boone struck out 16 and overcame nine errors behind him to post the win.

The Rise of the Buckeyes

Cleveland again got its own team in 1939, as the Cleveland Bears repre-sented the city in the Negro American League. Home games were played at Cleveland Stadium but there were only a few as the team had a record of 9–9 in the final standings. (Just like the Indians at the time, the lure of the big ballpark for special event-type contests likely was the approach.)

The next year, 1940, the Bears called League Park home, again following the Indians by choosing the smaller park rather than struggling with the high overhead costs at the downtown stadium. The home opener was played on Sunday, May 25, as the visiting St. Louis Bears won a doubleheader, 7–1 and 4–3. A crowd of 5100 watched, though many stayed home because of threat-ening weather. The following Sunday, the Kansas City Monarchs swept the Bears, 8–0 and 8–4. A week later, Cleveland finally prevailed, sweeping Indi-anapolis, 1–0 and 11–9. Preacher Henry earned the win in the opener with a four-hitter. But the operation again appeared to be shaky. On July 13, a *Call and Post* story by Ken Jessamy said that the Bears did not show up for a scheduled doubleheader against Birmingham at League Park. He cited high rental costs for the use of the ballpark (though they must have been less than the stadium a year earlier), injuries and bad management, reporting that as a result of these issues the team looked like a bunch of third-rate sandlotters. The Bears wound up with a record of 10–10 as Kansas City won the league with a 12–7 mark.

Black semi-pro teams were using League Park on occasion by 1941. A team called the Cleveland Giants played host to a team from Beloit, Wisconsin, in May before several hundred fans. The Cleveland White Sox, an operation headed up by Clevelander Wilbur Hayes, played a doubleheader with the Birmingham Black Barons at the park in June, losing 15–4 and 3–1 before 1200 fans. Later that month, on the 15th, there was a scheduled doubleheader between the Kansas City Monarchs and Chicago American Giants in Cleveland. There were hopes for a record crowd to see black baseball in Cleveland, but the games were rained out. That summer, Hayes and Erie, Pennsylvania, businessman Ernie Wright teamed up to put Cleveland back in the Negro American League. They contracted with the Indians for use of League Park that year on Sundays when the American League team was out-of-town. They used the nickname Stars after acquiring the Negro American League's St. Louis Stars and merging that team with Hayes's semi-pro club.

The combined squad debuted at League Park on August 3, when the Stars met Kansas City in a doubleheader. It was designated as Satchel Paige Day and 10,000 fans turned out to see the legendary hurler toss the second game for Kansas City as the Stars were swept. Ticket prices were 85 cents for box seats, 60 cents for general admission and 25 cents for kids.

In 1942, under the new name Cincinnati/Cleveland Buckeyes, the team played at various locations around the state, including League Park. On September 7 of that year, a tragic accident cost Buckeye pitcher Raymond Owens and catcher Ulysses Brown their lives. Returning from a late-season barnstorming game in Buffalo against the New York Black Yankees, their vehicle was struck by a truck on U.S. Route 20, just west of Geneva, Ohio.

For the next year, 1943, the team took up full-time residence in Cleveland with League Park as their home, going 25–20 on the season in the Negro American League. They added slugger Sam Jethroe, pitcher Willie Grace and player-manager Quincy Trouppe, who was also the team's catcher.

The team's League Park debut came before a "meager crowd" on May 2 in a scheduled exhibition doubleheader against the St. Louis Stars. Rain interfered, however, and the second game was canceled after the first game ended in a 1–1 tie in 11 innings. The home season was restricted to a series of home doubleheaders, beginning with a 3–0 and 4–2 sweep of the Cincinnati Clowns on May 30.

After splitting with the Kansas City Monarchs the following week, there was controversy at the next home date, June 20 versus Chicago. The visitors won both games but not before the umpire threw out two players, nearly causing a Chicago forfeit. Instead, team operator Wilbur Hayes convinced the arbiter to rescind the ejections so that the crowd wouldn't be denied the opportunity to see the games. The dispute caused a delay of 45 minutes.

Legendary Josh Gibson of the Homestead Grays homered over the right field wall on the next home date as the Grays swept a pair of games before 7500 fans. Next, on August 1, the Buckeyes swept Memphis, 7–1 and 1–0, as pitcher Eugene Bremer threw a one-hitter in the nightcap. A season-high crowd of 10,000 saw the games with Birmingham on August 29 and the home season ended with a sweep of Cincinnati on September 12. The *Call and Post* listed the season's total home attendance at 40,000.

Cleveland then went 40–41 in the 1944 campaign as Jethroe led the league in batting average and stolen bases. The team managed to play the more extensive schedule despite the wartime travel restrictions. The team's record was good enough for third place in the league.

Then, in 1945, the hiring of all-star backstop Trouppe as player/manager left the team poised for success. A crowd of over 10,000 watched the Buckeyes take a doubleheader from the Memphis Red Sox in their home opener on May 27 to begin the 1945 season. Controversy prevailed during game one of a June doubleheader against Chicago. With the score tied 1–1 in the 13th inning, the Buckeyes had the bases loaded with no one out. Parnell Woods hit a grounder to shortstop and Avelino Canizares was called safe on a close play at the plate to give Cleveland a 2–1 win. The Chicago players protested so vehemently that police came out to protect umpire Harry Walker. Chicago won the nightcap, 6–1, and Walker umpired again without incident.

The Buckeyes won the Negro American League's first-half title with a 31–9 record and continued to excel in the second half of the season. On September 2, the Buckeyes won a doubleheader from the Chicago American Giants, 6–2 and 10–0, at League Park with 5000 in attendance. The game was designated "Wilbur Hayes Day" and the Cleveland team executive was presented with a certificate for a 1946 automobile in recognition of his longtime promotion of sports in the black community.

The Buckeyes also wound up winning the second-half title with a 22–7 mark, sending the team and its combined 53–16 record straight to the 1945 Negro World Series against the Homestead Grays, winners of the Negro National League. The Grays featured legends Cool Papa Bell, Josh Gibson and Buck Leonard.

Game one took place at Cleveland Stadium (where the Buckeyes had also played occasional home regular season games) and the home team won, 2–1, before 6500 fans on Thursday night, September 13. The teams then played an exhibition game in Dayton on Friday night while the stadium hosted a Cleveland Rams football exhibition game and returned to Cleveland for game two at League Park on Sunday afternoon, September 16.

While St. Ignatius and Cathedral Latin were playing high school football at the stadium, a crowd of 10,000 showed up at League Park for baseball. Willie Grace homered for the Buckeyes in the eighth inning over the right-field screen, as Cleveland rallied to tie the score at two each. Pitcher Eugene Bremer came up with the bases loaded and two out in the ninth and drove in the winning run with a drive off the famous right-field wall to give the Buckeyes the 3–2 win. The fans rushed the field and carried Bremer on their shoulders in celebration.

The next day's game, scheduled at the Grays' home field in Pittsburgh, was rained out. The teams traveled to a neutral site, Washington, D.C., on Tuesday, where the Buckeyes won, 4–0, behind the pitching of Big George Jefferson. They next moved to Shibe Park in Philadelphia on Thursday and Cleveland completed the four-game sweep with a 5–0 win with Frank Carswell on the mound.

While posting a 26–27 record in 1946, another League Park oddity occurred as the Buckeyes became the only Negro League team with a white player, pitcher Eddie Klep, who began the season with the team but was released after just three appearances.

In 1947, the team had League Park all to itself with Bill Veeck having moved the entire Indians' schedule to the stadium. This made it possible for the Buckeyes to play an expanded league schedule and almost resulted in the addition of lights and night games to League Park. Veeck was reportedly supportive of a plan by Westinghouse which would have cost the Buckeyes $10,000 for equipment and $5000 for installation. Considering that it would have cost the team $2500 rental to take a single night game to the stadium, Wright and Hayes thought that the plan might pay off. The idea never came to fruition, however.

The Buckeyes enjoyed another great season in 1947 winning the Negro American League pennant with a record of 54–23. This time, they met the New York Cubans in the World Series. The first game, at the Polo Grounds, resulted in a 5–5 tie that was halted by rain. Game two was played at Yankee Stadium, where the Buckeyes took a 10–7 decision.

The Cubans then took control of the series, winning 9–4 in Philadelphia and 9–2 in Chicago. The next stop was in Cleveland and the Cubans won again, 6–0, at Cleveland Stadium to go up three games to one. On September

28, facing elimination, the Buckeyes took the field at League Park. Cleveland jumped out to a 5–0 lead but allowed New York to score in the sixth, seventh and eighth innings for a 6–5 win to wrap up the series, four games to one. The game drew a crowd of 4500 while the Indians were simultaneously closing out their regular season at the stadium with a 1–0 loss to Detroit before 27,617.

Despite the loss, the Buckeyes had a terrific year. A solid hitting team, they were led by Sam Jethroe, who led the league in batting (.356) as well as doubles, triples, runs scored and stolen bases. Five other regulars batted over .300 for the year. But interest in the Negro Leagues was beginning to wane as Jackie Robinson had broken the color barrier with Brooklyn of the National League and Larry Doby had integrated the American League with the Indians in 1947.

Old Satch

Satchel Paige, likely the most identifiable player in the history of Negro League baseball, had toiled off-and-on at League Park throughout his legendary career that had begun in 1927 with the Birmingham Black Barons. In a career that had seen him throw an amazing number of innings for an equally amazing number of teams, Paige had even hurled for the 1931 Cleveland Cubs.

He later reminisced about his days in Cleveland in his 1962 book, *Maybe I'll Pitch Forever*, and revealed his frustration with the color barrier. He said that he'd "look over at ... League Park. That was the big money there. All season long it burned me, playing there in the shadow of that stadium."[4] This comment apparently contributed to a misidentification of the location of the Cubs' home field as being "directly across the street from League Park" according to the wonderfully comprehensive 1989 *Ballparks of North America*, by Michael Benson. The park was not literally in the shadow of League Park. And Paige, of course, did get many opportunities in League Park over the years, but never as a major leaguer.

But in 1948, Paige did get his shot in the big leagues by signing with the Cleveland Indians on July 7, his 42nd birthday. Certainly past his prime, Old Satch still had the ability to be a key to the Indians' pennant run downtown at Cleveland Stadium. He had previously teamed up with star Cleveland pitcher Bob Feller to set up a series of off-season barnstorming games with other major and Negro Leaguers.

The sad irony of Paige's signing with the Indians was that it helped seal the fate of Negro League baseball in Cleveland and beyond. Paige compiled a record of 6–1 with a 2.47 ERA for the World Series champion Tribe. He made one appearance in the Series, pitching a hitless inning of relief against the Boston Braves.

This view shows the entire League Park area in October 1949 as the Buckeyes were about to return for their final games there in 1950. It's also easy to see how difficult parking must have been around the ballpark (Robert Runyan photograph, collection of Bruce Young).

Paige returned to the Indians in 1949 and pitched for the St. Louis Browns from 1951–53. In 1952, at age 46, he posted a record of 12–10 with a 3.07 ERA for a Browns team that finished in 7th place with a dismal record of 64–90! He came back for one final big league appearance on September 25, 1965, throwing three innings of shutout ball and allowing just one hit for the Kansas City Athletics at the age of 59. He was elected to the Baseball Hall of Fame in 1971.

The Buckeyes Fade

Opening day at League Park in 1948 saw Cleveland split a doubleheader with the Birmingham Black Barons before 6000 fans. Cleveland mayor Tom Burke, wearing a Buckeyes cap, threw out the first pitch. The pageantry included the Elks Drum and Bugle Corps and the Buckeye Jazz Band playing the national anthem. After a slow start on the field that year, the Buckeyes went on a streak of 16 wins in 17 outings, but the *Cleveland Call and Post* continued to lament the lack of crowd support for the team. The newspaper blamed the $1.50 ticket price that the team was now charging for all seats.

Meanwhile, the team was trying desperately to increase interest and enhance its reputation. An agreement was reached with television station WEWS to televise some of the team's games in 1948, starting with a doubleheader against the Memphis Red Sox on June 6. But the Buckeyes' landlord, Veeck and the Indians, nixed the deal according to the *Cleveland Call and Post* on May 15, saying that "because of the rent agreement, the Buckeyes could not give permission for installation of the television equipment in the park."[5] It's likely that Veeck was using a technicality that the Buckeyes' lease did not specifically allow for such telecasts since he did not want the additional competition to Indians' ticket sales or broadcasts.

Indians management apparently relented, however, as the *Call and Post* of June 12 reported that "more history was made when television station WEWS covered both games (of the doubleheader with Memphis) with Van Patrick handling the play-by-play and Paul Hodges doing the pre-game interviews. This marks the first time in Negro ball that a team has had simultaneous radio and television coverage."[6] Cleveland and Memphis split the twinbill. There were no additional telecasts, however, as the Buckeyes feared that the televised games would further erode their already dwindling attendance figures.

A week after the television test, on June 13, legendary Negro Leaguer Buck O'Neill, manager of the Kansas City Monarchs, brought his team to Cleveland for a doubleheader. Cleveland swept O'Neill's team, 6–5 and 6–2, before some 3000 fans.

Another highlight of the year came when a crowd of 6500 (including 500 kids admitted for free) turned out for a 4th of July doubleheader with the Indianapolis Clowns, the Buckeyes' biggest attendance of the year. That season also provided a chance for League Park fans to see a future all-time great when the Buckeyes played the Birmingham Black Barons. A teenaged outfielder with great power and speed named Willie Mays patrolled the League Park outfield for the Barons that year.

But the integration of the major leagues continued to take its toll on the Negro Leagues, especially in Cleveland, where the Indians were in the race for the American League pennant with former Negro League stars Satchel Paige and Larry Doby playing key roles. On September 5, the Buckeyes finished their home season with a doubleheader sweep of the Chicago American Giants, 5–0 and 3–1, but only 1100 fans turned out. The Buckeyes finished third of six teams in the league with a record of 41–42, but with the Indians having won the major league World Series that year, the Negro League team continued to slide toward oblivion.

So Hayes moved the Buckeyes to Louisville for the 1949 season, hoping for better attendance. The team did return to League Park one day in July that year, meeting the Indianapolis Clowns in a doubleheader that drew a crowd of 5500. Hayes admitted that Louisville was no better, so the Buckeyes returned for one last hurrah at League Park in 1950. But Jethroe had been signed away by the National League's Boston Braves, where he earned Rookie of the Year honors. More and more players were abandoning the Negro Leagues, and the leagues were garnering less and less attention as a result. The Buckeyes were unable to finish out the 1950 season, folding on July 6 with a record of 3–39. Negro League baseball in Cleveland was done, taking professional baseball from the venue for good and leaving League Park one step closer to extinction.[7]

7

Beyond Baseball

Some of the people ... who live or work nearby didn't even know the park was once the home of the Cleveland Indians, let alone such defunct teams as football's Cleveland Rams.—Grant Segall, *Cleveland Plain Dealer*

Multi-Purpose

The behemoth ballpark by Lake Erie, Cleveland Municipal Stadium, issued in an era of multi-purpose outdoor sports facilities that dominated the country for the next half century. It would host an extensive variety of events over the years, including some that its designers could never even have imagined. Cleveland Stadium's sheer size allowed for this flexibility, but the drawbacks of its size became evident almost right away as well, as evidenced by the failure of the 1932–33 shift of all Indians' home games there and by the sporadic use of the park for baseball that ensued between 1936 and 1946.

Likewise, League Park had quietly thrived in fulfilling a multi-purpose role of its own throughout its existence. Both boxing and football had significant histories at the park. Football especially grew with the park, which played host to many key games between teams at the high school, college and professional levels. Two NFL champion teams called League Park home. In addition, there was one other unusual usage of the park for baseball purposes.

Hollywood Calls

While the Cleveland Buckeyes had vacated League Park in 1949 for Louisville, the big leaguers did actually make a return of sorts for a couple of days that year. A feature film, "The Kid from Cleveland," was filmed in the city during the spring of 1949.

It was the story of a troubled teenaged "Kid," played by Russ Tamblyn, who had run away from home. In the movie, his life is turned around by a sportscaster and the Cleveland Indians team as they defend their 1948 world championship. The film featured most of the current Indians players as well as owner Bill Veeck, general manager Hank Greenberg and coach Tris Speaker, all playing themselves. Included are numerous scenes in and around Cleveland Municipal Stadium, along with actual game footage and highlights.

League Park gets an appearance about midway through the 89-minute Republic Pictures production. Exactly four minutes and one second of scenes made the final cut from League Park, which is used to fill in as the Tribe's spring training ballpark in Tucson, Arizona. Shots from behind the batting cage at home plate and down the left field line give good views of the double-decked third-base grandstand. And several shots from different angles in left field show the seating areas in the left-field bleachers and the pavilion seats beyond third base down the left-field line. Plenty of extras, largely neighborhood residents, can be seen in the stands, and there is dialogue by most of the Indians stars, including Bob Feller, Satchel Paige and Lou Boudreau as well as Veeck, Greenberg and Speaker.

Released on September 5, 1949, the movie was largely panned by critics. Players who appeared were not paid, but instead offered a portion of the profits. It is doubtful that there were any. Veeck once stated, "I have an unwritten law at home that I adhere to: I never allow my kids to mention or see that abortion." Boudreau added, "I would like to buy every print of it and burn it."[2] The movie was promoted with the slogan, "The Story Of ... A Kid ... A City ... And 30 Godfathers!," which was a reference to the team's roster. The slogan prompted Feller to quip, "Those Thirty Godfathers must have been the only people who ever saw it. At least that's what we hope."[3]

Tamblyn, "The Kid," did go on to appear in more critically acclaimed films later in life, such as "Seven Brides For Seven Brothers" and "West Side Story."

Boxing Days

While League Park is most certainly noted for baseball, boxing was the sport that challenged the National Pastime for general sporting interest during the park's heyday. Naturally, with the most seats of any venue in Cleveland until the stadium opened in 1931, that the site was used when big fights came to the city during the warm weather months.

The fighter most responsible for the increased popularity of the sport in Cleveland and the use of League Park for boxing was a featherweight champion named Johnny Kilbane. Born in Cleveland in 1889, Kilbane grew up on the city's west side and took up boxing at age 18 to help support his family. Having found success, he was able to get a title match with champion Abe Attell in Kansas City in 1910. He lost, but worked toward a rematch, finally getting it in February 1912 in California. He won a 20-round decision and

Cleveland favorite Johnny Kilbane is in action in the boxing ring at League Park in 1918. Seats were placed on the infield area while the ring itself appears to be located between the pitcher's mound and the first-base line. The grandstand shown is that just beyond first base, down the right-field line. Note the Indians' home dugout along the right side of the picture (Cleveland State University, Cleveland Press Collection).

returned home as a conquering hero. Attell, by the way, resurfaced as one of the gamblers involved with the Black Sox scandal of the 1919 World Series.

The celebratory parade for the Irishman Kilbane on St. Patrick's Day was witnessed by what was reported to be the largest gathering of people in the history of the city, estimated at 100,000. And, late in 1911, Mayor Herman Baehr ended a ban of boxing in the city, paving the way for Kilbane to fight in his hometown, first at Gray's Armory.

Kilbane retained his title for the next several years and, with the onset of World War I, became a boxing instructor in the U.S. Army in 1918. It was during this time that Kilbane debuted at League Park as part of a military benefit boxing card on July 6. The exhibition bouts were to support the soldier's recreational fund. Ten matches were slated that day, with Kilbane the only current champion on the card.

Most of the city's leading citizens attended, with many women also in attendance. Three bands were on hand and a crowd of nearly 8000 included uniformed soldiers and sailors, who were admitted free of charge. One hundred Red Cross workers were also in attendance. The bouts were filmed for distribution at various Army camps. The boxers involved received only railroad fare and hotel expenses, while ticket sellers and ushers donated their services. Nearly $13,000 was raised. Kilbane, who didn't take the bout very seriously, out-pointed Larry Hansen in their four-round match. Matt Brock also decisioned Johnny Dundee in their four-rounder, considered the best bout of the night.

Two years later, Kilbane was involved in his first real boxing card at League Park. On Wednesday night, July 28, 1920, Kilbane met Artie Root in a non-title bout. That afternoon, with the Indians in the heat of the pennant race, Jim Bagby had thrown a shutout as the Tribe defeated Boston. Temporary lighting and the ring were set up for the nighttime boxing card. The largest fight crowd in Cleveland to date, 14,000, saw Kilbane send Root to the canvas in the fifth round. Root survived the knockdown but lost the 10-round decision. Kilbane pocketed $10,000 for his winning effort.

The boxing matches at League Park continued in 1921. On May 25, a Wednesday night, Kilbane defeated British fighter Freddie Jacks before 7500 fight fans to retain his featherweight crown with a unanimous 10-round decision.

He returned to defend his title again at League Park on September 17 that year, when he was guaranteed $50,000 to face Baltimore's Danny Frush. Ticket prices ranged from $15 for ringside to $2, with a 10 percent war tax. Controversy surrounded the match, beginning when Kilbane initially refused to fight over a dispute about the judges selected by the Boxing Commission. The dispute was settled and Kilbane took to the ring. In the first round, Kilbane complained to the referee about a low blow, and Frush hit him again while he was complaining. Kilbane retaliated by kneeing Frush, who fell to the canvas. The referee refused to award a forfeit and Frush returned, only to be knocked down four times before being knocked out in the seventh round. Sixty policemen entered the ring to maintain order after the knockout.

After 12 years as world champion, longer than any featherweight in history, Kilbane was finally dethroned by Eugene Criqui on June 2, 1923, at New York's Polo Grounds and retired from the ring. He later used his popularity to be elected Cleveland's Clerk of Courts.

At least one other world championship was decided at League Park, that of the welterweight crown in 1930. Tommy Freeman, though born in Arkansas, had been adopted by Cleveland as its own. He faced "Young" Jack

Thompson on September 3 before 8000 fans. Although he was knocked down in the second round, Freeman battled back, knocking Thompson to one knee with a barrage of punches in the twelfth. Freeman scored the upset over the Californian with a 15-round decision to take the title.

Freeman won his next five bouts after that, but lost in a rematch with Thompson indoors at Cleveland Public Hall on April 14, 1931, on a 12-round technical knockout.

High School Football Arrives

Despite being built for baseball, League Park was used from its early years as a site for football games. High schools and other amateurs began playing football there before the turn of the century, when the park was still in its wooden configuration. The oddly shaped baseball field easily lent itself to the gridiron, which ran along the third-base line with end zones in front of the first-base seats and the left-field bleachers.

On November 21, 1896, Central High School and University School met at League Park to decide the interscholastic championship of Cleveland, the first football game on the grounds. Touchdowns at that time were worth 4 points and field goals were worth 5 points. The weather was rainy and the field quickly became a sea of mud. Central took an 8–0 lead at halftime (halves were 35 minutes long) and increased the lead to 12–0 before holding on to win, 12–9. The next week at League Park, the Collinwood YMCA team defeated the Cleveland Medical College by a score of 6–0. The game featured a 75-yard touchdown run and conversion kick. The game was played with 20-minute halves.

League Park continued to host prep football games in the ensuing years. One of the biggest took place in 1904 when East High and Central met in front of nearly 6000 fans. East High claimed that year's championship with a convincing 38–5 victory.

In 1919, St. Ignatius and Cathedral Latin met for just the second time. Latin overcame the muddy conditions to gain the 7–0 win. This began a string of Thanksgiving Day games between the two schools at the venue. The two longtime Cleveland powerhouses also scheduled key battles with other foes on the League Park gridiron.

The growing popularity of high school football in Cleveland during the 1920s continued to make League Park an attractive venue for big games because of its large seating capacity, chairback seats and excellent views of the field. In 1920, West Tech and East Tech met on November 27 to decide the city championship. After a scoreless first half, East Tech scored on a long touchdown run and won the game, 7–0, before 10,000 fans.

In 1921, the first intersectional high school football game in Cleveland was played on October 29 at League Park. West Tech beat Fitchburg, Massachusetts, 13–12, as Marty Karowski threw for one touchdown and ran for another in the fourth quarter for the win.

The biggest game that year, however, came a week later on November 5 when East Tech attempted to beat a powerful Toledo Scott team for the second year in a row. Newspapers had billed it as the most important scholastic game ever played in Cleveland. With a crowd of 13,000 looking on, the two teams battled to a 7–7 halftime tie. In the fourth quarter, a Scott field goal attempt was blocked and returned for a touchdown, giving East Tech a 14–7 win.

In 1922, Glenville High, led by the running and passing of future NFL Hall of Famer Benny Friedman, played East High at the ballpark on November 3. Friedman scored two touchdowns and an extra point as Glenville won, 13–0, before 15,000 spectators. Two years later, the big game was between Lakewood and West Tech. Despite a snowstorm, 10,000 came to watch the game as Lakewood won, 9–6.

After 1925, no high school games were played at League Park until 1930. On November 1 of that year, East Tech and East High clashed at the ballpark. With 10,000 fans watching, East Tech won by the score of 6–0. Two weeks later, East Tech returned to face West High before 8000, winning 18–0. By the fall of 1931, however, city-owned Cleveland Stadium had opened and that venue was a natural to take over many of the biggest high school games, especially those involving Cleveland public schools.

The Old College Try

College football also found its way to League Park during the 1920s. John Carroll University (known as St. Ignatius College until 1922) began playing the sport in 1920, using League Park as its home field until 1925. In 1923, John Carroll took over League Park's Thanksgiving Day tradition from the St. Ignatius and Cathedral Latin high schools, playing host to cross-town rival Baldwin-Wallace. John Carroll won in freezing rain, 25–0, as halfback Dick Bright scored every point in the game. In 1924, the Thanksgiving Day opponent was North Dakota and John Carroll won again, 28–0. Fordham, still a decade away from its most-famous "Seven Blocks of Granite" teams, came to League Park for the holiday game in 1925 and downed John Carroll, 13–7.

The four local football-playing colleges got together to form the Big Four Conference in 1933. Baldwin-Wallace, Case Tech, John Carroll and Western Reserve had finally decided that playing each other in football every year made sense. Western Reserve and Case, the two side-by-side institutions, had already taken their annual, late-season rivalry game to League Park in 1929.

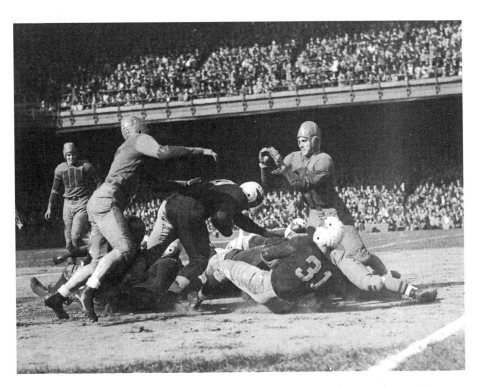

Leather helmets were still in vogue when this football action photograph was taken at League Park during the 1935 collegiate season. The visible grandstands are those running along the third-base line, in front of Linwood Avenue (Cleveland Public Library).

In 1930, when Ray Ride became the head coach at Case, John Carroll was coached by Ralph Vince, both of whom were graduates of Washington & Jefferson College in Pennsylvania. That relationship was the key to getting the four schools to overcome their differences and agree to play a full round-robin.

The formation of the Big Four made for immediate rivalries and elevated the interest of both the fans and the press in local college football. All-Big Four teams were to be selected at the end of the season by the coaches and local newspapers. The Campbell Trophy was to be presented to the league champion on the basis of two points for a victory and one for a tie.

League Park was one of the main venues for Big Four contests until 1942, when World War II largely interrupted intercollegiate athletics. It was generally used by Western Reserve as its home field during those years, and 18 of the 60 Big Four matchups took place at League Park. Only Cleveland Stadium, with 22 of the contests, hosted more. John Carroll called Cleveland

Stadium home during this time, while BW and Case Tech often used their on-campus fields. Those two teams would occasionally use League Park or the stadium when projected attendance dictated.

Amazingly, in the first year of competition, 1933, all four teams finished with one win, one loss and a tie in the head-to-head meetings. Overall, each school had a winning record that year: Baldwin-Wallace and Case at 5–3–1, John Carroll at 5–2–2 and Western Reserve at 4–3–1.

In 1934 Western Reserve went undefeated in the Big Four, winning games at League Park over each of its three conference rivals. The Red Cats nipped previously unbeaten Baldwin-Wallace, 8–6. BW star Kenny Noble was tackled in the end zone late in the game for a safety to provide the margin of victory. WRU shut down star John Carroll ball-carrier Mike Artale to prevail, 14–0, in front of a crowd of 13,000. Reserve then clinched the championship with a 21–13 win over Case before 10,000.

Ohio State Invades

The most notable game of that 1934 season was a non-conference game for Western Reserve against Ohio State at League Park. In January, Sam Willaman had resigned as Ohio State's head coach to take over at Western Reserve. Granted a full professorship at the WRU, he wound up with a salary increase. In addition, the Buckeyes agreed to meet the Red Cats on the first Saturday in November.

New OSU coach Francis Schmidt brought his team to Cleveland with a 3–1 record, having only lost to Illinois, 14–13. It was the first game for Ohio State in Cleveland since a 28–0 victory at Case Tech's Van Horn field in 1916. Ohio State had not played Western Reserve since 1913, a 14–8 Buckeye win in Columbus. Despite Reserve's undefeated status, Ohio State was a huge favorite to win. The Buckeye line averaged 207 pounds, outweighing Western Reserve by an average of 27 pounds per man.

Ohio State took the train to Terminal Tower in Cleveland and stayed overnight at the Lake Shore Hotel. The all-brass band also came from Columbus to support the Scarlet and Gray. In the spirit of friendly competition, Western Reserve planted a buckeye tree in front of Adelbert Library to mark the renewal of the rivalry. High school teams from the Cleveland area were invited to attend the game. Ticket prices ranged from $3.00 to $1.20.

Western Reserve took the opening kick and was quickly forced to punt. It took Ohio State just four plays to score. Dick Heekin ran in the first touchdown to begin a rout before 11,000 fans. Damon Wetzel then scored on a 41-yard run and quarterback Tippy Dye threw touchdown passes to John Bettridge and Frank Antenucci to make it 28–0 at halftime.

Football action goes across the baseball infield during a 1935 Western Reserve University home game versus Baldwin-Wallace College at League Park. Reserve took a legitimate shot at bringing big-time college football to Cleveland and League Park in the 1940s but gave up on the effort in the 1950s (Cleveland Public Library).

The second half was even worse for Western Reserve. Ohio State added three touchdowns in the third period and four more in the fourth to win, 76–0. Ohio State gained 482 rushing yards and 224 passing while holding the Red Cats to 101 total yards. The margin of victory led to complaints that the Buckeyes had run up the score.

Big Four Heyday

The 1935 Big Four championship was decided by Baldwin-Wallace and Western Reserve in front of 21,000 at League Park, the largest Big Four Conference crowd ever at the facility. Baldwin-Wallace came into the game with a 3–0 record, having outscored Buffalo, John Carroll and Bowling Green by a combined score of 129–6. The team of BW coach Ray Watts, with stars such as Ken Noble, Norm Schoen and Dick Van Alman, was referred to as the "Aerial Circus." The Yellow Jackets wound up as college football's highest-scoring team that year, with an average of 43.8 points per game. Western Reserve had what may have been the best football team in school history. Led

A packed lower deck and bleacher area shows part of the total attendance of 18,483 at a college football game inside League Park in 1938. Western Reserve University utilized League Park for most of its home games in the 1930s and 1940s. This one was against crosstown rival John Carroll. The NFL Rams, having used League Park in 1937, played elsewhere from 1938–1941 before returning for their final four seasons in Cleveland, 1942–1945, then moving to Los Angeles, and ultimately St. Louis (Cleveland State University, Cleveland Press Collection).

by running backs Ray Zeh and Vic Ippolito, they had defeated Hillsdale, Cornell and Buffalo by a combined score of 120–19. The teams were tied at 14 at halftime, but the Red Cats pulled away in the second half to win, 27–14. The crowd was also the largest yet to see a football game involving local schools.

As John Carroll and Case Tech struggled in 1936, the big game again was Baldwin-Wallace versus Western Reserve at League Park. And once again the teams were undefeated when they met. The Red Cats were 4–0, including a 59–0 win over Findlay and a 40–0 pasting of Bowling Green. Baldwin-Wallace was 3–0, coming off of a 19–7 win in frigid conditions at Syracuse.

A gathering of 18,000 came for the match-up in rainy conditions. The rain may have helped neutralize BW's wide-open offense. Western Reserve scored on its first possession to go up 7–0 and never trailed in the contest, winning 20–6. It turned out to be BW's only loss of the season as the Yellow

Jackets went 7–1. Western Reserve went 10–0 on the season, outscoring its opponents 244–28.

Western Reserve continued its dominance of the Big Four in 1937. The Red Cats went undefeated in the conference and finished 8–2 overall. Baldwin-Wallace was bested by WRU at League Park once again, this time by a score of 21–7 in front of 13,000. The conference season ended with a Reserve victory over their neighboring rival Case Tech, 6–0, before 17,000 fans at League Park.

The following year, 1938, Western Reserve coach Bill Edwards once again had a powerful squad, shutting out Baldwin-Wallace 40–0 in front of 8000 at League Park. A much-improved John Carroll team faced the Red Cats in November in a critical Big Four showdown. A paid crowd of 18,321, second best for a Big Four game at League Park, was on hand to see Reserve stars like receiver Al Litwak, running backs Johnnie Ries and Steve Belichek and punter Johnny Andrews take on the Blue Streaks with Lou Sulzer, Jim Morgan and Eddie Arsenault, a running back from Maine who also starred on the JCU hockey team.

Dick Booth of the Red Cats raced 76 yards for a touchdown on just the second play of the game and Western Reserve led, 7–0. An Arsenault interception in the second period set up a touchdown run by Bill Young for the Blue Streaks, but the extra point was missed and Reserve was still ahead, 7–6. Just before halftime, John Carroll blocked a punt out of the end zone for a safety to take an 8–7 lead.

Reserve got a 13-yard touchdown run by Ries to take a 14–8 lead in the third quarter. In the final period, the Red Cats pulled away with an 80-yard touchdown drive and an interception return for a TD and a 27–8 win. Twelve days later, on Thanksgiving Day, the Red Cats capped an undefeated Big Four season at League Park, beating the Case Tech Rough Riders, 13–3, before 10,000 fans in the annual holiday match-up.

Having gone undefeated in Big Four games since going 1–1–1 in the 1933 inaugural year, Western Reserve finally lost a pair Big Four games in 1939, 8–7 to Baldwin-Wallace and 6–0 to John Carroll, though neither game took place at League Park. John Carroll won the league at 3–0 and was 7–1 overall. Each of the conference schools finished with overall winning records that year with Baldwin-Wallace 6–2, Western Reserve 5–3–1 and Case Tech 5–3. Western Reserve again won the rivalry game with Case, 18–0, at League Park with 12,000 fans in attendance.

John Carroll and Baldwin-Wallace slumped in 1940, leaving neighbors Case Tech and Western Reserve to meet in a showdown for the league crown at League Park. Case came in at 6–1, having lost only at Carnegie Tech, while WRU was also 6–1, with the lone setback at Dayton. Reserve had won the four previous Saturdays at League Park, defeating Miami 47–6, Boston University 19–0, Ohio University 6–0 and John Carroll 12–0.

The Thanksgiving Day battle between Case and Reserve turned out to be one of the most exciting football games ever played at League Park. A crowd of 13,365 watched in ideal weather conditions as Johnny Ries ran 73 yards for a touchdown in the first period to put the Red Cats ahead 6–0. A goal-line stand prevented WRU from extending the lead and then Bob Melreit scored on a 2-yard run for Case. The extra point put the Rough Riders up 7–6 at the half. Ries threw a touchdown pass of 23 yards to put Western Reserve back in front, 12–7, in the third, but Melreit again ran for a touchdown and Case regained the lead, 14–12, going into the final quarter.

The score stayed that way through the period, but Reserve had the ball late with a chance to take the lead. Coach Bill Edwards called on Ernie Eros, who had been taken off the field with a third-quarter injury, to try a 32-yard field goal. The kick wobbled over the crossbar to give Reserve a 15–14 win and the Big Four championship. Western Reserve was rewarded with an invitation to the Sun Bowl in El Paso, Texas, where the Red Cats defeated Arizona State, 26–13, on New Year's Day, 1941.

In the 1941 season, Western Reserve looked to again repeat as champions. The Red Cats defeated John Carroll, 27–20, at Cleveland Stadium and Baldwin-Wallace, 19–0, at League Park to set up another showdown against Case for the title. The Rough Riders were undefeated and high ticket demand caused the game to be switched to Cleveland Stadium. It was a wise move, as an all-time Big Four record crowd of 38,827 turned out, more than could be accommodated at League Park, for Reserve's 26–6 win.

Reserve moved its home games away from League Park to Shaw Stadium in 1942, which turned out to be the final season for the conference. WRU won the outright crown again, its eighth in the ten years of competition. The Litkenhous rating system placed the league as the 12th strongest in the country but, like many schools around the country, John Carroll and Western Reserve elected to shut down their programs for the duration of the World War II. And, as a result, the Big Four wound up shutting down too ... forever.

Red Cats Aim High

Western Reserve clearly had been the dominant college football program in the city during the Big Four days, with its eight outright league titles and another shared crown during the league's ten years of existence. Highlights were the perfect 10–0 season of 1936, another undefeated campaign of 9–0 in 1938, and the 8–2 season of 1940, which included the Sun Bowl victory. The Red Cats were 26–3–1 in head-to-head Big Four games and 75–14–4 overall during that era. So when football resumed at Western Reserve in 1946, the institution had set its sights on a higher level of competition and began an upgrade toward a national schedule. The Red Cats went 4–3–2 in their return season that year, playing their home schedule at Shaw Stadium. But with the Indians having vacated League Park in 1947, WRU took the opportunity to become a prime tenant of the ballpark that fall. Among the foes at home were Ohio University and Cincinnati, as the team went 4–5. Road games included contests with Rutgers and Duquesne.

Meanwhile in 1947, the *Pittsburgh Courier* Charity Fund Football Classic was played at the park to benefit the Cleveland NAACP. The October 4 game pitted Wilberforce against Kentucky State. After a scoreless first half, Andy Bibb ran for a pair of Wilberforce touchdowns and his team went on to a 34–6 win before 8000 fans.

Also that year, John Carroll used League Park for a home game for the final time. The Blue Streaks, playing their home games at Shaw Stadium, expected a big crowd for their October 18th game with Baldwin-Wallace. So the game was shifted, but drew only 8000, as JCU topped BW, 28–19. Carl Taseff, who went on to an extensive career as an NFL player and assistant coach, scored two touchdowns to lead the victors. Fullback Lee Tressel, later BW's storied coach and the father of eventual Ohio State head coach Jim Tressel, scored one of the touchdowns for the Yellow Jackets.

The next year, 1948, Western Reserve had an even more ambitious schedule in its attempt to bring big-time college football to Cleveland and League Park, playing home games against Pittsburgh, Kent State and Miami of Ohio. Road contests included the likes of West Virginia, Brown and Western Michigan, as well as a return game at Cincinnati. Reserve also kept the Case Tech rivalry alive during this stretch with a Thanksgiving Day game at League Park, but the Red Cats dropped John Carroll and Baldwin-Wallace from their schedule. The tough schedule took its toll on WRU, as the Cats went just 1–8–1, with the lone win over Butler, 6–0, at League Park on October 9.

In 1949, Ohio, Brown, Western Michigan and West Virginia all returned the previous year's games with contests at League Park. But the Cats could only salvage a 7–7 tie with Ohio from those four games. And the West Virginia game, on Saturday, November 19, drew less than a thousand fans, according to the *Plain Dealer* report. WRU did lead that game, 13–0, before falling, 21–13. Among the wins that season were games at Kent State and Butler, as well as a 30–0 rout of Case Tech to close out the year and ensure local supremacy on Thanksgiving. Mayor Tom Burke and Governor Frank Lausche were among the 12,500 in attendance for the game with Case, which gave Reserve a final record of 4–5–1.

After the 1949 season, the Red Cats left aging League Park for good,

Western Reserve, which later merged with Case Tech to form Case Western Reserve University, abandoned League Park after the 1949 season. This is a program cover from that final season. The Red Cats tied this game, 7–7, but lost each of their other home games that year to Brown, Western Michigan and West Virginia (Image property of Case Western Reserve University Archives).

returning to Shaw Stadium before moving on campus to Clarke Field in 1951. By 1955, Western Reserve completely abandoned its big-time aspirations, reducing the scope and length of its schedule dramatically.

Pro Ball and the Early NFL

Professional football in Cleveland got its start at League Park on October 8, 1916. A team called the Cleveland Indians of the Ohio League defeated the Carlisle Indians, 39–7, before 3500 fans, some sitting in temporary bleachers on the south side of the field and in front of the famous right field wall.

When the National Football League was formed in 1920 (initially under the banner of the American Professional Football Association), Cleveland joined the loop under new team owner Jimmy O'Donnell. Renamed the Cleveland Tigers and using League Park as its home, Cleveland went 2–4–2 on the season, placing tenth among the 14 teams in the league. The team's first home game was on Sunday, October 31, a 7–0 win over the Columbus Panhandles. The remaining home games were played on the next three Sundays.

In 1921, the team acquired perhaps the greatest athlete of all-time, Native American Jim Thorpe, who took over as player-coach. The season opened at home on October 16, with Columbus again providing the opposition. Thorpe scored on a long touchdown run in the first quarter and, with the team up 27–0 in the second, he was able to sit out the rest of the game. The Tigers went on to a 35–9 win.

The Cincinnati Celts invaded League Park the following week. Thorpe left the game after being injured while making a catch, but Cleveland still won, 28–0. The team's other League Park contest was a 7–0 loss to the Canton Bulldogs on November 13. A 3–5 final record was good for 11th place among the 21 teams but it was not good enough for the team to continue and Cleveland was out of pro football in 1922.

Cleveland jeweler Samuel Deutsch formed a new franchise called the Indians in 1923, again setting up shop at League Park. Cleveland carried a 3–0–3 record into its season-ending game with the Canton Bulldogs, which were also undefeated at 7–0–1, so the November 25 match-up was billed as the league championship. A crowd of 18,000 on a cloudy, mild day saw Canton jump to a 20–3 lead en route to a 46–10 win. The Bulldogs played and won three more games to finish the season 11–0–1, their second straight undefeated season.

Then, Deutsch used the "if you can't beat 'em, join 'em" approach, purchasing the Canton team and combining them with his Indians squad to become the Cleveland Bulldogs in 1924. The team went 7–1–1, good for first place and the championship of the 18-team NFL. With the unbalanced schedule, coach Guy Chamberlin's team posted a winning percentage of .875, edging out the Chicago Bears (6–1–4, .857), Frankford Yellow Jackets (11–2–1, .846) and the Duluth Kelleys (5–1–0, .833) for the title. Frankford (just outside of Philadelphia) had handed Cleveland both blemishes on its record, a 3–3 tie at Frankford and a 12–7 loss at League Park on November 16. The Cleveland team was otherwise often dominant on its way to the championship, defeating Rochester 59–0, Dayton 35–0 and Milwaukee 53–10.

In the unsettled world of pro football in that era, teams came and went. So in 1925, the Cleveland franchise was originally intended to be called the Collegians but it again became known as the Bulldogs. This happened despite the fact that nearby Canton had also regained a team in the league, likewise going with the Bulldogs nickname. Weather played havoc with Cleveland's 1925 season. The game scheduled at League Park on October 25 versus Canton was cancelled because of rain and mud. A day earlier, a scholastic game between West Tech and East Tech had rendered the field unplayable. Plans were made to move the game to November 11, but the Bulldogs ended up playing a game at Detroit that day instead. A scheduled game at League Park on November 15 with Frankford was also postponed due to weather and was finally made up to close the season on December 20.

Cleveland finally did play host to Canton on December 6, winning 6–0. Indians center fielder Tris Speaker attended the game and saw the home team score on a touchdown run in the third quarter to gain the victory. The team finished 5–8–1, for 12th place out of 20 teams. Cleveland again dropped out of the NFL after that season.

With the demise of the NFL team, League Park took a hiatus from pro football for a decade. Other teams represented Cleveland during three of those seasons, but the teams utilized Luna Park or Cleveland Municipal Stadium for their home contests.

The Rams Take the Stage

In 1936, however, a team in the second incarnation of the American Football League took up residence at League Park under an ownership group headed by Cleveland attorney Homer Marshman of Waite Hill, in suburban Lake County. The team was nicknamed the Rams, to the approval of the Cleveland sporting press, which liked the brevity of the name and its ability to fit easily into headlines. The owners also liked that the nickname echoed that of then-collegiate power Fordham.

After four years without a team, pro football returned to Cleveland on October 11, 1936, when the Rams met the Syracuse Braves at League Park.

Clad in scarlet and gray with a stampeding ram named "Swifty" as its mascot, a crowd of 5000 saw the home team win, 26–0. The following week, the Rams lost, 9–0, to Boston before 7000 fans. The team went on to post a 5–2–2 record for a second-place finish in the six-team league behind the Boston Shamrocks.

While the league returned for a second season in 1937, Cleveland was not part of it. The NFL had granted Marshman a franchise in February for $10,000, allowing the Rams to move to the more established and respected league. Cleveland won out over Los Angeles and Houston for the NFL spot, likely due to travel considerations. The team colors were switched to red and black and the team trained for the season in Marshman's home of Lake County at Lake Erie College in Painesville under the direction of coach Hugh Bezdek.

With the baseball Indians scheduled to begin their second-to-last home series of the year on Saturday, September 11, at League Park, the Rams' first NFL game on Friday night, September 10 was scheduled on the lakefront at Cleveland Stadium against the Detroit Lions. The Rams lost, 28–0.

After the opener, Rams' home games moved to League Park, with the first game there on October 3, a 6–0 loss to the Chicago Cardinals before a crowd of 10,400. The Chicago Bears, featuring Bronko Nagurski, invaded League Park the following week. Under the direction of fabled coach George Halas, the visitors endured in the mud and rain to win, 20–2. The bad weather held the crowd to only 5000. The Rams continued to struggle throughout the season, finishing the year with a record of 1–10, fifth and last in the NFL's West Division. Visits by the Green Bay Packers and Washington Redskins, with star Sammy Baugh, rounded out the League Park slate. A highlight was Cleveland's number one draft choice, fullback Johnny Drake of Purdue, who was named the league's Rookie of the Year. The Rams averaged 8900 fans at home with a top ticket price of $2.20.

In 1938, the Rams played their home games at Shaw Stadium in East Cleveland, now wearing blue and yellow uniforms. From 1939 through 1941, home games were played downtown at Municipal Stadium. None of those teams finished higher than fourth place in the division, with a best mark of 5–5–1 in 1939. Prior to the 1941 season, Dan Reeves purchased the team for $135,000. He made a grandstand play, hiring former baseball umpire and general manager Billy Evans of the Cleveland Indians baseball team as G.M. of the Rams. The move did not work, as the team went 2–9.

League Park again became the Rams' home field in 1942 and the team responded with a best-yet third-place finish and a record of 5–6 under coach Dutch Clark, who had taken over in 1939. Games at League Park included wins over the Cardinals and Lions along with losses to the Packers and Bears. The first home game of the year, a win over the Philadelphia Eagles on September 20, was played at Akron's Rubber Bowl since there was still a week left in the Indians' baseball season at League Park.

Due to World War II, the Rams suspended operations for the 1943 season, leaving the West Division with four teams. Meanwhile, Philadelphia and Pittsburgh merged for the year, leaving the East with four as well.

Cleveland resumed play in 1944 with games again at League Park. Chili Walsh was named general manager and Buff Donelli took over as head coach. The team began its season 3–0, including a 19–7 home opener win over the Chicago Bears on October 8. But the team won only one more time in a schedule that saw the team play seven of its ten games on the road. The only other home games were November losses to Green Bay and Detroit.

NFL Champions

As the 1945 season approached and World War II wound down, rumors were already circulating that Cleveland taxicab magnate Arthur McBride was planning to put a Cleveland team into a new league in 1946, the All-America Football Conference. But the Rams were undeterred and poised for a big season. G.M. Chili Walsh fired Donelli as head coach and hired his own brother, Adam Walsh, in his place. Rookie quarterback Bob Waterfield, out of UCLA, took over under center after two years in the Army. Waterfield brought along his bride, Hollywood starlet Jane Russell.

Back-to-back shutout wins over the Cardinals, 21–0, and Bears, 17–0, at League Park opened the season. The team stayed undefeated with a 27–14 win at Green Bay and a 41–21 victory over the Bears in Chicago. The streak was snapped at Philadelphia on October 28, 28–14, but the Rams rebounded with a 21–17 win over the New York Giants at the Polo Grounds the following week. That win, coupled with a Green Bay loss to the Bears, put Cleveland alone in first place at 5–1 as the Packers dropped to second place at 4–2.

A showdown was at hand as Green Bay was scheduled to visit League Park on the following Sunday, November 11. Temporary, wooden bleacher seating was added in the right field area to help accommodate a crowd of 28,000 fans at the first sellout of a professional football game in Cleveland history. A small, additional press box was added behind and above those seats as well. The overflow crowd was thrilled from the outset as Fred Gehrke of the Rams raced 72 yards for a touchdown on the very first play from scrimmage. He added a 42-yard TD run and Bob Waterfield threw an 84-yard touchdown pass to Jim Benton as Cleveland built a 20–7 first-quarter lead. No further scoring occurred and the Rams improved their first-place record to 6–1. During the game, a portion of the temporary bleachers from the Flood Chair Rental Company collapsed under the weight and movement of the large

The Cleveland Rams mostly used League Park for pro football from their formation in 1936 until the team moved to Los Angeles following its 1945 NFL championship season. A temporary press box was constructed in front of the fabled right-field wall in order to allow a covered sideline view of the field, shown here in 1945. A temporary game clock was also placed in front of the center-field scoreboard. The franchise still exists, now playing in St. Louis after first moving to Los Angeles (Cleveland Public Library).

crowd. The only serious injury was a broken leg. After the collapse, fans from those seats stood along the sidelines.

After two more wins, over the Cardinals in Chicago and a division-clincher over the Lions in Detroit on Thanksgiving, the Rams played their final game at League Park on December 2. The Rams closed out a 9–1 regular season with a 20–7 win over the Boston Yanks before 18,470 fans. Benton caught eight passes in the game to bring his season total to a league-leading 45. The team would play host to the East Division champion Washington Redskins in two weeks for the NFL Championship.

There had been pressure to move the Green Bay game to much larger

Cleveland Stadium, but the Rams had a lease for their games at League Park. The championship game was not covered by the lease, so this game was moved

to the lakefront. Played in bitterly cold weather before a crowd of 32,178, league MVP Bob Waterfield directed the Rams to a 15–14 victory over the Washington Redskins.

Despite having won the championship, the Rams left Cleveland for Los Angeles the following season, as owner Dan Reeves returned his star quarterback, Waterfield, to the site of his college heroics. It was a match that made monetary sense, especially with the debut of McBride's new team in the fledgling AAFC now set for the 1946 season. There was opposition to the relocation by some NFL owners, but Reeves threatened to disband the team if they blocked the move.

In addition, the new AAFC team, the Browns, had a lease with Cleveland Stadium, which was much more appealing to the growing sport of pro football because of its larger capacity. The new Browns team went on to dominate the AAFC for its four years of existence and the team was

This is a poster promoting the movie, *The Kid from Cleveland*, which was partially filmed at League Park following the departure of the Indians in 1949. The old ballpark served as a stand-in for the team's spring training site in Tucson for the film.

absorbed into the NFL in 1950. That year the Browns and Rams met in the NFL championship game at Cleveland with the Browns winning, 30–28.

The result of the establishment of the Browns and the relocation of the Rams was that pro football actually vacated League Park a year before Bill Veeck moved his baseball Indians to the city-owned, downtown stadium.

8

Decline and Rebirth

For all of the modifications, after the Indians, Buckeyes and Browns left, the playing surface was, and still is, there. Kids can still play on the field today in the footsteps of Speaker, Feller, Wambsganss, Jethroe, Jim Brown and other legends.—Morris Eckhouse and Greg Crouse, *Where Cleveland Played*

The City Takes Over

For nearly 20 years, League Park had been a thorn in the side for the city of Cleveland. The privately owned stadium, although small and outdated, competed for events that Cleveland Stadium could have hosted, giving more return to the city coffers on the investment it had made in the huge edifice.

But by the summer of 1950, League Park's usefulness had diminished. The Indians were entrenched downtown, having drawn a record 2.6 million baseball fans for their 1948 World Series championship year, a major league record so impressive that it was bettered just once in the next 28 years (by the Los Angeles Dodgers). Pro football also had moved to Cleveland Stadium with the establishment of the Browns in 1946. Big-time college football had vacated League Park when Western Reserve University looked elsewhere after the 1949 season. And the final League Park tenant, the Negro League baseball Buckeyes, closed up shop mid-season in 1950.

Bill Veeck had sold the Indians and the team's assets, including League Park, following the 1949 season for a then-staggering $22 million. The new owners, a group headed by Ellis Ryan, were able to work a deal to rid themselves of the team's old home in March 1950 as part of the agreement for the team's new lease of Cleveland Stadium. The city paid the ball club $150,000 for League Park, with the intention of turning the field into a site for the amateur games in its recreational leagues. Once and for all, the city of Cleveland was going to eliminate the privately owned, competing ballpark. After the demise of the Buckeyes in late 1950, the city placed advertisements for bids to demolish all but the lower deck area from near first base and wrapping behind home plate to near third.

Demolition of the seating areas down the right-field foul line begins late in 1950. Portions of the roof covering the upper deck in that part of the park had already been removed (Cleveland State University, Cleveland Press Collection).

Meanwhile, the Hough neighborhood, which had benefited for so many decades from the events and activity that accompanied League Park, quickly headed into decline. One positive of the deal with the city was that, unlike most old ballparks whose land would be reused, League Park's footprint and playing field would remain, as the location made the transition to a new life

Workers from the Newman Company take a lunch break atop the steps to the old Indians' dugout during the 1951 transformation of the former big league stadium into a site for amateur sports for the city of Cleveland. Exactly when the individual seats were removed between 1951 and 1960 is unknown (Cleveland State University, Cleveland Press Collection).

as a park for recreational purposes and amateur sports. It also provided a rare opportunity for both youths and adults to play on the same field where a virtual who's who of sports had competed from 1891 to 1950. No such opportunity was made available to League Park's contemporaries such as Forbes Field or Shibe Park. Most of the former ballpark sites were marked as historical settings, but none of them offered a new generation the chance to continue to play on that very ground.

Only Pieces Remain

Mother Nature had actually begun demolition of League Park when a 53-mile-an-hour winter wind and storm blew through Cleveland on February 19, 1948. A 150-foot section of the wall from next to the centerfield scoreboard to the space behind the bleachers in left center field was toppled, leaving the

Sherwin-Williams Paints advertising sign above the wall twisted and destroyed as well. Groundskeeper Harold Bossard and his crew pulled down the sign and section of the exterior wall, with the damage estimated at $10,000.

Then, after the city had taken over ownership, in October 1950 a contract was awarded to the Schirmer Peterson Company to demolish and remove the upper deck, pavilion and bleachers of League Park for $49,500.[1] The plan was to leave the lower-deck chairback seats in place but there is no evidence as to exactly when they were removed ... eventually, photos show just the concrete risers remaining. That lower deck concrete then served as a seating area.

Prior to the main demolition, advertisements ran in Cleveland newspapers offering the sale of steel, lumber and other miscellaneous items, and even 13,000 individual seats. (Interestingly, several rows of the seats turned up in a Vermont barn in 2010.) One such demolition ad even touted that the entire steel structure could be dismantled and re-assembled as a stadium. There were no takers.

Even the famous right-field wall was removed in favor of a common chain link fence. Eventually, a second backstop and infield were added in deep center field, facing toward the original home plate, so that two youth games could be played at once on the grounds. An optimistic story that accompanied a photo of the demolition in progress in the *Cleveland Press* predicted that "Youngsters will play softball and bounce on teeter-totters where Joe Sewell scooped hot grounders."[2] A playground and basketball court filled the area between the ticket and office building and the first base stands along 66th Street. A swimming pool later went into the area where the stands had been located deep in the left-field corner. The number of high school games dwindled.

The site's big league baseball days were chronicled and recounted during this time, as the *Cleveland Press* ran an extensive series of articles in 1953 by sportswriter Frank Gibbons that relived many stories and history from the Park.

In 1957, the office/ticket building at the corner of East 66th and Lexington was remodeled into League Park Center at a cost of $65,000. The space became home to a city service area for youth activities as a result. The city of Cleveland

Opposite page, top: A crumpled Sherwin-Williams advertising sign is part of the damage done to League Park during a storm in February 1948. The ballpark was still serving as the home of the Cleveland Buckeyes and the Western Reserve University football team at the time, although the Indians had moved permanently downtown following the 1946 season (Cleveland State University, Cleveland Press Collection). *Bottom:* Not only were the pavilion seats gone by 1951, but the entire upper deck had been eliminated as well. The excavation had put the playing field in disarray, but the city of Cleveland would restore it for what was planned to be a premier recreation field (Cleveland State University, Cleveland Press Collection).

From 1951 to 1961, the lower-deck concrete seating area wrapping around the baselines remained intact. This picture is from 1961, just before the remaining seating area, everything beyond the dotted line, was demolished. The foreground section was retained because the Cleveland Browns were practicing at the site at that time, utilizing the old Indians clubhouse beneath that section of seats. That final piece would remain until 2002 (Cleveland State University, Cleveland Press Collection).

contributed $25,000, the Cleveland Foundation $16,000 and the remainder came from the Neighborhood Settlement Association, which sponsored a ceremony on May 24 to mark the renovation. This project included the enclosure of the front ticket window area.

The entire Hough neighborhood, which extends from East 55th Street to East 106th Street west to east, and from Superior to Euclid Avenues north to south, likely suffered from further and more rapid decline with the shift of League Park from a sporting venue to a park/playground space. From 1950, the final year of the Cleveland Buckeyes, Hough's population dropped from 65,694 to just 25,330 in 1960. Meanwhile, the non-white population went from 5 percent to 74 percent over that same decade as traditional, middle-class residents fled the area for the quickly expanding and developing suburbs.

By 1960, with Elizabeth Lewis as director of League Park Center, the *Cleveland Call and Post* ran a story about how the building was busy serving youths of the neighborhood and their families. Reading and writing programs as well as sewing and craft classes were being offered in the old Indians offices. The site was also being used for programs of the Volunteer Leader Corps and Junior Achievement.

In 1961, the concrete seating area behind home plate and down the third

By the summer of 1951, only the lower-deck grandstand and seats wrapping around from first to third base remained. This view of those remaining sections is aided by the collapsed perimeter wall to the ballpark, which had been behind the left-field bleachers. This wall was first damaged by a winter storm in 1948 (Cleveland State University, Cleveland Press Collection).

base line was demolished, leaving only the first-base lower-deck concrete risers and the old Indians clubhouse underneath intact. It was said that expanded playground facilities would replace the removed seating bowl area. This also opened up space where the city even tried putting an ice skating surface on the hallowed ground during the winters of 1961–62 and 1962–63, reminiscent of the baseball team's attempt to do the same way back in winter 1901–02. These efforts also foreshadowed the modern day ball club's "Snow Days" promotion of ice skating and sledding at Progressive Field, which began in the winter of 2010–11. As they say, "What goes around comes around."

The Browns Practice Here

The 1961 grandstand reduction had left only the first-base seating area standing. More importantly, that space contained the shabby remains of the

All of the individual lower-deck seats had been removed and only the concrete risers remained around the League Park diamond when this father and son visited the site of baseball history in 1960 (Cleveland State University, Cleveland Press Collection).

Indians clubhouse, which had been used for Cleveland Browns practices since 1952. Decades later, long-time Browns trainer Leo Murphy reminisced about the conditions. "There were five showers, one urinal, one potty, one sink, one telephone and the trainer's room was like a telephone booth."[3] State-of-the-art facilities built for a baseball team in 1910 obviously did not suit a National Football League team some fifty years later.

Nevertheless, the field itself continued to be tended to until the Browns left after the 1965 NFL season. It was a last hurrah for the field, as the Browns were the dominant pro football team of the era. Their roster included eventual Hall of Famers such as Jim Brown, Otto Graham, Lou Groza and Paul Warfield among the many greats who honed their talents daily on the legendary turf. But in addition to the deteriorating and inadequate locker room, the lack of parking in an increasingly rough neighborhood was also a concern. In bad weather, legendary coach Paul Brown was known to drive his car right onto the field in order to supervise practice, reportedly to the disdain of owner Art Modell, who had purchased the team in 1961.

With League Park down to just that small portion of the old first base lower deck, the signature corner ticket and office building, and the brick wall that connected to the building and ran behind the remaining grandstand along East 66th Street, the building was literally a shadow of its former self.

After the Browns left, the playing field itself degenerated. Fewer amateur games took place on the field as the neighborhood's reputation and safety continued to decline. The site was now relegated to occasional community events and the like, such as the "Soul of Hough" show on July 18, 1966. This event featured 23 artists and sculptors, including 19 from the Hough area, along with a jazz concert, rock and roll band

A wrecking ball destroys part of the lower-deck grandstand during the 1961 demolition. The final, small seating area that remained would stand for over 40 more years and into the next century (Cleveland State University, Cleveland Press Collection).

and dancers, which was attended by 400 people.

That same night, just blocks away at East 79th and Hough Avenue, an incident at the 79ers Bar triggered race riots in the neighborhood, similar to what was happening elsewhere around the country during that turbulent era. It took until July 24 for order to be restored by the Cleveland police and Ohio National Guard. The riots further damaged the area's reputation and kept many away from League Park and its neighborhood.

A Restoration Attempt

Irony abounded as League Park decayed. Downtown at the Stadium, an interior fence had long since been added to the playing field in order to create home runs, while old League Park's famous, high wall had been created many decades earlier in order to help prevent them. Meanwhile, the Indians had gone from a park that was criticized for being too small to one that was regularly chided for being too large. League Park's lack of lights contributed to its downfall, but as the novelty of lights wore off and with decades of mediocre teams, Indians' attendance often languished near the bottom of the American League during the 1960s and 1970s.

By 1979, League Park's remaining seating section was becoming badly weathered and the concrete had begun to chip and decay. But legendary sports editor Hal Lebovitz of the *Cleveland Plain Dealer* used a series of columns to help promote a plan to revitalize League Park. Perhaps Lebovitz was inspired by a full-page story written by sportswriter Bob Dolgan that ran in the paper's news section in 1976. Hal no doubt had a soft spot in his heart for the old place and Dolgan's piece detailed the dilapidated state of the park at that time. A photo of the unkempt, weed-filled field with an old tire lying out near second base told it all.

The story described how a tiny, 45 × 18 foot basketball court had been put into a room in the old ticket/office building and had the Head Start social program was offering youth dances there every other Friday night. But it was more than the neglect of the grounds or the status of the building that was described. Ultimately, the story exposed the lack of appreciation for all of the great feats and events that had happened there.

And perhaps it was the Dolgan story that inspired Peter Jedick to write a small booklet about the place that came out in 1978. Just 29 years old, Jedick was born after the Indians had moved out, but that didn't deter him from authoring the 4500-word pamphlet that sold for $1.95. The publication even related a Dolgan line (also used earlier in this book) about fans at League Field being close enough to hear the players curse and be sprayed by their tobacco juice. The booklet was clearly popular; after the first run of 1000 copies sold out, it went back for several additional printings over the years.

The book also set the stage for Lebovitz to write about the "mystique" and "nostalgia" that League Park still conjured up in the minds of the many residents who had played or watched games there. He reported that he was flooded with responses and comments whenever he wrote about the old ballyard.

Lebovitz went on to report that the League Park Restoration Committee had set aside Saturday, August 25, 1979, as League Park Day and that the Cleveland Landmark Commission and Planning Commission had approved the site as a Cleveland landmark, meaning that a plaque would be placed on the grounds. Plans were being formulated to upgrade the field, restore the remaining seating area and do additional improvements with funds raised from the August event and federal matching grant money, which was available because the site had already been listed that year on the National Register of Historic Places. Former city councilman John Cimperman, head of the Cleveland Landmarks Commission, had taken over as committee chairman. The goal was to raise $125,000 and then apply for matching funds, making for a total of $250,000.

Although hopes for an old-timers' game never materialized, there was a memorabilia display and sale, amateur games, music by Sam Finger and his Dixie Dandies, and an antique car parade to Cleveland Municipal Stadium for that night's Indians game. Bill Wambsganss, who executed the unassisted triple play in the 1920 World Series, was among several former players to attend, along with Luke Sewell, Roy Weatherly and Al Milnar. Former Yankee Red Ruffing also appeared. Two youth games were held and souvenir programs, t-shirts and pennants were sold.

The highlight of the event was the unveiling of the large bronze Ohio Historical Marker denoting the site. Cimperman presided over the ceremony, along with Mayor Dennis Kucinich, while

Top: Mayor Dennis Kucinich, flanked by his wife Sandy and Cleveland Landmarks Commission head John Cimperman, led the festivities at a 1979 League Park Day event designed to kick off a restoration plan at the field. The site was registered that year on the National Register of Historic Places. *Bottom:* Bill Wambsganss, who turned the unassisted triple play in the 1920 World Series, returned to League Park for the 1979 celebration, addressing the crowd and describing one more time how he did it (photographs by Ken Krsolovic).

Indians team president Gabe Paul represented the current Indians. Wambsganss, 85 years old, recounted just how he turned the famous triple play from

Top: The exterior of the old signature League Park building at the corner of 66th and Lexington had received a coat of paint for the 1979 celebration day event, covering its brick exterior. *Bottom:* A view down the first-base line toward home plate shows the final remaining piece of concrete risers from the League Park grandstand. This section was from behind the Indians' old dugout and covered the remains of the team's clubhouse (photographs by Ken Krsolovic).

the exact spot on the field. It was a nice event, but any momentum from it quickly faded.

Try, Try Again

In 1985, *Plain Dealer* news columnist Bill Hickey longed for the excitement of League Park and called for the construction of a similar park downtown instead of the then-popular plan for a multi-purpose domed stadium. The

A look at the architect's drawing for the modest proposed renovation of 1979, which failed despite the promotion of *Cleveland Plain Dealer* sports editor Hal Lebovitz (photograph by Ken Krsolovic).

paper then reported in early 1986 that the heavy bronze historic marker had been knocked to the ground sometime that winter and was being stored in a closet inside the office building. By opening day in early April, it had still not been remounted. The paper again recounted the story of the park in a article on the front page of its Features Section, this time accompanied by Bob Feller's reminiscence and photos. The plaque was fixed, but the park continued to languish.

In 1988, Hough–area city councilwoman Fannie Lewis led another effort to make something happen. She had the support of another *Plain Dealer* columnist, Brent Larkin, who bemoaned the fact that League Park was graffiti-covered and crumbling. Cimperman was still calling for the $250,000 to clean and repair the remaining grandstand, restore the locker room and create a museum. Councilwoman Lewis expressed anger that the city had failed to move forward on any of the plans and declared that she would demand the support of City Hall.

But League Park reached its 100th anniversary in 1991 and there was still no progress. The milestone was only commemorated by a series of additional media stories about its anniversary and an accompanying event, organized by Morris Eckhouse and Allen Pfenninger of the Society of American Baseball Research. About 50 fans watched on a rainy day as Feller and another longtime Tribe pitcher, Mel Harder, returned to celebrate the centennial on May 1, 1991, by throwing ceremonial pitches, just as Cy Young had done to christen the place on May 1, 1891. Councilwoman Lewis once more spoke of her dream of having League Park serve as an anchor for a return to prosperity for the

Top: In 2002, the final piece of grandstand was removed. Steel girder braces were added to the remaining wall in order to keep it from falling, with the stands no longer there to hold it up (Photograph by Tim Dembowski). *Bottom:* All-time great Bob Feller and mayor Jane Campbell appeared at League Park for the demolition of the final section of concrete grandstand (Photograph by Tim Dembowski).

Here is one last look at the interior of the old home team clubhouse before its destruction in 2002. The space had been sealed for decades (photograph by Tim Dembowski).

neighborhood, much as it had done when the Indians called it home. She again delivered the message of her hope for a restored office building, bleachers and museum underneath the concrete stands, along with a repaired playing field. But one news story about the event painted a pretty grim picture of the park and its surroundings. Administrative assistant Yvonne Williamson of League Park Center (now operated by the United Way funding) told of having been robbed at gunpoint in the building, as well as numerous other break-ins and even a rape near the remaining grandstand earlier in that 100th anniversary year.

Nevertheless, Lewis kept at it. In 1993, as the Indians were playing their final season in Cleveland Stadium and new Jacobs Field was being built, she got the support of mayor Michael White. He hinged his backing on the hopes that Cleveland State University's NCAA Division I program would make a remodeled League Park the home field for its baseball team. White intended to request funding from the state for the project with the college taking over maintenance of a remodeled field. But CSU, just two miles and a five-minute drive away, showed little, if any, interest in the site and neighborhood. Instead, Cleveland State continued to use various fields and ballparks much farther from campus over the ensuing years and in 2011 announced an end to the 79-

year-old program, citing the lack of a suitable nearby facility as its primary reason for dropping the sport.

Meanwhile, there was still hope for League Park. New housing had begun appearing throughout the area, including developments called Lexington Village and Renaissance Place. Joseph Marinucci, Cleveland's economic development director, thought that the heightened awareness of Cleveland's stadium history might spur the project. And while the old ballpark was, in fact, featured on various paraphernalia and memorabilia (including everything from lithographs and pins to beer cans) during the new ballpark's construction, still no progress occurred at the League Park site. Ed Feke, a neighborhood planner in the city's Community Development Department at the time, called for a formal study to look at the grandstand and the potential for a museum beneath it. But once again the ideas did not come to fruition.

Then, in 2002, mayor Jane Campbell had the final grandstand section and locker room space beneath demolished, likely in response to its unsafe, and presumably now unfixable, condition. The brick wall remained, with new girders installed to anchor and reinforce it. But the now-decrepit backstop behind home plate, placed there when the seating behind home had been removed in 1961, was also razed. Campbell did, however, give her support to architect Paul Volpe's $13 million plan for a new 4000-seat grandstand wrapping around the baselines, accompanied by a museum to League Park history, conference rooms, a picnic area and community park. She set aside $1.7 million of city dollars for the project, scheduled to take place over the next three years, but once again the project stalled.

Five years later, new mayor Frank Jackson presented a plan costing $8.5 million, including $5 million from the sale of city bonds in 2008 and 2009 to repair the site. This revised design by Volpe's firm, City Architecture, called for a 2500-seat stand and for renovation of the building, the wall, and the tunnel connecting the dugout beneath the first base stands that had been demolished five years earlier. In addition to fixing the field, this plan included the installation of a replica of the famous right-field wall. The museum was gone, but space inside the office building could still be used for this purpose, it was said. Fannie Lewis, still a city council member, said that she was unaware of the scaled-down plan and still favored the museum, but that "We're going to get it done one way or another."[4]

Restoration at Hand?

Fannie Lewis died on August 11, 2008, at the age of 82. She had served on Cleveland's city council since 1980 but she could not get League Park rebuilt during her lifetime. Hal Lebovitz had died in 2005. Yet hopes for restoration did not die with them.

In June 2007, David Jones had visited the site and became enamored with its history and significance. He created a website, leaguepark.org, as a repository of trivia and information about the ballpark, while also establishing a non-profit organization, the League Park Society, in August 2008 with a goal of helping to preserve and restore the grounds. The society held and promoted events in support of the effort, including a ceremony in 2008 marking the centennial the Addie Joss perfect game as well as one in 2010 for the 100th anniversary of

Top: This Ohio Historical Marker was installed at the site as part of the 1979 League Park Day celebration. Now somewhat weathered, and having survived an attack by vandals, the sign still graces the property. *Bottom:* The razing of the final section of League Park's grandstand exposed the steps and tunnel from the home dugout to the locker room, which had been inaccessible for many years. The underground space is still visible today as one of the last remnants of the 1910 park construction. The remaining wall along East 66th Street can be seen as well (photographs by Ken Krsolovic).

A sign signifying the planned renovation of the League Park sight went up in 2011 after Cleveland City Council had approved the spending of $387,000 to hire an architectural firm for the latest of many attempts at reviving the site (photograph by Ken Krsolovic).

the park's reopening as a concrete-and-steel edifice. The group also touted occasional games played on the field by a team called the Cleveland Blues, who play "vintage-style" baseball, under rules from 1864, which was, of course, well before the League Park site was actually used for baseball. But the efforts of the "Society" and updates to its website tailed off in the second decade of the new century.

Perhaps the most promising news yet came on February 7, 2011, when Cleveland's city council approved the spending of $387,000 to hire an architectural firm to create plans and oversee renovation of the site. The city simultaneously committed $5 million for the project's first phase, a renovation of

Opposite page, top: The back side of League Park's ticket/office building, as it appeared in 2011. Notice the doors on the upper levels of the building that once connected straight from the offices to the right-field grandstand. *Bottom:* League Park's signature building once again shows its brick face, rather than a painted surface. But as of 2011, the building was unused, with most of its windows broken (photographs by Ken Krsolovic).

This view of League Park's remaining exterior wall that runs along East 66th Street shows some of the girder work that was installed in 2002 to support the structure.

the building, wall and field, scheduled for completion in 2012. An additional $3.5 million of private money is in the plans for phase two, which would include a new seating area, locker rooms, concession stand, etc. Major League Baseball's "RBI" program, Reviving Baseball in Inner Cities, has been approached for funding. Councilman T.J. Dow, who took over Lewis's ward after her death, picked up on her effort. At long last, on October 27, 2012, ground was broken for the renovation of the site and reestablishment of a premier baseball field. It is expected to be complete by September 2013.

So perhaps more than memories will remain at the corner of East 66th Street and Lexington Avenue on Cleveland's near East Side. And although there are fewer and fewer people alive who remember the place in its heyday, or even in its declining years, there is clearly something special about the ballpark that stood there.

Whatever the future holds, there can be no dispute that a great deal of major league baseball history took place on this Midwestern city block. League Park also was a part of the very first days of the National Football League and it is one of only four former Negro League ballparks that still exist in some form (along with Hinchliff Stadium in Paterson, N.J., Rickwood Field in Birmingham and Bush Stadium in Indianapolis). When the grandstand was being knocked down in 1951, the *Cleveland Press* predicted that "...in years to come it will be difficult to remember that Lefty Grove and Ty Cobb and the baseball greats of yesteryear played here."[5]

Let us hope that the newspaper's prophecy may yet be averted. The fabled grounds and legends of League Park deserve to be remembered and to be forever treasured.

Appendices

A—League Park and Its Teams by Year

YEAR	TEAM	LEAGUE	W-L	PCT.	GB	PLACE	TOTAL	RANK
1891	Spiders	National	65–74	.468	22½	5th	132,000	6th
1892	Spiders	National	93–56	.624	8½	2nd	139,928	7th
1893	Spiders	National	73–53	.570	12½	3rd	130,000	9th
1894	Spiders	National	68–61	.527	21½	6th	82,000	11th
1895	Spiders	National	84–46	.646	3	2nd	143,000	11th
1896	Spiders	National	80–48	.625	9½	2nd	152,000	12th
1897	Spiders	National	69–62	.527	23½	5th	115,250	12th
1898	Spiders	National	81–68	.544	21	5th	70,496	12th
1899	Spiders	National	20–134	.130	84	12th	6,088	12th
1900	Lake Shores	American*	63–73	.463	19½	6th	unknown	
1901	Blues	American	54–82	.397	29	7th	131,380	8th
1902	Bronchos	American	69–67	.507	14	5th	275,395	4th
1903	Naps	American	77–63	.550	15	3rd	311,280	4th
1904	Naps	American	86–65	.570	7½	4th	264,749	5th
1905	Naps	American	76–78	.494	19	5th	316,306	5th
1906	Naps	American	89–64	.582	5	3rd	325,733	6th
1907	Naps	American	85–67	.559	8	4th	382,046	5th
1908	Naps	American	90–64	.584	½	2nd	422,262	6th
1909	Naps	American	71–82	.464	27½	6th	354,627	7th
1910	Naps	American	71–81	.467	32	5th	293,456	6th
1911	Naps	American	80–73	.523	22	3rd	406,296	5th
1912	Naps	American	75–78	.490	30½	5th	336,844	6th
1913	Naps	American	86–66	.566	9½	3rd	541,000	3rd
1914	Naps	American	51–102	.333	48½	8th	185,997	8th
	Bearcats	Amer. Assoc.*	82–81	.503	14½	5th	99,732	5th
1915	Indians	American	57–95	.375	44½	7th	159,285	7th
	Spiders	Amer. Assoc.*	67–82	.450	22½	7th	86,977	5th
1916	Indians	American	77–77	.500	14	6th	492,106	4th
1917	Indians	American	88–66	.571	12	3rd	477,298	2nd
1918	Indians	American	73–54	.575	2½	2nd	295,515	1st
1919	Indians	American	84–55	.604	3½	2nd	538,135	4th
1920	Indians	American	98–56	.636	—	1st	912,832	2nd
1921	Indians	American	94–60	.610	4½	2nd	748,705	2nd
1922	Indians	American	78–76	.507	16	4th	528,145	5th
1923	Indians	American	82–71	.536	16½	3rd	558,856	4th
1924	Indians	American	67–86	.438	24½	6th	481,905	7th

YEAR	TEAM	LEAGUE	W-L	PCT.	GB	PLACE	TOTAL	RANK
1925	Indians	American	70–84	.455	27½	6th	419,005	5th
1926	Indians	American	88–66	.571	3	2nd	627,426	6th
1927	Indians	American	66–87	.431	43½	6th	373,138	7th
1928	Indians	American	62–92	.403	39	7th	375,907	7th
1929	Indians	American	81–71	.533	24	3rd	536,210	4th
1930	Indians	American	81–73	.526	21	4th	528,483	5th
1931	Indians	American	78–76	.506	30	4th	483,027	4th
1932	Indians	American	87–65	.572	19	4th	468,953†	2nd
1934	Indians	American	85–69	.552	16	3rd	391,338	4th
	Red Sox	Negro National	4–25	.138	17	6th	unknown	
1935	Indians	American	82–71	.536	12	3rd	397,615	5th
1936	Indians	American	80–74	.519	22½	5th	500,391†	4th
1937	Indians	American	83–71	.539	19	4th	564,849†	4th
1938	Indians	American	86–66	.566	13	3rd	652,006†	3rd
1939	Indians	American	87–67	.565	20½	3rd	563,926†	5th
1940	Indians	American	89–65	.578	1	2nd	902,576†	3rd
	Bears	Negro American	10–10	.500	2½	3rd-T	unknown	
1941	Indians	American	75–79	.487	26	4th-T	745,948†	2nd
1942	Indians	American	75–79	.487	28	4th	459,447†	4th
1943	Indians	American	82–71	.536	15½	3rd	438,894†	5th
	Buckeyes	Negro American	25–20	.556	‡	‡	40,000	‡
1944	Indians	American	72–82	.468	17	5th-T	475,272†	8th
	Buckeyes	Negro American	40–41	.494	13½	3rd	unknown	
1945	Indians	American	73–72	.503	11	5th	558,182†	6th
	Buckeyes	Negro American	56–13	.768	—	1st	unknown	
1946	Indians	American	68–86	.442	36	6th	1,057,289†	4th
	Buckeyes	Negro American	14–17	.452	11	4th	unknown	
1947	Buckeyes	Negro American	54–23	.701	—	1st	unknown	
1948	Buckeyes	Negro American	41–42	.494	17½	3rd	unknown	
1950	Buckeyes	Negro American	3–39	.071	folded July 6		unknown	

*— Indicates minor league team
†— Attendance total for games at both League Park and Cleveland Municipal Stadium.
‡— Standings not recorded

Notes

All leagues were 8-team leagues except the National League from 1982 to 1899 which had 12 teams, and the Negro Leagues with six teams.

Games at Cleveland Stadium: July 31, 1932, through 1933 season; August 2, 1936; Sundays and holidays May 30 to September 1937 and April 1938 to June 1939; all games in 1940 after August 17; and Sundays, holidays and night games June 27, 1939, to September 1946.

B—Box Scores from Memorable Games

The First Game at League Park — Friday, May 1, 1891

CINCINNATI	AB	R	H	RBI	PO	A	E
McPhee, 2b	4	0	0	0	2	6	0
Latham, 3b	4	1	2	3	5	1	1
Marr, rf	3	0	0	0	0	0	2
Holliday, lf	4	0	3	0	0	1	0
Reilly, 1b	4	0	1	0	14	1	2
Slattery, cf	4	0	2	0	2	0	0
Smith, ss	4	0	1	0	0	5	5
Keenan, c	4	1	1	0	1	2	0
Duryea, p	1	0	0	0	0	2	0
Rhines, p	2	1	0	0	0	1	0
TOTALS	34	3	10	3	24	19	5

CLEVELAND	AB	R	H	RBI	PO	A	E
McAleer, lf	5	1	2	0	2	0	0
McKean, ss	5	1	2	1	4	1	0
Davis, cf	4	3	0	0	4	0	0
Childs, 2b	4	1	2	4	2	1	1
Johnson, rf	4	1	2	1	1	0	0
Alvord, 3b	5	0	1	0	1	0	0
Virtue, 1b	4	2	2	1	9	1	0
Zimmer, c	3	2	2	1	8	4	0
Young, p	3	1	1	1	1	4	0
TOTALS	37	12	14	9	27	11	1

Cincinnati	000 000 030—	3	10	5
Cleveland	200 132 04X—	12	14	1

Doubles—McAleer, Childs, Zimmer 2, Holliday, Keenan. Triples—Virtue 2. Home Runs—Latham. Sacrifice Hits—McAleer, Childs, Johnson, Virtue, Young. Stolen Base—Johnson. Double Plays—Latham (unassisted), McKean to Virtue.

CINCINNATI	IP	H	R	ER	BB	SO
Duryea (L)	—	—	—	—	1	—
Rhines	—	—	—	—	3	—
Young (W)	9	10	3	1	1	—

Wild Pitch-Rhines.
Umpire-Powers. Time—1:58. Attendance—9000.

National League Championship Game One — Monday, October 17, 1892

BOSTON	AB	R	H	RBI	PO	A	E
Long, ss	4	0	1	0	2	6	0
BOSTON	AB	R	H	RBI	PO	A	E
McCarthy, rf	4	0	1	0	0	0	0
Duffy, cf	4	0	1	0	1	0	0
Kelly, c	4	0	0	0	8	2	0
Nash, 3b	4	0	1	0	1	2	0
Lowe, lf	4	0	0	0	2	0	0
Tucker, 1b	4	0	0	0	15	0	0
Quinn, 2b	4	0	1	0	3	5	0
Stivetts, p	4	0	0	0	1	4	0
TOTALS	36	0	5	0	33	19	0

CLEVELAND	AB	R	H	RBI	PO	A	E
Childs, 2b	3	0	0	0	2	4	1
Burkett, lf	4	0	2	0	0	0	0
Davis, 3b	4	0	1	0	1	3	0
McKean, ss	3	0	1	0	2	1	0
Virtue, 1b	4	0	0	0	15	0	0
McAleer, cf	3	0	0	0	3	0	0
O'Connor, rf	4	0	0	0	3	0	0
Zimmer, c	4	0	0	0	7	3	1
Young, p	4	0	0	0	0	4	0
TOTALS	33	0	4	0	33	15	2

Boston	000 000 000 00 — 0	4	0
Cleveland	000 000 000 00 — 0	5	2

Sacrifice Hits—Virtue, Tucker. Stolen Bases—McAleer, Duffy. Double Plays—Stivetts to Tucker, Long to Quinn to Kelly. Left on Base—Cleveland 4, Boston 3.

BOSTON	IP	H	R	ER	BB	SO
Stivetts	11	4	0	0	4	7

CLEVELAND	IP	H	R	ER	BB	SO
Young	11	5	0	0	0	6

Passed Ball—Zimmer.
Umpires—Emslie and Snyder. Time—2:00. Attendance—6000.

National League Championship Game Two — Tuesday, October 18, 1892

BOSTON	AB	R	H	RBI	PO	A	E
Long, ss	5	2	1	—	0	4	0

McCarthy, rf	5	1	2	—	2	1	0
Duffy, cf	5	1	3	—	3	0	0
Kelly, c	4	0	0	—	0	2	0
Nash, 3b	4	0	1	—	0	3	0
Lowe, lf	4	0	1	—	1	0	1

BOSTON	AB	R	H	RBI	PO	A	E
Tucker, 1b	4	0	2	—	17	0	0
Quinn, 2b	3	0	0	—	3	2	0
Staley, p	4	0	0	—	1	4	0
TOTALS	38	4	10	—	27	16	1

CLEVELAND	AB	R	H	RBI	PO	A	E
Childs, 2b	3	0	0	—	3	0	0
Burkett, lf	4	0	1	—	1	0	0
Davis, 3b	1	0	0	—	0	0	0
Tebeau, 3b	3	0	0	—	2	0	1
McKean, ss	4	1	2	—	2	5	0
Virtue, 1b	4	0	1	—	6	1	1
McAleer, cf	4	0	2	—	2	0	0
O'Connor, rf	4	1	1	—	2	1	0
Zimmer, c	4	1	3	—	8	0	0
Clarkson, p	4	0	1	—	0	2	0
TOTALS	35	3	11	—	26*	9	2

*Kelly out on interference

Boston	101 010 010 —	4	10	1
Cleveland	001 100 001 —	3	11	2

Doubles— McAleer, Zimmer, Duffy. Triples— Zimmer, Duffy-2. Sacrifice Hits— Burkett, Virtue, O'Connor, Clarkson, McCarthy, Duffy. Stolen Bases— Kelly, Nash. Double Play — McCarthy to Tucker. Left on Base — Cleveland 6, Boston 8.

BOSTON	IP	H	R	ER	BB	SO
Staley (W)	9	11	3	3	1	0

CLEVELAND	IP	H	R	ER	BB	SO
Clarkson (L)	9	10	4	2	1	6

Umpires— McQuaid (H), Gaffney (B). Time — 1:35. Attendance — 6700.

National League Championship G a m e Three — Wednesday, October 19, 1892

BOSTON	AB	R	H	RBI	PO	A	E
Long, ss	4	0	1	—	4	2	1
McCarthy, rf	4	1	2	—	1	0	0
Duffy, cf	4	0	1	—	2	1	0

Ganzel, c	4	0	2	—	7	1	0
Nash, 3b	4	0	0	—	0	2	1
Lowe, lf	4	1	1	—	2	0	0
Tucker, 1b	3	0	0	—	8	0	1
Quinn, 2b	3	0	1	—	2	2	0
Stivetts, p	3	1	1	—	1	1	0
TOTALS	33	3	9	—	27	9	3

CLEVELAND	AB	R	H	RBI	PO	A	E
Childs, 2b	3	1	1	—	3	3	0
Burkett, lf	4	1	2	—	1	0	0
Tebeau, 3b	4	0	0	—	1	0	0
McKean, ss	4	0	2	—	1	5	0
Virtue, 1b	4	0	0	—	11	0	0
McAleer, cf	4	0	1	—	3	0	0
O'Connor, rf	4	0	1	—	2	0	0
Zimmer, c	4	0	0	—	2	1	0
Young, p	3	0	0	—	0	1	0
Davis, ph	1	0	0	—	0	0	0
TOTALS	35	2	7	—	24	10	0

Cleveland	200 000 000 —	2	7	0
Boston	110 000 10X —	3	9	3

Doubles—Burkett, Quinn, Stivetts. Sacrifice Hits—McAleer, O'Connor, Tucker, Stivetts. Stolen Bases—McKean, McCarthy. Left on Base — Cleveland 7, Boston 6.

BOSTON	IP	H	R	ER	BB	SO
Stivetts (W)	9	7	2	2	1	6

CLEVELAND	IP	H	R	ER	BB	SO
Young (L)	8	9	3	3	0	0

Umpires— Snyder, Emslie. Time — 1:30. Attendance — NA.

Temple Cut Game One — Friday, October 2, 1895

BALTIMORE	AB	R	H	RBI	PO	A	E
McGraw, 3b	4	2	3	—	0	1	0
Keeler, rf	5	0	2	—	2	0	0
Jennings, ss	4	1	1	—	0	8	0
Kelley, lf	4	0	3	—	1	0	0
Brodie, cf	4	0	0	—	1	0	0
Gleason, 2b	4	0	2	—	3	1	0
Carey, 1b	4	0	0	—	10	1	0
Robinson, c	4	1	2	—	6	0	0
McMahon, p	4	0	0	—	2	3	0
TOTALS	37	4	13	—	26	14	0

CLEVELAND	AB	R	H	RBI	PO	A	E
Burkett, lf	4	1	1	—	0	0	0
McKean, ss	4	0	3	—	4	5	0
Childs, 2b	5	1	1	—	3	3	1
McAleer, cf	5	0	1	—	2	0	0
O. Tebeau, 1b	5	2	2	—	14	0	0
Zimmer, c	4	0	2	—	1	2	0
Blake, rf	4	0	2	—	3	0	0
McGarr, 3b	4	1	1	—	0	1	0

CLEVELAND	AB	R	H	RBI	PO	A	E
Young, p	4	0	1	—	0	6	0
TOTALS	39	5	14	—	27	17	1

Baltimore	000 001 021 —	4	13	0		
Cleveland	000 011 012 —	5	14	1		

Two out when winning run scored

Doubles— McKean, Blake, Tebeau, Burkett, McGraw, Robinson. Triple— McKean. Sacrifice Hit— Burkett. Stolen Base— McGarr. Double Play— McKean to Tebeau. Left on Base— Cleveland 5, Baltimore 4.

BALTIMORE	IP	H	R	ER	BB	SO
McMahon (L)	8.2	14	5	5	2	1

CLEVELAND	IP	H	R	ER	BB	SO
Young (W)	9	13	4	4	1	0

Passed Ball— Robinson.

Umpires— Keefe, McDonald. Time— 2:15. Attendance— 6000.

Temple Cup Game Two — Saturday, October 3, 1895

BALTIMORE	AB	R	H	RBI	PO	A	E
McGraw, 3b	4	0	0	—	1	0	0
Keeler, rf	3	0	1	—	2	0	0
Jennings, ss	4	1	1	—	1	6	1
Kelley, lf	3	1	0	—	3	0	0
Brodie, cf	4	0	1	—	2	1	0
Gleason, 2b	4	0	0	—	3	2	0
Carey, 1b	3	0	2	—	10	1	1
Clarke, c	3	0	1	—	1	1	0
Hoffer, p	3	0	0	—	1	0	1
TOTALS	31	2	6	—	24	11	3

CLEVELAND	AB	R	H	RBI	PO	A	E
Burkett, lf	5	1	4	—	2	0	0
McKean, ss	4	1	1	—	4	8	1
Childs, 2b	3	1	0	—	3	2	0
McAleer, cf	3	1	0	—	1	1	1
O. Tebeau, 1b	4	1	1	—	11	0	0
Zimmer, c	3	1	2	—	4	2	0
Blake, rf	4	0	0	—	2	1	0
McGarr, 3b	4	0	2	—	0	1	0
Cuppy, p	3	1	1	—	0	2	0
TOTALS	33	7	11	—	27	17	2

Baltimore	010 001 000 —	2	6	3		
Cleveland	300 012 10X —	7	11	2		

Doubles— Zimmer, McGarr, Cuppy, Burkett. Sacrifice Hits— Childs, Cuppy. Stolen Bases— Burkett, McKean. Hit By Pitch— McAleer. Left on Base— Cleveland 6, Baltimore 4.

BALTIMORE	IP	H	R	ER	BB	SO
Hoffer (L)	8	11	7	3	2	2

CLEVELAND	IP	H	R	ER	BB	SO
Cuppy (W)	9	6	2	1	2	0

Wild Pitch— Hoffer. Passed Ball— Clarke. Umpires— Keefe, McDonald. Time— 2:15. Attendance— 10,000.

Temple Cup Game Three — Monday, October 5, 1895

BALTIMORE	AB	R	H	RBI	PO	A	E
McGraw, 3b	4	0	2	—	0	0	0
Keeler, rf	4	1	0	—	2	0	0
Jennings, ss	3	0	2	—	5	2	0
Kelley, lf	4	0	1	—	2	1	0
Brodie, cf	4	0	0	—	1	0	0
Gleason, 2b	4	0	0	—	1	3	0
Carey, 1b	4	0	1	—	9	1	0
Robinson, c	4	0	1	—	3	1	1
McMahon, p	3	0	0	—	0	4	0
TOTALS	34	1	7	—	24	12	1

CLEVELAND	AB	R	H	RBI	PO	A	E
Burkett, lf	3	0	2	—	0	0	0
McKean, ss	4	1	0	—	4	6	1
Childs, 2b	4	1	2	—	4	8	0
McAleer, cf	4	1	2	—	1	0	0
O. Tebeau, 1b	4	0	1	—	13	0	0
Zimmer, c	3	1	1	—	4	1	0
Blake, rf	3	1	1	—	0	0	0
McGarr, 3b	4	0	2	—	1	1	0
Young, p	4	1	1	—	0	2	0
TOTALS	33	7	12	—	27	18	1

Baltimore	000 000 010 — 1	7	1		
Cleveland	300 000 31X — 7	12	1		

Doubles— Childs, Zimmer, Blake, McGarr. Sacrifice Hits— Blake, Burkett. Stolen Base— McKean. Left on Base— Cleveland 5, Baltimore 7.

BALTIMORE	IP	H	R	ER	BB	SO
McMahon (L)	8	12	7	7	1	1

CLEVELAND	IP	H	R	ER	BB	SO
Young (W)	9	7	1	1	1	1

Umpires— McDonald, Hurst. Time— 1:45. Attendance— 12,000.

Cy Young's No Hitter — Saturday,
September 18, 1897

CINCINNATI	AB	R	H	RBI	PO	A	E
Holliday, rf	4	0	0	0	1	0	0
Hoy, cf	4	0	0	0	2	0	0
McPhee, 2b	3	0	0	0	1	6	0
Beckley, 1b	3	0	0	0	15	0	0
Corcoran, ss	3	0	0	0	1	3	0
Irwin, 3b	3	0	0	0	1	3	0
Burke, lf	3	0	0	0	1	1	1
Schriver, c	1	0	0	0	2	0	0
Rhines, p	1	0	0	0	0	2	0
Ritchey, ph	1	0	0	0	0	0	0
TOTALS	28	0	0	0	24	15	1

CLEVELAND	AB	R	H	RBI	PO	A	E
Burkett, lf	4	0	1	—	2	0	0
Childs, 2b	3	2	2	—	0	4	0
Wallace, 3b	4	0	0	—	2	0	2
O'Connor, 1b	4	1	2	—	13	0	0
McKean, ss	4	1	0	—	3	3	1
Pickering, cf	3	1	1	—	2	0	0
Belden, rf	3	1	2	—	1	0	0
Zimmer, c	2	0	0	—	3	1	0
Young, p	3	0	0	—	1	3	0
TOTALS	30	6	8	—	27	11	3

Cincinnati   000 000 000 —   0   0   1
Cleveland   200 100 03X —   6   8   3

Double— Childs. Sacrifice Hit— Zimmer. Stolen Bases— Childs, Pickering, Corcoran. Left on Base— Cincinnati 2, Cleveland 5.

CINCINNATI	IP	H	R	ER	BB	SO
Rhines (L)	8	8	6	—	4	1

CLEVELAND	IP	H	R	ER	BB	SO
Young (W)	9	0	0	0	1	3

Wild Pitch— Rhines.
Umpire— Kelley. Time— 1:35. Attendance— 2,500

Temple Cup Game Four — Friday,
October 8, 1897

BALTIMORE	AB	R	H	RBI	PO	A	E
McGraw, 3b	4	0	0	—	0	1	0
Keeler, rf	4	1	3	—	0	0	0
BALTIMORE	AB	R	H	RBI	PO	A	E
Jennings, ss	4	1	1	—	2	5	1
Kelley, lf	4	1	1	—	1	0	0
Doyle, 1b	4	1	2	—	9	2	0
Reitz, 2b	4	0	1	—	2	1	0
Brodie, cf	3	0	0	—	2	0	0
Robinson, c	3	0	0	—	10	1	0
Corbett, p	3	1	3	—	1	4	0
TOTALS	33	5	11	—	27	14	1

CLEVELAND	AB	R	H	RBI	PO	A	E
Burkett, lf	4	0	0	0	3	0	0
McKean, ss	4	0	1	0	1	3	0
Childs, 2b	2	0	1	0	3	1	0
McAleer, cf	4	0	0	0	3	1	0
O'Connor, 1b	3	0	0	0	9	0	0
Zimmer, c	3	0	0	0	2	1	1
McGarr, 3b	4	0	1	0	0	2	0
Blake, rf	3	0	0	0	3	0	0
Cuppy, p	3	0	1	0	0	2	0
Wallace, ph	1	0	0	0	0	0	0
TOTALS	31	0	4	0	24	10	1

Cleveland   000 000 000 —   0   4   1
Baltimore   000 000 23X —   5   11   1

Doubles— Corbett, Jennings, Keeler, Kelley. Stolen Bases— McKean, McGarr, Blake, Childs, Doyle. Double Play— McAleer to O'Connor.

BALTIMORE	IP	H	R	ER	BB	SO
Corbett (W)	9	4	0	0	5	6

CLEVELAND	IP	H	R	ER	BB	SO
Cuppy (L)	8	11	5	4	0	1

Umpires— Emslie, Sheridan. Time— 2:10. Attendance— 2000.

First American League Game at

L e a g u e Park — Monday, April 29, 1901

MILWAUKEE	AB	R	H	RBI	PO	A	E
Waldron, rf	5	0	1	—	2	0	0
Gilbert, 2b	4	0	0	—	0	0	1
Haliman, lf	3	1	1	—	3	1	0
Anderson, 1b	4	0	1	—	6	0	0
Conroy, ss	4	1	0	—	6	3	0
Duffy, cf	3	0	1	—	1	0	0
Burke, 3b	4	1	2	—	2	1	2
Leahy, c	4	0	1	—	4	1	0
Hawley, p	4	0	1	—	0	2	0
TOTALS	35	3	8	—	24	8	3

CLEVELAND	AB	R	H	RBI	PO	A	E
Pickering, rf	4	1	1	—	1	0	1
McCarthy, lf	4	1	1	—	1	0	2
Genins, cf	4	1	1	—	4	0	0
LaChance, 1b	4	1	3	—	14	0	0
Bradley, 3b	3	0	1	—	1	4	0
Beck, 2b	4	0	0	—	2	0	0
Haliman, ss	4	0	1	—	4	5	2
Yeager, c	2	0	1	—	0	1	0
Hoffer, p	3	0	0	—	0	4	0
TOTALS	32	4	9	—	27	14	5

Milwaukee	011 100 000 —	3	8	3
Cleveland	000 100 021 —	4	9	5

Doubles— Bradley, Pickering, Haliman. Triple — McCarthy. Sacrifice Hit — Duffy. Stolen Bases— LaChance, Conroy. Double Plays— Conroy to Leahy, Haliman to Burke. Hit By Pitch — Bradley. Left on Base — Cleveland 6, Milwaukee 6.

MILWAUKEE	IP	H	R	ER	BB	SO
Hawley (L)	8	9	4	—	1	2

CLEVELAND	IP	H	R	ER	BB	SO
Hoffer (W)	9	8	3	—	0	1

Umpires— Sheridan, Mannaseau. Time — NA. Attendance — 7500.

The Greatest Comeback — T h u r s d a y , May 23, 1901

WASHINGTON	AB	R	H	RBI	PO	A	E
Farrell, lf	6	1	0	—	0	0	0
Dungan, rf	5	2	2	—	6	0	0
Quinn, 2b	5	1	2	—	3	2	0
Foster, lf	5	1	3	—	2	0	1
Everitt, 1b	3	1	0	—	12	1	0
Grady, c	4	2	2	—	4	0	1
Clingman, ss	4	2	2	—	3	7	0
Coughlin, 3b	3	3	2	—	0	0	0
Patton, p	4	2	2	—	1	2	0
Lee, p	0	0	0	—	0	0	0
TOTALS	40	13	14	—	26	12	1

CLEVELAND	AB	R	H	RBI	PO	A	E
Pickering, rf	6	1	1	—	0	0	0
McCarthy, lf	5	2	2	—	6	0	0
Bradley, 3b	5	2	4	—	2	2	2
LaChance, 1b	5	1	3	—	12	0	0
Wood, c	4	1	1	—	2	0	1
Schiebeck, ss	5	2	4	—	0	1	1

CLEVELAND	AB	R	H	RBI	PO	A	E
Genins, cf	4	1	1	—	4	0	0
Egan, 2b	4	2	1	—	0	5	0
Hoffer, p	4	1	1	—	1	4	0
Beck, ph	1	1	1	—	0	0	0
TOTALS	43	14	19	—	27	12	4

Washington	050 130 202 —	13	14	2
Cleveland	000 040 019 —	14	19	4

Two out when winning run scored

Doubles— Schiebeck, Beck, Coughlin. Triple — Dungan. Sacrifice Hits— Patton, Everett, Clingman, Coughlin. Stolen Bases— Grady, Clingman. Double Play— Clingman to Quinn. Clingman to Quinn to Everitt. Left on Base — Cleveland 7, Washington 7.

WASHINGTON	IP	H	R	ER	BB	SO
Patton	8.2	16	11	—	2	2
Lee (L)	0	3	3	—	1	1

CLEVELAND	IP	H	R	ER	BB	SO
Hoffer (W)	9	14	13	3	3	0

Hit By Pitch — Patton. Passed Ball- Grady. Umpire — Cantillon. Time — 2:00. Attendance — 1250.

Bob Rhoads No-Hitter — Friday September 18, 1908

BOSTON	AB	R	H	RBI	PO	A	E
Niles, 2b	4	0	0	—	2	1	0

Lord, 3b	4	0	0	—	0	2	0
Speaker, cf	3	0	0	—	0	0	0
Gessler, rf	1	1	0	—	1	0	1
Thoney, lf	2	0	0	—	2	0	0
Wagner, ss	3	0	0	—	4	7	1
Stahl, 1b	3	0	0	—	9	0	0
Donahue, c	3	0	0	—	5	1	1
Arellanes, p	3	0	0	—	1	0	0
TOTALS	26	1	0	—	24	11	3

CLEVELAND	AB	R	H	RBI	PO	A	E
Goode, rf	4	1	1	—	0	0	0
Bradley, 3b	4	0	0	—	1	1	1
Hinchman, lf	4	0	0	—	1	0	0
Lajoie, 2b	4	1	1	—	3	7	1
Stovall, 1b	3	0	1	—	16	2	0
Bemis, c	3	0	1	—	2	1	0
Birmingham, cf	3	0	0	—	2	0	0

CLEVELAND	AB	R	H	RBI	PO	A	E
Perring, ss	3	0	0	—	1	2	0
Rhoads, p	3	0	1	—	1	6	0
TOTALS	31	2	5	—	27	19	2

Boston	010 000 000 —	1	0	3
Cleveland	000 100 01X —	2	5	2

Triples—Rhoads, Lajoie. Sacrifice Hits—Thoney 2, Gessler 2. Left on Base—Cleveland 6, Boston 5.

BOSTON	IP	H	R	ER	BB	SO
Arellanes (L)	8	5	2	—	0	5

CLEVELAND	IP	H	R	ER	BB	SO
Roads (W)	9	0	1	—	2	2

Hit By Pitch—Rhoads. Wild Pitch—Rhoads, Arellanes.
Umpire—Connolly. Time—1:30. Attendance—6950.

Addie Joss' Perfect Game — Friday, October 2, 1908

CHICAGO	AB	R	H	RBI	PO	A	E
Hahn, rf	3	0	0	0	1	0	0
Jones, cf	3	0	0	0	0	0	0
Isbell, 1b	3	0	0	0	7	1	1
Dougherty, lf	3	0	0	0	0	0	0
Davis, 2b	3	0	0	0	1	0	0
Parent, ss	3	0	0	0	0	3	0
Schreck, c	2	0	0	0	12	1	0
White, ph	1	0	0	0	0	0	0
Tannehill, 3b	2	0	0	0	0	0	0
Donohue, ph	1	0	0	0	0	0	0
Walsh, p	2	0	0	0	1	3	0
Anderson, ph	1	0	0	0	0	0	0
TOTALS	27	0	0	0	24	8	1

CLEVELAND	AB	R	H	RBI	PO	A	E
Goode, rf	4	0	0	0	1	0	0
Bradley, 3b	4	0	0	0	0	1	0
Hinchman, lf	3	0	0	0	3	0	0
Lajoie, 2b	3	0	1	0	2	8	0
Stoval, 1b	3	0	0	0	16	0	0
Clarke, c	3	0	0	0	4	1	0
Birmingham, cf	4	1	2	0	0	0	0
Perring, ss	2	0	1	0	1	1	0
Joss, p	3	0	0	0	0	5	0
TOTALS	27	0	0	0	24	8	1

Chicago	000 000 000 —	0	0	1
Cleveland	001 000 00X —	1	4	0

Stolen Bases—Birmingham-2, Lajoie, Perring.
Left on Base—Cleveland-4, Chicago-0.

CHICAGO	IP	H	R	ER	BB	SO
Walsh (L)	8	4	1	0	1	15

CLEVELAND	IP	H	R	ER	BB	SO
Joss (W)	9	0	0	0	0	3

Wild Pitch—Walsh-1.
Umpires—Connolly, O'Loughlin. Time—1:40. Attendance—11,000.

First Game in Concrete and Steel League Park — Thursday, April 21, 1910

DETROIT	AB	R	H	RBI	PO	A	E
McIntyre, lf	4	0	1	—	4	0	0
Bush, ss	4	0	0	—	0	6	0
Cobb, rf	4	0	0	—	2	0	0
Crawford, cf	4	1	2	—	0	0	0
Delehanty, 2b	4	1	1	—	2	1	0
Moriarty, 3b	3	1	0	—	1	4	0
T. Jones, 1b	4	0	2	—	17	0	0
Stanage, c	3	1	1	—	1	2	0
Willett, p	3	1	1	—	0	4	0
TOTALS	33	5	8	—	27	17	0

CLEVELAND	AB	R	H	RBI	PO	A	E

Krueger, lf	3	0	0	0	2	0	0
Bradley, 3b	4	0	1	0	2	2	0
Turner, 2b	4	0	0	0	2	3	1
Lajoie, 1b	4	0	1	0	9	0	0
Lord, rf	4	0	0	0	1	0	0
Clarke, c	3	0	2	0	6	1	0
Birmingham, cf	3	0	0	0	3	0	0
Ball, ss	3	0	0	0	1	1	0
Young, p	3	0	1	0	1	5	0
TOTALS	31	0	5	0	27	12	1

Detroit	002 000 300 —	5	8	0
Cleveland	000 000 000 —	0	5	1

Doubles — Stanage, McIntyre, Clarke, Young. Sacrifice Hit — Stanage. Stolen Base — Crawford. Left on Base — Cleveland-7, Detroit-4.

DETROIT	IP	H	R	ER	BB	SO
Willett (W)	9	5	0	0	2	0

CLEVELAND	IP	H	R	ER	BB	SO
Young (L)	9	8	5	—	2	6

Hit by Pitch — by Willett (Birmingham). Umpires — Sheridan, Kerin. Time — 1:31. Attendance — 18,832.

Addie Joss Benefit All-Star Game — Monday, July 24, 1911

ALL-STARS	AB	R	H	RBI	PO	A	E
Speaker, cf	2	1	2	—	0	0	0
Milan, cf	3	1	2	—	3	0	0
Collins, 2b	5	1	2	—	3	6	0
Cobb, rf	4	0	2	—	1	0	0
Baker, 3b	4	1	1	—	0	1	0
Crawford, lf	4	0	1	—	0	0	0
Chase, 1b	3	1	3	—	17	1	0
Wallace, ss	3	0	0	—	1	7	0
Street, c	2	0	1	—	1	0	0
Livingstone, c	2	0	1	—	1	0	0
Wood, p	0	0	0	—	0	0	0
Johnson, p	1	0	0	—	0	1	0
Ford, p	2	0	0	—	0	1	0
TOTALS	35	5	15	—	27	17	0

CLEVELAND	AB	R	H	RBI	PO	A	E
Graney, lf	4	0	1	—	0	0	0
Olson, ss	4	1	2	—	2	6	1
Jackson, rf	2	0	0	—	0	0	0
Butcher, rf	2	0	1	—	1	0	0
Stovall, 1b	2	1	1	—	2	2	0
Lajoie, 1b	2	0	0	—	6	0	0
Birmingham, cf	4	0	1	—	9	3	1
Ball, 2b	4	0	0	—	3	1	0
Turner, 3b	3	0	1	—	2	1	0
Smith, c	1	0	0	—	0	2	0
Easterly, c	3	0	0	—	2	0	0
Young, p	0	0	0	—	0	0	0
Kaler, p	1	0	0	—	0	0	0
Blanding, p	1	1	1	—	0	0	0
Griggs, ph	1	0	0	—	0	0	0
TOTALS	34	3	8	—	27	15	2

All-Stars	210 100 100 —	5	15	0
Cleveland	010 000 020 —	3	8	2

Doubles — Birmingham, Speaker, Milan, Blanding. Triples — Collins, Olson. Sacrifice Flies — Wood, Chase. Stolen Bases — Speaker, Graney, Milan, Livingstone. Double Play — Olson to Ball to Stovall. Left on Base — Cleveland-5, All-Stars-1.

ALL-STARS	IP	H	R	ER	BB	SO
Wood (W)	2	2	1	1	0	0
Johnson	3	1	0	0	0	1
Ford	4	5	2	2	1	1

CLEVELAND	IP	H	R	ER	BB	SO
Young (L)	3	6	3	—	0	0
Kaler	3	4	1	—	1	0

CLEVELAND	IP	H	R	ER	BB	SO
Blanding	3	5	1	—	0	2

Time — 1:32. Umpires — Egan, Connally. Attendance — 15,281.

Nap Lajoie's 3000th Hit — Sunday, September 27, 1914

NEW YORK	AB	R	H	RBI	PO	A	E
Maisel, 3b	3	1	1	—	0	0	0
Hartzell, lf	4	0	1	—	5	0	0
Cook, rf	2	0	0	—	2	0	0
Cree, cf	4	0	1	—	1	1	0
Mullen, 1b	4	0	1	—	8	2	0
Peckinpaugh, ss	4	1	0	—	1	2	0
Sweeney, c	4	0	1	—	5	3	0
Boone, 2b	4	1	2	—	2	3	0
McHale, p	2	0	0	—	0	2	0
Daley, ph	1	0	0	—	0	0	0
Brown, p	0	0	0	—	0	0	0
Truesdale, ph	1	0	0	—	0	0	0

TOTALS	33	3	7	—	24	13	0

CLEVELAND	AB	R	H	RBI	PO	A	E
Smith, cf	4	1	2	—	2	0	0
Chapman, ss	2	0	0	—	8	2	1
Johnston, 1b	4	0	0	—	7	0	0
Leibold, rf	4	0	0	—	0	0	0
Lajoie, 2b	3	2	2	—	1	5	0
Graney, lf	2	1	1	—	3	0	1
Barbare, 3b	3	1	1	—	1	2	0
Egan, c	3	0	1	—	5	2	0
Morton, p	2	0	0	—	0	0	0
TOTALS	27	5	7	—	27	11	2

New York	101 000 100 —	3	7	0
Cleveland	100 031 00X —	5	7	2

Doubles—Smith, Lajoie 2. Sacrifice Hits—Chapman, Morton. Sacrifice Fly—Chapman. Double Play—Egan to Lajoie. Left on Base—Cleveland 2, New York 6.

NEW YORK	IP	H	R	ER	BB	SO
McHale (W)	6	7	5	—	1	4
Brown	2	0	0	0	0	1

CLEVELAND	IP	H	R	ER	BB	SO
Morton (L)	9	7	3	—	2	5

Hit By Pitch—Morton. Passed Ball—Sweeney. Umpires—Dinneen, Egan. Time—1:48. Attendance—NA.

1920 World Series Game Four — Saturday, October 9, 1920

BROOKLYN	AB	R	H	RBI	PO	A	E
Olson, ss	4	0	1	0	1	3	0
J. Johnston, 3b	4	1	2	0	1	0	0
Neis, pr	0	0	0	0	0	0	0
Griffith, rf	4	0	1	1	1	0	0
Wheat, lf	4	0	0	0	0	0	1
Myers, cf	3	0	0	0	6	1	0
Konetchy, 1b	2	0	0	0	5	0	0
Kilduff, 2b	3	0	1	0	2	3	0
Miller, c	3	0	0	0	7	0	0
Cadore, p	0	0	0	0	1	0	0
Mamaux, p	1	0	0	0	0	0	0
Marquard, p	0	0	0	0	0	1	0
Lamar, ph	1	0	0	0	0	0	0
Pfeffer, p	1	0	0	0	0	0	0
TOTALS	30	1	5	1	24	8	1

CLEVELAND	AB	R	H	RBI	PO	A	E

Jamieson, lf	2	0	0	0	1	0	0
Evans, ph-lf	3	0	1	0	0	0	0
Wambsganss, 2b	4	2	1	2	4	6	0
Speaker, cf	5	2	2	0	3	0	0
Smith, rf	1	0	1	1	1	0	0
Burns, ph-1b	2	0	1	2	7	0	1
Gardner, 3b	3	0	1	1	2	3	0
D. Johnston, 1b	1	0	0	0	4	0	0
Wood, ph-rf	2	0	0	0	0	0	0
Graney, ph-rf	1	0	0	0	0	0	0
Sewell, ss	4	0	2	0	1	7	1
O'Neill, c	2	0	1	0	4	0	0
Coveleski, p	4	1	1	0	0	2	0
TOTALS	34	5	12	5	27	18	2

Brooklyn	000 100 000 —	1	5	1
Cleveland	202 001 00X —	5	12	2

Double—Griffith. Sacrifice Fly—Gardner. Double Plays—Myers to Olson to Kilduff, Sewell to Wambsganss to Burns, Gardner to Wambsganss to Burns. Left on Base—Brooklyn-3, Cleveland-10.

BROOKLYN	IP	H	R	ER	BB	SO
Cadore (L)	1	4	2	2	1	1
Mamaux	1	2	2	2	0	1
Marquard	3	2	0	0	1	2
Pfeffer	3	4	1	1	2	1

CLEVELAND	IP	H	R	ER	BB	SO
Coveleski (W)	9	5	1	1	1	4

Wild Pitch—Pfeffer
Umpires—Dinneen (H), Klem (1), Connolly (2), O'Day (3). Time—1:54. Attendance—25,734.

1920 World Series Game Five — Sunday, October 10, 1920

BROOKLYN	AB	R	H	RBI	PO	A	E
Olson, ss	4	0	2	0	3	5	0
Sheehan, 3b	3	0	1	0	1	1	1
Griffith, rf	4	0	0	0	0	0	0
Wheat, lf	4	1	2	0	3	0	0
Myers, cf	4	0	2	0	0	0	0
Konetchy, 1b	4	0	2	1	9	2	0
Kilduff, 2b	4	0	1	0	5	6	0
Miller, c	2	0	2	0	0	1	0
Krueger, c	2	0	1	0	2	1	0
Grimes, p	1	0	0	0	0	1	0
Mitchell, p	2	0	0	0	1	0	0
TOTALS	34	1	3	1	24	17	1

CLEVELAND	AB	R	H	RBI	PO	A	E
Jamieson, lf	4	1	2	0	2	1	0
Graney, lf	1	0	0	0	0	0	0
Wambsganss, 2b	5	1	1	0	7	2	0
Speaker, cf	3	2	1	0	1	0	0
E. Smith, rf	4	1	3	4	0	0	0
Gardner, 3b	4	0	1	1	2	2	1
D. Johnston, 1b	3	1	2	0	9	1	0
Sewell, ss	3	0	0	0	2	4	0
O'Neill, c	2	1	0	0	3	1	1
Thomas, c	0	0	0	0	1	0	0
Bagby, p	4	1	2	3	0	2	0
TOTALS	33	8	12	8	27	13	2

Brooklyn	000 000 001 —				1	13	1
Cleveland	400 310 00X —				8	12	2

Triples — Konetchy, E. Smith. Home Runs — E. Smith, Bagby. Sacrifice Hits — Sheehan, D. Johnston. Double Plays — Olson to Kilduff to Konetchy, Jamieson to O'Neill, Gardner to Wambsganss to Johnston, Johnston to Sewell to Johnston. Triple Play — Wambsganss (unassisted). Left on Base — Brooklyn-7, Cleveland-6.

BROOKLYN	IP	H	R	ER	BB	SO
Grimes (L)	3.1	9	7	7	1	0
Mitchell	4.2	3	1	0	3	1

CLEVELAND	IP	H	R	ER	BB	SO
Bagby (W)	9	13	1	1	0	3

Wild Pitch — Bagby. Passed Ball — Miller. Umpires — Klem (H), Connolly (1), O'Day (2), Dinneen (3). Time — 1:49. Attendance — 26,884.

1920 World Series Game Six — Monday, October 11, 1920

BROOKLYN	AB	R	H	RBI	PO	A	E
Olson, ss	4	0	1	0	4	1	0
Sheehan, 3b	4	0	0	0	0	3	0
Neis, rf	2	0	0	0	3	0	0
Krueger, ph	1	0	0	0	0	0	0
Griffith, rf	0	0	0	0	0	0	0
Wheat, lf	4	0	0	0	2	0	0
Myers, cf	4	0	1	0	1	0	0
Konetchy, 1b	3	0	1	0	9	1	0
McCabe, pr	0	0	0	0	0	0	0
Kilduff, 2b	4	0	0	0	2	2	0
Miller, c	3	0	0	0	3	3	0
S. Smith, p	3	0	0	0	0	2	0
TOTALS	32	0	3	0	24	12	0

CLEVELAND	AB	R	H	RBI	PO	A	E
Evans, lf	4	0	3	0	4	0	0
Wambsganss, 2b	4	0	0	0	1	2	0
Speaker, cf	3	1	1	0	3	0	0
Burns, 1b	2	0	1	1	10	0	0
Gardner, 3b	3	0	0	0	2	2	1
Wood, rf	3	0	1	0	2	0	0
Sewell, ss	3	0	1	0	2	3	2
O'Neill, c	3	0	0	0	3	2	0
Mails, p	3	0	0	0	0	1	0
TOTALS	28	1	7	1	27	10	3

Brooklyn	000 000 000 —				0	3	0
Cleveland	000 001 00X —				1	7	3

Doubles — Burns, Olson. Left on Base — Brooklyn-7, Cleveland-4.

BROOKLYN	IP	H	R	ER	BB	SO
S. Smith (L)	8	7	1	1	1	1

CLEVELAND	IP	H	R	ER	BB	SO
Mails (W)	9	3	0	0	2	4

Umpires — Connolly (H), O'Day (1), Dinneen (2), Klem (3). Time — 1:34. Attendance — 27,194.

1920 World Series Game Seven — Tuesday, October 12, 1920

BROOKLYN	AB	R	H	RBI	PO	A	E
Olson, ss	4	0	0	0	1	1	0
Sheehan, 3b	4	0	1	0	2	1	1
Griffith, rf	4	0	0	0	3	0	0
Wheat, lf	4	0	2	0	3	0	0
Myers, cf	4	0	0	0	3	0	0
Konetchy, 1b	4	0	1	0	8	0	0
Kilduff, 2b	3	0	0	0	1	4	0
Miller, c	2	0	0	0	2	1	0
Lamar, ph	1	0	0	0	0	0	0
Krueger, c	0	0	0	0	1	0	0
Grimes, p	2	0	1	0	0	2	1
Schmandt, ph	1	0	0	0	0	0	0
Mamaux, p	0	0	0	0	0	0	0
TOTALS	33	0	5	0	24	9	2

CLEVELAND	AB	R	H	RBI	PO	A	E
Jamieson, lf	4	1	2	0	3	0	0
Wambsganss, 2b	4	0	1	0	5	3	0
Speaker, cf	3	0	1	0	3	0	0

E. Smith, rf   3 0 0 0 3 1 0
Gardner, 3b   4 1 1 0 1 3 0
D. Johnston, 1b   2 0 1 0 11 1 0
Sewell, ss   4 0 0 0 0 6 2
O'Neill, c   4 0 1 0 1 0 0
Coveleski, p   3 1 0 0 0 1 1
TOTALS   31 3 7 0 27 15 3

Brooklyn   000 000 000 —   0 5 2
Cleveland   000 110 10X —   3 7 3

Doubles— O'Neill, Jamieson. Triple— Speaker. Stolen Bases— D. Johnston, Jamieson. Left on Base — Brooklyn-6, Cleveland-8.

BROOKLYN	IP	H	R	ER	BB	SO
Grimes (L)	7	7	3	2	4	2
Mamaux	1	0	0	0	0	1

CLEVELAND	IP	H	R	ER	BB	SO
Covelskie (W)	9	5	0	0	0	1

Umpires— O'Day (H), Dinneen (1), Klem (2), Connolly (3). Time — 1:55. Attendance — 27,525.

Tris Speaker's 300th Hit — Sunday, May 17, 1925

WASHINGTON	AB	R	H	RBI	PO	A	E
Rice, rf	4	2	2	—	0	0	0

WASHINGTON	AB	R	H	RBI	PO	A	E
S. Harris, 2b	3	0	1	—	7	2	0
J. Harris, lf-1b	4	0	1	—	2	0	0
Goslin, cf-lf	4	0	1	—	3	0	0
Shirley, 1b	3	0	0	—	10	0	0
McNeely, cf	3	0	0	—	1	0	0
Bluege, 3b	3	0	1	—	0	3	0
Peckinpaugh, ss	4	0	1	—	1	4	0
Ruel, c	4	0	1	—	3	0	0
Zachary, p	2	0	0	—	0	5	0
TOTALS	32	2	8	—	27	14	0

CLEVELAND	AB	R	H	RBI	PO	A	E
Jamieson, lf	4	0	0	—	1	1	1
Lutzke, 3b	4	0	1	—	1	4	0
Speaker, cf	4	0	3	—	3	0	0
Knode, pr	0	1	0	—	0	0	0
J. Sewell, ss	3	0	0	—	3	4	1
L. Sewell, rf	4	0	2	—	6	1	0
Lee, rf	3	0	1	—	0	0	0
Burns, 1b	4	0	1	—	11	1	0
Fewster, 2b	2	0	0	—	1	2	1

Klugman, 2b   1 0 0 — 1 0 0
Uhle, p   3 0 1 — 0 2 0
TOTALS   32 1 9 — 27 14 3

Washington   001 000 010 —   2 8 0
Cleveland   000 000 001 —   1 9 3

Doubles— Rice, Goslin, Lutzke, Speaker, Burns, L. Sewell. Sacrifice Hits— Zachary, S. Harris, Lee. Double Plays— Peckinpaugh to S. Harris, S. Harris to Shirley, Bluege to S. Harris to Shirley, Fewster to J. Sewell to Burns. Left on Base — Washington 6, Cleveland 6.

WASHINGTON	IP	H	R	ER	BB	SO
Zachary (W)	9	9	1	—	0	1

CLEVELAND	IP	H	R	ER	BB	SO
Uhle (L)	9	8	2	—	1	6

Hit By Pitch — Zachary.

Umpires— Geisel, Moriarty, Rowland. Time — 1:45. Attendance — 20,000.

Babe Ruth's 500th Home Run — Sunday, August 11, 1929

NEW YORK	AB	R	H	RBI	PO	A	E
Combs, cf	4	0	0	0	3	1	0
Robertson, 3b	5	0	0	0	1	1	0
Gehrig, 1b	3	2	1	1	9	0	1

NEW YORK	AB	R	H	RBI	PO	A	E
Ruth, rf	4	2	2	1	2	0	0
Lazzeri, 2b	3	0	0	0	2	2	1
Meusel, lf	4	0	1	2	3	0	1
Dickey, c	3	0	2	0	2	1	0
Lary, pr	0	0	0	0	0	0	0
Koenig, ss	4	1	1	0	2	3	1
Wells, p	3	0	1	0	0	1	0
Sherid, p	0	0	0	0	0	0	0
Durst, ph	1	0	0	0	0	0	0
TOTALS	34	5	8	4	24	9	4

CLEVELAND	AB	R	H	RBI	PO	A	E
Morgan, rf	5	1	0	0	1	0	0
J. Sewell, 3b	5	0	1	1	1	2	0
Averill, cf	5	2	3	1	3	0	0
Fonseca, 1b	4	1	2	0	14	4	0
Falk, lf	2	0	1	1	1	1	0
Hodapp, 2b	4	1	2	2	0	7	0
Gardner, ss	4	0	1	0	1	3	1
L. Sewell, c	4	1	2	1	3	0	0
Hudlin, p	4	0	1	0	3	2	0

TOTALS	37	6	13	6	27	17	1
New York	010 112 000 —	5	8	4			
Cleveland	000 312 00X —	6	13	1			

Doubles—Meusel, Averill. Home Runs—Ruth, Gehrig. Sacrifice Hit—Falk. Double Play—Combs to Gehrig. Left on Base—New York-6, Cleveland-9.

NEW YORK	IP	H	R	ER	BB	SO
Wells (L)	5.2	12	6	4	1	1
Sherid	2.1	1	0	0	0	0

CLEVELAND	IP	H	R	ER	BB	SO
Hudlin (W)	9	8	5	4	4	2

Umpires—Nallin (H), Dinneen (1), McGowan (3). Time—2:00. Attendance—25,000.

Wes Ferrell's No-Hitter and Homer—Wednesday, April 29, 1931

ST. LOUIS	AB	R	H	RBI	PO	A	E
Levey, ss	2	0	0	0	0	0	0
Burns, 1b	4	0	0	0	6	3	0
Goslin, lf	3	0	0	0	7	0	0
Kress, rf	4	0	0	0	1	0	0
Schulte, cf	4	0	0	0	1	0	0
Storti, 3b	3	0	0	0	1	2	0
Melillo, 2b	3	0	0	0	3	3	0
ST. LOUIS	AB	R	H	RBI	PO	A	E
R. Ferrell, c	3	0	0	0	2	0	0
Gray, p	2	0	0	0	3	2	0
Waddey, ph	1	0	0	0	0	0	0
Stiles, p	0	0	0	0	0	0	0
TOTALS	29	0	0	0	24	10	0

CLEVELAND	AB	R	H	RBI	PO	A	E
Burnett, 3b	4	2	2	0	1	3	0
Fonseca, 1b	4	0	1	1	2	3	0
Averill, cf	5	1	2	2	1	0	0
Hodapp, 2b	4	0	1	1	2	3	0
Vosmik, lf	4	0	1	0	1	0	0
Falk, rf	4	0	0	0	0	0	0
Hunnefield	4	2	2	0	2	3	3
Sewell, c	3	2	1	1	8	0	0
W. Ferrell, p	4	2	2	4	0	2	0
TOTALS	36	9	13	9	27	11	3

Doubles—Hunnefield, Vosmik, W. Ferrell. Home Runs—W. Ferrell, Averill. Sacrifice Hit—Fonseca. Double Play—Burnett to Fonseca. Left on Base—St. Louis-5, Cleveland-6.

St. Louis	000 000 000 —	0	0	0
Cleveland	011 200 23X —	9	13	3

ST. LOUIS	IP	H	R	ER	BB	SO
Gray (L)	7	10	6	6	0	1
Stiles	1	3	3	3	2	0

CLEVELAND	IP	H	R	ER	BB	SO
W. Ferrell (W)	9	0	0	0	3	8

Umpires—Geisel (H), Moriarty (1), Hildebrand (3). Time—NA. Attendance—4,000.

The Longest Game at League Park—July 10, 1932

PHILADELPHIA	AB	R	H	RBI	PO	A	E
Haas, rf	9	3	2	0	7	1	0
Cramer, cf	8	2	2	1	5	0	0
Dykes, 3b	10	2	3	4	0	7	0
Simmons, lf	9	4	5	2	1	1	0
Foxx, 1b	9	4	6	8	19	2	0
McNair, ss	10	0	2	1	6	3	0
Hoving, c	4	0	0	0	1	0	0
Madjeski, c	5	0	0	0	9	1	0
Williams, 2b	8	1	2	0	5	9	0
Krause, p	1	0	0	0	0	1	0
Rommell, p	7	2	3	1	1	5	1
TOTALS	80	18	25	17	54	30	1

CLEVELAND	AB	R	H	RBI	PO	A	E
Porter, rf	10	3	3	2	3	0	0
Burnett, ss	11	4	9	2	5	5	1
Averill, c	9	3	5	4	4	1	1
Vosmik, lf	10	2	2	1	8	1	0
Morgan, 1b	11	1	5	4	15	0	1
Myatt, c	7	2	1	0	10	1	0
Cissell, 2b	9	1	4	3	4	5	2
Kamm, 3b	7	1	2	0	5	6	0
Hudlin, p	0	0	0	0	0	0	0
Ferrell, p	5	0	0	0	0	0	0
TOTALS	83	17	33	16	54	22	5

Philadelphia 201 201 702 000 000 201 18 25 1
Cleveland 300 311 601 000 000 200 17 33 5

Doubles—Burnett-2, Myuatt, Cissell, Vosmik, Morgan-2, Haas, Dykes, Kamm, Porter, McNair, Foxx. Triple—Williams. Home Runs—Foxx-3, Averill. Stolen Base—Cissell.

Sacrifice Hits— Kamm, Ferrell. Double Play — Williams to McNair to Foxx, Burnett to Cissell to Morgan, Kamm to Cissell to Morgan, Williams to Madjewski to Foxx. Left on Base — Philadelphia-15, Cleveland-24.

PHILADELPHIA	IP	H	R	ER	BB	SO
Krause	1	4	3	3	1	0
Rommel (W)	17	29	14	13	9	7

CLEVELAND	IP	H	R	ER	BB	SO
Brown	6.2	13	8	7	1	3
Hudlin	0	0	2	2	2	0
Ferrell (L)	11.1	12	8	6	4	7

Wild Pitches— Rommel-2.

Umpires— Hildebrand (H), Owens (B). Time — 4:05. Attendance — 10,000.

Fifteen Inning Complete Game Duel — August 24, 1935

PHILADELPHIA	AB	R	H	RBI	PO	A	E
Finney, rf	6	0	1	0	1	0	0
Cramer, cf	6	0	3	0	4	0	0
Johnson, lf	5	0	1	0	3	0	0
Foxx, 1b	5	0	1	0	12	2	0
Higgins, 3b	6	0	1	0	2	1	0
McNair, ss	6	0	0	0	8	6	0
Warstler, 2b	6	0	1	0	5	10	0
Richards, c	6	0	0	0	8	4	0
Turbeville, p	5	0	0	0	1	1	0
TOTALS	51	0	8	0	44	24	0

CLEVELAND	AB	R	H	RBI	PO	A	E
Galatzer, rf	4	1	1	0	1	0	0
Averill, cf	5	1	1	2	7	0	0
Vosmik, lf	3	0	0	0	5	0	0
Trosky, 1b	5	0	1	0	17	1	0
Hale, 3b	5	0	2	0	1	4	0
Knickerbocker,ss	4	0	2	0	1	6	1
Brenzel, c	3	0	0	0	5	1	0
Hughes, ph	1	0	0	0	0	0	0
Phillips, c	2	0	0	0	1	0	0
Berger, 2b	5	0	2	0	5	5	0
Hudlin, p	4	0	0	0	2	2	0
TOTALS	42	2	9	2	45	19	1

Philadelphia 000 000 000 000 000 — 0 8 0
Cleveland   000 000 000 000 002 — 2 9 1

Doubles— Hale, Trosky. Home Run — Averill.

Sacrifice Hits— Vosmik, Turbeville, Johnson. Stolen Base — Higgins. Double Plays— Brenzel to Berger, McNair to Foxx-2, Warstler to McNair to Foxx-2, Higgins to Warstler to Foxx, McNair to Warstler to Foxx. Left on Base — Philadelphia-9, Cleveland-10.

PHILADELPHIA	IP	H	R	ER	BB	SO
Turbeville (L)	14.2	9	2	2	13	6

CLEVELAND	IP	H	R	ER	BB	SO
Hudlin (W)	15	8	0	0	1	6

Wild Pitches— Turbeville-3.

Umpires— Kolls (H), Owens (B). Time — NA. Attendance — NA.

Bob Feller's Exhibition Debut — Monday, July 6, 1936

ST. LOUIS	AB	R	H	RBI	PO	A	E
Moore, cf	5	2	1	0	2	0	0
S. Martin, 2b	1	0	0	0	5	2	0
King, 2b	2	0	1	0	3	2	0
J. Martin, rf	4	0	0	1	0	0	0
Mize, ph	1	0	0	0	0	0	0
Medwick, lf	1	0	1	1	1	0	0
Fullis, lf	1	0	0	0	1	0	0
Collins, 1b	3	0	0	0	5	0	1
Davis, 1b	1	1	0	0	4	0	0
Ogrodowski, c	5	1	2	1	1	0	0
Durocher, ss	2	0	2	0	1	2	0
Gelbert, 3b	3	0	1	2	1	2	1
Garibaldi, 3b	4	0	0	0	2	4	0
Munns, p	4	1	1	0	0	0	0
TOTALS	37	6	9	5	24	12	2

CLEVELAND	AB	R	H	RBI	PO	A	E
Hughes, 2b	5	1	2	0	2	1	0
Hale, 3b	1	0	0	0	0	1	0
Gugler, 3b	1	0	0	0	0	1	0
Averill, cf	2	0	1	1	1	0	0
Galatzer, cf	2	2	1	0	1	0	0
Trosky, 1b	4	0	0	0	5	0	0
Weatherly, rf-lf	3	2	2	1	2	0	0
Vosmik, lf	2	0	0	0	1	0	0
Campbell, rf	1	1	1	1	0	0	0
Knickerbocker, ss	1	0	0	0	1	2	0
Berger, ss	3	1	1	1	1	1	1
O'Neill, c	1	0	0	0	7	0	0
Sullivan, ph	1	0	1	0	0	0	0
Becker, c	2	0	1	1	4	1	0

Uhle, p	1	0	0	0	0	0	0
Feller, p	1	0	0	0	0	0	0
Kardow, p	2	0	0	0	0	0	0
TOTALS	33	7	10	5	27	7	1

St. Louis	001 010 103 —	6	9	2
Cleveland	100 101 04X —	7	10	1

Doubles—Sullivan, Ogrodowski, Weatherly, Becker. Home Run—Weatherly. Stolen Bases—S. Martin-2, Moore-2, Hughes, Garibaldi, Campbell, Berger. Double Plays—S. Martin to Collins, Durocher to S. Martin to Collins. Left on Base–

ST. LOUIS	*IP*	*H*	*R*	*ER*	*BB*	*SO*
Munns (L)	8	10	7	—	4	1

CLEVELAND	*IP*	*H*	*R*	*ER*	*BB*	*SO*
Uhle	3	2	1	—	2	2
Feller	3	2	1	—	1	8
Kardow (W)	3	5	4	—	3	0

Wild Pitches—Munns-2. Passed Ball—O'Neill.

Umpires—Ormsby, Owens. Time—2:03. Attendance—3, 500.

Bob Feller's First Major League Start — Sunday, August 23, 1936

ST. LOUIS	*AB*	*R*	*H*	*RBI*	*PO*	*A*	*E*
Lary, ss	4	1	1	0	3	3	0
Clift, 3b	2	0	1	0	2	1	0
Solters, lf	4	0	0	0	0	0	0
Bell, rf	4	0	2	1	1	0	0
West, cf	4	0	0	0	0	0	0
Bottomley, 1b	3	0	1	0	7	1	0
ST. LOUIS	*AB*	*R*	*H*	*RBI*	*PO*	*A*	*E*
Bejma, 2b	4	0	0	0	1	2	1
Giuliani, c	4	0	1	0	8	1	0
Caldwell, p	2	0	0	0	2	3	0
Coleman, ph	1	0	0	0	0	0	0
Van Atta, p	0	0	0	0	0	0	0
Liebhardt, p	0	0	0	0	0	0	0
Pepper, ph	1	0	0	0	0	0	0
TOTALS	33	1	6	1	24	11	1

CLEVELAND	*AB*	*R*	*H*	*RBI*	*PO*	*A*	*E*
Hughes, 2b	4	1	1	0	0	1	1
Hale, 3b	2	1	0	0	3	1	0
Averill, cf	3	1	1	0	1	0	0

CLEVELAND						
Trosky, 1b	4	1	4	2	5	0	0
Weatherly, rf	3	0	0	0	2	0	0
Vosmik, lf	4	0	1	2	1	0	0
George, c	4	0	1	0	15	1	0
Knickerbocker, ss	4	0	0	0	0	1	0
Feller, p	3	0	1	0	0	0	0
TOTALS	31	4	9	4	27	4	1

St. Louis	000 001 000 —	1	6	1
Cleveland	000 003 10X —	4	9	1

Doubles—Bell, Lary, Trosky. Left on Base—St. Louis-9, Cleveland-7. Double Play—Caldwell to Lary. Stolen Base—Clift.

ST. LOUIS	*IP*	*H*	*R*	*ER*	*BB*	*SO*
Caldwell (L)	6	6	3	3	3	4
Van Atta	1	2	1	1	1	1
Liebhardt	1	1	0	0	0	0

CLEVELAND	*IP*	*H*	*R*	*ER*	*BB*	*SO*
Feller (W)	9	6	1	1	4	15

Wild Pitches—Feller-4.

Umpires—Geisel (H), Ormsby (1), Basil (3). Time—X. Attendance—9000.

Bob Feller Ties Dizzy Dean's Major League Strikeout Record — Sunday, September 13, 1936

PHILADELPHIA	*AB*	*R*	*H*	*RBI*	*PO*	*A*	*E*
Finney, cf	1	1	0	0	1	0	0
Puccinelli, rf	2	0	0	0	1	0	0
Moses, rf-cf	2	1	1	0	5	0	0
Dean, 1b	3	0	1	1	7	0	0
Johnson, lf	4	0	0	0	4	0	0
Higgins, 3b	2	0	0	0	0	1	0
Luby, 2b	4	0	0	0	0	5	0
PHILADELPHIA	*AB*	*R*	*H*	*RBI*	*PO*	*A*	*E*
Peters, ss	4	0	0	0	3	1	1
Hayes, c	4	0	0	0	3	1	0
Gumpert, p	3	0	0	0	0	0	0
Moss, ph	0	0	0	0	0	0	0
TOTALS	29	2	2	1	24	8	1

CLEVELAND	*AB*	*R*	*H*	*RBI*	*PO*	*A*	*E*
Hughes, 2b	3	2	1	0	0	2	0
Knickerbocker, ss	2	2	1	0	0	1	0
Averill, cf	2	1	1	2	1	0	0

	AB	R	H	RBI	PO	A	E
Trosky, 1b	4	0	2	0	5	0	0
Weatherly, rf	4	0	0	1	2	0	0
Hale, 3b	4	0	0	0	0	0	0
Heath, lf	3	0	1	0	2	0	0
George, c	4	0	1	0	17	0	0
Feller, p	4	0	0	0	0	0	0
TOTALS	30	5	7	3	27	3	0

Doubles— Averill, Hughes. Hit By Pitch— Moses. Sacrifice Hit — Knickerbocker. Double Play — Luby to Peters to Dean. Left on Base — Philadelphia-10, Cleveland-7.

			R	H	E
Philadelphia	002 000 000 —		2	2	1
Cleveland	202 000 10X —		5	7	1

PHILADELPHIA	IP	H	R	ER	BB	SO
Gumpert (L)	8	7	5	3	5	2

CLEVELAND	IP	H	R	ER	BB	SO
Feller (W)	9	2	2	2	9	17

Balk — Gumpert. Wild Pitch — Feller.

Umpires— Kolls (H), Johnston (1), Owens (3). Time — NA. Attendance — 6500.

Joe DiMaggio's 56th Consecutive Game Hitting Safely — Wednesday, July 16, 1941

NEW YORK	AB	R	H	RBI	PO	A	E
Sturm, 1b	5	0	0	0	8	1	0
Rolfe, 3b	4	0	0	0	2	2	0
Heinrich, rf	4	1	0	0	2	1	0
DiMaggio, cf	4	3	3	0	3	0	0
Gordon, 2b	4	2	2	1	2	3	0
Rosar, c	5	1	3	5	5	1	0
Keller, lf	3	3	2	1	4	0	0
Rizzuto, ss	5	0	1	2	0	2	0
Donald, p	4	0	0	0	1	0	0
TOTALS	38	10	11	9	27	10	0

CLEVELAND	AB	R	H	RBI	PO	A	E
Boudreau, ss	4	1	1	0	2	1	0
Keltner, 3b	4	0	1	0	0	3	0
Weatherly, cf	3	0	0	0	2	0	0
Heath, rf	4	1	2	1	5	0	0
Trosky, 1b	3	0	1	1	7	1	1
Campbell, lf	4	0	0	0	2	0	0
Mack, 2b	3	1	1	0	3	3	0

	AB	R	H	RBI	PO	A	E
Bell, ph	1	0	0	0	0	0	0
Desautels, c	3	0	0	0	6	0	0
Walker, ph	1	0	1	0	0	0	0
Milnar, p	2	0	1	1	0	1	0
Krakauskas, p	1	0	0	0	0	0	0
Rosenthal, ph	0	0	0	0	0	0	0
TOTALS	33	3	8	3	27	9	1

Doubles— Mack, Rosar-2, Rizzuto, DiMaggio, Walker. Triple — Keller. Home Runs— Keller, Heath. Double Play — Rosar to Rolfe. Left on Base — New York-8, Cleveland-7.

			R	H	E
New York	200 140 012 —		10	11	0
Cleveland	110 001 000 —		3	8	1

NEW YORK	IP	H	R	ER	BB	SO
Donald (W)	9	8	3	3	4	5

CLEVELAND	IP	H	R	ER	BB	SO
Milnar (L)	5	8	7	7	4	3
Krakauskas	4	3	3	2	3	3

Umpires— Stewart (H), Summer (1), Rue (3). Time — 2:17. Attendance — 15,000.

1945 Negro Leagues World Series Game Two — Sunday, September 16, 1945

HOMESTEAD	AB	R	H	RBI	PO	A	E
Bell, lf	4	1	1	—	2	0	0
Benjamin, cf	3	0	1	—	1	0	0
Hoskins, rf	4	0	1	—	2	0	0
Leonard, 1b	4	1	2	—	6	1	0
Gibson, c	4	0	1	—	5	0	0
Bankhead, ss	4	0	0	—	3	1	0
Battles, 3b	1	0	0	—	0	0	0
Jackson, 2b	3	0	1	—	3	3	1
Wright, p	3	0	0	—	1	4	0
Wilson, 3b	3	0	0	—	1	1	0
TOTALS	33	2	7	—	24	10	1

CLEVELAND	AB	R	H	RBI	PO	A	E
Canazires, ss	4	0	2	0	2	5	0
Ware, 1b	3	0	0	0	16	0	0
Jethroe, cf	4	0	1	0	2	0	0

CLEVELAND	AB	R	H	RBI	PO	A	E
Woods, 3b	4	0	0	0	0	2	0
Grace, rf	4	1	1	2	3	0	0
Troupe, c	4	1	1	0	0	1	0
Armour, lf	3	2	1	0	1	0	0

Cowan, 2b	3	0	0	3	4	0
Bremer, p	3	0	2	2	0	6	0
TOTALS	35	4	8	4	27	18	0

Homestead	000 110 000 —	2	7	1
Cleveland	000 000 202 —	4	8	0

Doubles— Gibson, Armour, Troupe, Bremer. Home Run — Grace. Stolen Base — Armour. Sacrifice Hit — Benjamin.

HOMESTEAD	IP	H	R	ER	BB	SO
Wright (L)	8	8	4	—	3	5

CLEVELAND	IP	H	R	ER	BB	SO
Bremer (W)	9	7	2	2	2	1

Umpires— NA. Time— NA. Attendance — 10,000.

Ted Williams' Only Inside-the-Park
Homer Clinches Red Sox Pennant
— Friday, September 13, 1946

BOSTON	AB	R	H	RBI	PO	A	E
D. DiMaggio, cf	3	0	0	0	0	0	0
Pesky, ss	3	0	1	0	2	5	0
Williams, lf	3	1	1	1	2	0	0
Doerr, 2b	4	0	0	0	3	4	0
York, 1b	3	0	0	0	10	1	0
McBride, rf	4	0	0	0	6	0	0
Wagner, c	4	0	0	0	4	0	0
Gutteridge, 3b	2	0	0	0	0	0	0
Hughson, p	3	0	0	0	0	3	0
TOTALS	29	1	2	1	27	13	0

CLEVLEAND	AB	R	H	RBI	PO	A	E
Mackiewicz, cf	3	0	0	0	4	0	0
Ross, 3b	4	0	0	0	1	2	0
Seerey, lf	3	0	1	0	1	0	0
Edwards, rf	4	0	0	0	3	0	0
Fleming, 1b	4	0	0	0	8	3	0
Boudreau, ss	3	0	0	0	0	2	0
Mack, 2b	3	0	1	0	3	1	0
Hegan, c	3	0	0	0	6	0	0
Embree, p	2	0	1	0	1	3	1
TOTALS	29	0	3	0	27	11	1

Boston	100 000 000 —	1	2	0
Cleveland	000 000 000 —	0	3	1

Home Run — Williams. Sacrifice Hits— Mackiewicz, Gutteridge. Left on Base — Boston-6,

Cleveland-5.

BOSTON	IP	H	R	ER	BB	SO
Hughson (W)	9	3	0	0	2	4

CLEVELAND	IP	H	R	ER	BB	SO
Embree (L)	9	2	1	1	4	3

Umpires— Grieve (H), Paparella (1), Hubbard (3). Time— 1:28. Attendance — 3295.

Final Major League Game at L e a g u e Park — Saturday, September 21, 1946

DETROIT	AB	R	H	RBI	PO	A	E
Lake, ss	5	1	1	0	1	4	0
Kell, 3b	6	2	2	0	2	3	0
Evers, cf	6	0	1	1	1	0	0
Greenberg, 1b	3	1	1	1	15	1	0
Wakefield, lf	5	1	1	1	4	0	0
Cullenbine, rf	4	0	1	0	1	1	0
Bloodworth, 2b	4	0	0	0	2	5	0
Tebbets, c	5	0	0	0	6	2	0
Trout, p	4	0	2	0	1	1	0
TOTALS	42	5	9	3	33	17	0

CLEVELAND	AB	R	H	RBI	PO	A	E
Moss, 3b	6	0	1	0	2	3	2
Conway, ss	5	0	1	0	4	2	0
Robinson, 1b	4	0	2	0	11	0	0
Edwards, rf	3	1	1	0	1	0	0
Mitchell, cf	5	2	2	1	5	0	0
Seerey, lf	3	0	0	0	3	0	0
Mack, 2b	2	0	1	0	0	1	0
Fleming, ph	1	0	1	0	0	0	0
Meyer, 2b	2	0	0	0	3	2	0
Weigel, c	2	0	0	0	3	0	0
Wasdell, ph	1	0	0	1	0	0	0
Jordan, c	2	1	1	0	1	1	0
Kuzava, p	3	0	0	0	0	3	1
Becker, ph	1	0	1	1	0	0	0
Gromek, pr	0	0	0	0	0	0	0
Berry, p	0	0	0	0	0	0	0
Lemon, p	0	0	0	0	0	0	0
Woodling, ph	1	0	1	0	0	0	0
TOTALS	41	3	12	3	33	12	3

Detroit	011 010 000 02 —	5	9	0
Cleveland	000 002 010 00 —	3	12	3

Doubles— Edwards, Mitchell. Triples— Mack,

Kell. Stolen Base—Jordan. Sacrifice Hits—Robinson, Bloodworth. Double Plays—Bloodworth to Lake to Greenberg, Meyer to Robinson, Bloodworth to Greenberg. Left on Base—Detroit-13, Cleveland-11.

DETROIT	IP	H	R	ER	BB	SO
Trout (W)	11	12	3	3	5	6

CLEVELAND	IP	H	R	ER	BB	SO
Kuzava	8	4	3	1	7	3
Berry (L)	2.2	5	2	2	1	0
Lemon	0.1	0	0	0	0	0

Wild Pitch—Lemon.

Umpires—Rue (H), Passarella, (1), Berry (3). Time—2:40. Attendance—2772.

C—Dunn Field Pointers

Dunn Field
POINTERS

DUNN FIELD POINTERS

Published by

THE CLEVELAND BASEBALL COMPANY

IN ORDER THAT PATRONS MAY
SECURE THE MAXIMUM SERVICE
WITH THE MINIMUM EFFORT

CLEVELAND, OHIO

To Our Patrons

 DESIRE to express my appreciation of the liberal support which has been accorded my efforts to provide Cleveland with its first World's Championship club and to pledge a continuation of the policy which has brought this result.

I regret that the limited capacity of Dunn Field makes it impossible to provide box and reserved seat accommodations for all who desire same on big days, but we shall continue our policy of making improvements wherever possible and revising our plan of operation in order that our patrons may secure the accommodations provided for their comfort.

The changes inaugurated during the coming season will include the daily reservation of seven rows of seats on the main floor of the grand stand immediately back of the boxes, the addition of 202 additional box seats, a plan for checking up the boxes at the end of the fifth inning which will eliminate the annoyance to which our box patrons were subjected last season, and a complete new season box plan.

The following pages of this brochure are descriptive of the entrances to Dunn Field, and the color scheme of box and reserved seat tickets, and are designed to convey to our patrons information that will enable them to take full advantage of the service we desire to render with the minimum of effort and confusion.   J. C. DUNN, *President*
The Cleveland Baseball Company

Dunn Field Entrances

Payne Avenue and Wade Park cars pass the main entrance to Dunn Field, which is located at the corner of East 66th Street and Lexington Avenue.

The box seat tickets ($1.36), the reserved seat tickets ($1.13) and the pavilion admission tickets (68 cents) are always sold at this location; and turnstiles for these priced tickets are operated directly back of these ticket offices.

The grand stand admission tickets (90 cents) are always sold at the corner of East 66th Street and Linwood Avenue and turnstiles are operated at this location for tickets at this price. Grand stand admission tickets entitle the holders to any seat back of the posts on the main floor, and when these seats are filled they can pass up the stairway at either first or third base end of the grand stand to seats in the upper deck of the first and third base pavilions. When these seats are all occupied, the same ticket is sold for standing room on the main floor of the grand stand.

Owing to the fact that every seat in the grand stand will be reserved and sold in advance for the Opening Game, the above entrance information will not apply for the Opening Game. Holders of Opening Game tickets will need to inform themselves in regard to the entrance arrangements for that game without regard to the information which will apply for all the other games of the season.

Opening Game Information

In order to meet the advance demand for Opening Game tickets, we have decided to reserve every seat in the grand stand for this occasion. To avoid confusion at the entrances this reservation of the entire stand will make it necessary to handle the holders of the Upper Deck reserved seat tickets through the Linwood entrance, in the same manner as was done during the World's Series games. Opening Game tickets will have these special entrance requirements designated on each ticket and this information should not be confused with our regular entrance arrangements for the other games of the season, which are fully described in the following pages of this brochure.

Opening Game Grand Stand entrances will be as follows: Stile No. 1, Season Box Holders, East 66th Street near Lexington Avenue. Stiles 2 and 3, Box Tickets (red, green and lilac), Lexington Avenue and East 66th Street. Stiles 4, 5 and 6, Main Floor (yellow), Lexington Avenue and East 66th Street. Stiles 16, 17, 18, 19, 20 and 21, Upper Deck (white, pink and blue), East 66th Street and Linwood Avenue.

Opening Game box and reserved seat tickets are good for the opening game until same is played, making it unnecessary for our patrons to be put to the trouble of exchanging their tickets in the event of a postponement because of rain. This arrangement makes it necessary to have a special rain check on the opening game **box and reserve tickets**, the conditions of which are different from the rain checks on the tickets for all the other games of the season. Patrons should read the conditions of this special rain check carefully in order to understand what must be done provided they are unable to attend the game on a postponed date.

General Admission rain checks for the Opening Game are good for any future game of the season. **This special form of rain check applies to the box and reserve tickets only.**

Color Scheme in Box and Reserve Tickets

To avoid confusion and to facilitate the work of our ushers, a color scheme for the box and reserved tickets has been in operation for several years. The value of this color scheme was demonstrated by the absence of confusion in handling the World's Series crowds.

The Upper Deck Boxes, Main Floor Boxes, Upper Deck Reserved Seats, Main Floor Reserved Seats, First Base Upper Deck Reserved Seats and Third Base Upper Deck Reserved Seats are all designated by a specific color of ticket. This color scheme facilitates the work of our ticket sellers, and enables the ushers to seat our patrons with the minimum of confusion.

An increased familiarity with, and understanding of, this color scheme will enable our patrons to purchase their tickets in advance more intelligently, and will greatly increase the efficiency of our ushers. This color scheme, in connection with the tickets, is fully explained on the following pages.

VIEW OF INFIELD FROM UPPER GRAND STAND, FIRST BASE SIDE—**RED AND WHITE TICKETS.**   [7]

Do You Know the Color You Want?

RED TICKETS

Upper Deck Box Tickets (red) are on sale for every game of the season. These tickets call for seats in the two rows of boxes around the front of the upper deck of the grand stand and sell for $1.36 each, exclusive of war tax, which is 14 cents additional, making a total of $1.50 each. These boxes vary in size, and contain, four, six, eight and nine seats, according to location. For view of infield from these seats, see cuts on pages 5 and 7.

GREEN TICKETS

Main Floor Box Tickets (green) are for sale for every game of the season. These tickets call for seats in the three rows of boxes around the front of the main floor of the grand stand and sell for $1.36 each, exclusive of the war tax, which is 14 cents additional, making a total price of $1.50 each. These boxes contain four and eight seats each. For view of infield from these seats see cut on page 9.

VIEW OF INFIELD FROM MAIN FLOOR, THIRD BASE SIDE—GREEN AND YELLOW TICKETS. [9]

The Color of Your Ticket Means Something

YELLOW TICKETS

Main Floor Reserved Tickets (yellow) are on sale for every game of the season. These tickets call for seats in the first seven rows immediately back of the boxes on the main floor of the grand stand and sell for $1.13 each, exclusive of the war tax, which is 12 cents additional, making a total price of $1.25 each. For view of infield from these seats see cut on page 9.

LILAC TICKETS

Auto Box Tickets (lilac) are on sale for every game of the season and call for seats in boxes X, Y and Z in the rear of the first base side of the main floor of the grand stand, and sell for $1.13 each, exclusive of the war tax, which is 12 cents additional, making a total price of $1.25 each. During the week, coupons for these seats are sold at the exchange stile in the first base end of the grand stand, but on Sundays and Holidays these tickets will be sold at the windows on the outside of the park.

VIEW OF INFIELD FROM FIRST BASE UPPER PAVILION—**PINK TICKETS.**   [11]

The Color Scheme Helps You

WHITE TICKETS

The Upper Deck Reserved Tickets (white) are on sale for the Opening Game, all Sunday and Holiday games, and for such other games as the advance demand for reserved seats may make necessary. These tickets sell at all times for $1.13 each, exclusive of the war tax, which is 12 cents additional, making a total price of $1.25 each. On week days the seats in this section of the grand stand are not reserved but the price of admission is the same and a general admission ticket is sold to this part of the stand, and purchasers of these tickets are permitted to make their own selection of seats anywhere in this section back of the boxes. For view of infield, from these seats, see cuts on pages 5 and 7.

PINK TICKETS

First Base Upper Deck Reserved Tickets (pink) are on sale for the Opening Game, Sunday and Holiday games, and for such other games as the advance demand for reserved seats may make necessary. These tickets call for seats in the four sections of the First Base Upper Deck nearest the grand stand, and sell at all times for $1.13 each, exclusive of the war tax, which is 12 cents additional, making a total price of $1.25 each. For view of infield from these seats see cut on page 11.

BLUE TICKETS

Third Base Upper Deck Reserved Tickets (blue) are on sale for the Opening Game, Sunday and Holiday games, and for such other games as the advance demand for reserved seats may make necessary. These tickets call for seats in the four sections of the Third Base Upper Deck nearest the grand stand, and sell at all times for $1.13 each, exclusive of the war tax, which is 12 cents additional, making a total price of $1.25 each. For view of infield from these seats see cut on page 13.

VIEW OF INFIELD FROM THIRD BASE UPPER PAVILION

Dunn Field Admission Prices

A recapitulation of the foregoing ticket information is herewith presented together with the prices of the general admission tickets to the grand stand, pavilions and bleachers. The attention of our patrons is called to the fact that in the future the price of all box seats at Dunn Field will be $1.36, exclusive of the war tax, and the price of all reserved seats will be $1.13, exclusive of the war tax. This makes the total price of a box seat $1.50 and the total price of a reserved seat $1.25. The various admission prices to Dunn Field and their official designation and color of tickets are indicated below:

	Color	Price	War Tax	Total Price
Upper Deck Box Tickets	Red	$1.36	$0.14	$1.50
Main Floor Box Tickets	Green	1.36	.14	1.50
Auto Box Tickets	Lilac	1.13	.12	1.25
Main Floor Reserve Tickets	Yellow	1.13	.12	1.25
Upper Deck Reserve Tickets	White	1.13	.12	1.25
First Base Upper Deck Reserve Tickets	Pink	1.13	.12	1.25
Third Base Upper Deck Reserve Tickets	Blue	1.13	.12	1.25
Grand Stand Gen. Admission (Not Reserved)		.90	.10	1.00
Pavilion Admission		.68	.07	.75
Bleacher Admission		.45	.05	.50

TICKETS ORDERED BY MAIL

Mail orders for box and reserve tickets, when accompanied by check, bank draft, postoffice or express money order, are given prompt attention, and, if received in time, are filled before the tickets are placed on public sale. Mail orders should be addressed to The Cleveland Baseball Company, East 66th Street and Lexington Avenue, Cleveland, Ohio.

GRAND STAND UPPER PAVILION BOXES, FIRST BASE SIDE—**RED TICKETS.**   [15]

Advance Ticket Sales

Box and reserve tickets are on sale at our down town ticket office about one week in advance. Occasionally the advance demand for these tickets for some special series is so great that we are compelled to place them on sale more than a week in advance. This advance sale of tickets enables our patrons to avoid the confusion and delay at the ticket windows when they come to the game.

Tickets Ordered by Telephone

Telephone orders for tickets will be accepted for all ordinary week day games and tickets so ordered will be held at Window No. 1 until fifteen minutes of the time the game is advertised to start. **Telephone orders are not accepted for the Sunday and Holiday games and we must reserve the right to refuse to accept telephone orders for any game at our discretion, when the advance sale is so heavy that the acceptance of telephone orders would be an injustice to the great majority of our patrons.**

Ticket Scalping

There is a local ordinance against "ticket scalping." The maximum penalty provided under this ordinance is a fine of $50.00 and costs. The Cleveland Baseball Company is bitterly opposed to the "scalping" of its tickets and will not only assist in the prosecution of anyone arrested for this practice, but in addition to this will endeavor to bar from Dunn Field anyone who has been found guilty of this practice.

GRAND STAND UPPER PAVILION BOXES, THIRD BASE SIDE—**RED TICKETS.**

Sunday Morning Advance Sale Rules

Telephone orders for box and reserved seat tickets for Sunday games will not be accepted on Sunday morning. Such service can only be furnished to a few of our patrons at the expense of the vast majority.

Tickets for the Sunday games are placed on sale at Window No. 1 at 9:00 o'clock Sunday morning. In the interest of public convenience, we feel that our patrons will agree with us that those, who have postponed the purchase of tickets until Sunday morning, should come to Dunn Field and secure them instead of asking for a reservation over the phone and thereby causing a lot of congestion at the main entrance just a few minutes before the time for starting the game.

General Admission Information

We are convinced that many of our patrons would be better satisfied with their accommodations at Dunn Field if they would make a study of the situation and patronize our grand stand general admission entrance at the corner of East 66th Street and Linwood Avenue more than they did last season. On many days our patrons lined up at the reserved seat ticket windows and insisted upon paying the reserved seat price when they could have secured better seats at the general admission price. The last six or seven hundred reserve tickets sold for any game are always in the last four rows in the Upper Deck and these tickets are often sold at the Main Entrance windows when much more desirable seats are available to the purchasers of grand stand general admission tickets.

MAIN FLOOR BOXES, FIRST BASE SIDE.—GREEN TICKETS.   11

Better Protection for Box Seat Patrons

Many of our patrons encroached upon the rights of those purchasing box seat accommodations last season. This evil attained such proportions that it has been found necessary to inaugurate a new plan for the supervision of the box seats which will absolutely protect the purchasers of box tickets in their rights.

At the close of the fifth inning each day our ushers will visit all the boxes and collect the seat coupons from those occupying same. Anyone who is unable to give the usher a box seat coupon will be compelled to vacate the boxes. We feel that our box patrons will gladly co-operate with us in putting this plan into effect because of the relief from the annoyance of interlopers which it will afford.

Another plan to eliminate this evil will be the absolute discontinuance of the sale of extra chairs for boxes. Except in a very few cases this practice of selling extra chairs for boxes cannot be done without encroaching upon the rights of someone not interested in the matter and the only solution of the problem is the discontinuance of the practice entirely. No extra chairs will be available to the ushers and infraction of this rule will be considered sufficient grounds for the discharge of the usher.

MAIN FLOOR BOXES, THIRD BASE SIDE.—GREEN TICKETS.

[21]

New Season Box Plan

The adoption of the new rules to better protect our box patrons in their rights, makes necessary an entirely new season box plan, which will function properly with the new arrangement.

Under the new Season Box Plan the purchaser will be furnished a dated admission ticket with seat coupon attached for every seat in his box for every game of the season. There will be no more "identification books" or "book admission tickets."

The price of a single box seat for the season under this revised plan will be $96.25. This price will cover a single admission and a seat coupon for each game of the season, as well as the war tax for each game in accordance with the provisions of the revenue act. Under the new plan the cost of the various sized boxes for the season will be as follows:

	Four Seat Box	Six Seat Box	Eight Seat Box
War Tax	$ 43.12	$ 64.68	$ 86.24
308 admissions and seat coupons @ $1.11	341.88	. . . .	. . . .
462 admissions and seat coupons @ 1.11	. . . .	512.82	. . . .
616 admissions and seat coupons @ 1.11	. . . .	. . . .	683.76
Total cost including admissions to every game for all seats owned	$385.00	$577.50	$770.00

Anyone interested in the purchase of a season box will be furnished with more detailed information in regard to the plan upon application.

New Ladies' Day Arrangement

Every Friday, during the championship season, on which a game is scheduled, is known as "Ladies' Day." On all days so designated, ladies are admitted to the grand stand free of charge, upon payment of the war tax of ten cents. It is not necessary for ladies to be escorted by gentlemen in order to take advantage of this courtesy. This free admission on "Ladies' Days" applies only to the general admission seats. Ladies desiring to occupy box or reserved seats on these special "Ladies' Days" will be required to purchase the admission ticket as well as the seat coupon, just as they would have to do on any other day of the week. **The plan of selling seat coupons to ladies on these special days has been discontinued. Under this revised plan, which makes free admission on "Ladies' Day" strictly a general admission proposition, a special ladies' entrance will be operated at the corner of Linwood Avenue and East 66th Street on these days for all ladies who desire to take advantage of the free admission to the unreserved seats in the grand stand. No special ladies' gate will be operated at the main entrance at the corner of Lexington Avenue and East 66th Street.**

Downtown Ticket Office

The downtown ticket office will be continued at The Pyle and Allen Company's Cigar Store, 312 East Superior Avenue. Realizing that the facilities at our down town office proved inadequate last season, we have arranged with The Pyle and Allen Company to build a ticket booth in the front part of their store, access to which will be through a special entrance. This new arrangement will enable our downtown representatives to handle the advance sale of tickets with greater efficiency and we feel sure that our patrons will have no occasion to repeat the complaints which were registered against the poor arrangements in connection with our downtown ticket office last season.

The experience of the 1920 season proved that it is impossible for the club to make any iron clad rules, in connection with its downtown sale. Ordinarily box and reserve tickets for week day games will be on sale at the downtown office about a week in advance, and tickets for the Sunday games will be placed on sale Tuesday morning. **Whenever there is an unusual interest in any game or series of games, tickets will be placed on sale just as soon as the demand for same justifies such action. In cases of this kind announcement will be made in the daily papers.**

Chapter Notes

Chapter 1

1. Early ballpark locations and details largely from Franklin Lewis, *The Cleveland Indians* (New York: G.P. Putnam's Sons, 1946; reprint, Kent, OH: Kent State University Press, 2006), and Michael Benson, *Ballparks of North America* (Jefferson, NC: McFarland, 1989; softcover, 2009).
2. Benson, *Ballparks of North America*, 105.
3. *Cleveland Plain Dealer*, May 1, 1891.
4. *Cleveland Plain Dealer*, May 2, 1891.
5. *Cleveland Plain Dealer*, October 3, 1895.
6. *Cleveland Plain Dealer*, July 10, 1897.
7. Information on Sunday play and game sites can be found in Charlie Bevis, *Sunday Baseball: The Major Leagues' Struggle to Play Baseball on the Lord's Day, 1876–1934* (Jefferson, NC: McFarland, 2003), and Benson, *Ballparks of North America*.
8. For more information on Louis Sockalexis, see Brian McDonald, *Indian Summer: The Forgotten Story of Louis Sockalexis, the First Native American in Major League Baseball* (Emmaus, PA: Rodale, 2003), and David L. Fleitz, *Louis Sockalexis: The First Cleveland Indian* (Jefferson, NC: McFarland, 2002).
9. *Cleveland Leader*, March 28, 1899.
10. *Cleveland Leader*, May 2, 1899.
11. *Cleveland Plain Dealer*, July 31, 1899.
12. *Cleveland Plain Dealer*, August 13, 1899.
13. *Cleveland Plain Dealer*, August 23, 1899.
14. *Cleveland Leader*, August 23, 1899.
15. *Cleveland Plain Dealer*, August 25, 1899.
16. The story of the team and season can be found in J. Thomas Hetrick, *Misfits! The Cleveland Spiders of 1899* (Jefferson, NC: McFarland, 1991; softcover, Clifton, VA: Pocol Press, 2000).
17. The formation of the early American League is chronicled in Norman Macht, *Connie Mack and the Early Years of Baseball* (Lincoln: University of Nebraska Press, 2007).
18. *Cleveland Press*, April 4, 1900.
19. *Cleveland Leader*, April 28, 1903.
20. *Cleveland Leader*, October 3, 1907.
21. *Cleveland Press*, October 2, 1908.
22. Further information on the Joss game and other perfect games can be found in James Buckley, Jr., *Perfect: The Inside Story of Baseball's Sixteen Perfect Games* (Chicago: Triumph, 2002), and Michael Coffey, *27 Men Out: Baseball's Perfect Games* (New York: Atria Books, 2004).
23. Harold Helfer, "The Sign That Cost the Tribe a Flag," *Baseball Digest* 13, no. 5 (1954): 47. Accessed through the "Cleveland Indians" clippings file at the Ernie Harwell Sports Collection, Detroit Public Library.
24. *Cleveland Plain Dealer*, September 8, 1909.
25. Ibid.

Chapter 2

1. *Cleveland Press*, April 21, 1910.
2. *Elyria* (Ohio) *Evening Telegram*, December 6, 1909.

3. Ibid.

4. *Chicago Daily Tribune*, December 19, 1909.

5. *Cleveland Plain Dealer*, September 11, 1910.

6. *Cleveland Plain Dealer*, October 10, 1910.

7. The 1908 American League batting race is examined in Cait Murphy, *"Crazy '08{in}: How a Cast of Cranks, Rogues, Boneheads, and Magnates Created the Greatest Year in Baseball* (New York: HarperCollins, 2007).

8. Michael Coffey, *27 Men Out* (New York: Atria, 2004).

9. Reed Browning, *Cy Young: A Baseball Life* (Amherst: University of Massachusetts Press, 2000), 190.

10. *Cleveland News*, July 23, 1911.

11. Addie Joss' complete story is told in Scott Longert, *Addie Joss: King of Pitchers* (Cleveland: Society for American Baseball Research, 1998).

12. *Cleveland Press*, September 10, 1910.

13. For Jackson's biography, see David L. Fleitz, *Shoeless: The Life and Times of Joe Jackson* (Jefferson, NC: McFarland, 2001).

14. *Cleveland Plain Dealer*, May 16, 1911.

15. *Cleveland Plain Dealer*, October 4, 1911.

16. *Cleveland Plain Dealer*, May 19, 1913.

17. *Cleveland News*, June 21, 1914.

18. *Cleveland Plain Dealer*, May 24, 1915.

19. *Cleveland Plain Dealer*, August 9, 1915.

20. *Cleveland Plain Dealer*, April 9, 1916.

21. Two biographies have been published on Speaker in recent years. See Charles Alexander, *Spoke: A Biography of Tris Speaker* (Dallas: Southern Methodist University Press, 2007), and Timothy Gay, *Tris Speaker: The Rough-And-Tumble Life Of A Baseball Legend* (Lincoln: University of Nebraska Press, 2005).

22. *Cleveland Plain Dealer*, August 30, 1919.

Chapter 3

1. Curt Smith, *Storied Stadiums: Baseball's History through Its Ballparks* (New York: Carroll & Graf, 2001), p. 94

2. Mike Sowell, *The Pitch That Killed* (New York: Macmillan, 1989), p. 154.

3. *Cleveland Press*, April 13, 1920.

4. See Sowell's *The Pitch That Killed* for more information on Chapman and his death.

5. *Cleveland Press*, September 1, 1920.

6. *Washington Post*, September 28, 1920.

7. For more information about the 1920 World Series, see Josh Leventhal, *The World Series: An Illustrated Encyclopedia of the Fall Classic* (New York: Black Dog and Leventhal, 2001); for a full account of the Indians' season, see Gary Webster, *Tris Speaker and the 1920 Indians* (Jefferson, NC: McFarland, 2012).

8. *Cleveland Plain Dealer*, October 13, 1920.

Chapter 4

1. *Cleveland Press*, April 21, 1921.

2. *Cleveland News*, May 17, 1921.

3. *Baseball When the Grass Was Real: Baseball from the Twenties to the Forties Told by the Men Who Played It* (New York: Coward, McCann and Geoghegan, 1975), 17–19.

4. *Cleveland Plain Dealer*, July 28, 1928.

5. *Cleveland Press*, June 6, 1918.

6. *Cleveland Plain Dealer*, May 15, 1921.

7. *Cleveland Plain Dealer*, August 11, 1929.

8. *Cleveland Plain Dealer*, April 23, 1930.

9. *Cleveland Plain Dealer*, May 28, 1930.

Chapter 5

1. *Cleveland Press*, April 20, 1932.
2. *Milwaukee Journal*, December 26, 1933.
3. *New York Times*, October 14, 1933.
4. *Cleveland Plain Dealer*, June 2, 1936.
5. *Cleveland Plain Dealer*, March 14, 1936.
6. *Cleveland Plain Dealer*, August 29, 1939.
7. *Cleveland Plain Dealer*, August 14, 1940.
8. *The Sporting News*, April 20, 1944.
9. *The Sporting News*, June 10, 1937.
10. See Michael Seidel, *Streak: Joe DiMaggio and the Summer of '41* (New York: McGraw-Hill, 1988; reprint, Lincoln: University of Nebraska Press, 2002).
11. *Cleveland Plain Dealer*, August 8, 1943.
12. Bill Veeck's story is best told in the book he wrote with Ed Linn, *Veeck — As in Wreck* (New York: G.P. Putnam's Sons, 1962; reprint, Chicago: University of Chicago Press, 2001).

Chapter 6

1. *Cleveland Call and Post*, May 26, 1934.
2. *Cleveland Call and Post*, June 16, 1934.
3. *Chicago Defender*, July 24, 1931.
4. Larry Tye, *Satchel: The Life and Times of an American Legend* (New York: Random House, 2009), p. 52.
5. *Call and Post*, May 15, 1948.
6. *Call and Post*, June 12, 1948.
7. The complete story of black baseball in Cleveland is available in Stephanie Liscio, *Integrating Cleveland Baseball: Media Activism, the Integration of the Indians and the Demise of the Negro League Buckeyes* (Jefferson, NC: McFarland, 2010).

Chapter 7

1. Hal Erickson, *The Baseball Filmography, 1915 through 2001* (Jefferson, NC: McFarland, 2002; softcover, 2010), p. 265
2. Ibid.
3. Ibid.

Chapter 8

1. *Cleveland Plain Dealer*, October 26, 1950.
2. *Cleveland Press*, September 20, 1951.
3. *Cleveland Plain Dealer*, July 15, 1992.
4. *Cleveland Plain Dealer*, June 9, 2007.
5. *Cleveland Press*, September 20, 1951.

Bibliography

Special Collections

Charles W. Mears and Eugene C. Murdock
Collections, Cleveland Public Library
Ernie Harwell Sports Collection, Detroit
Public Library

Newspapers and Magazines

Carroll (Ohio) *News*
Chicago Defender
Chicago Tribune
Cleveland Call and Post
Cleveland Gazette
Cleveland Leader
Cleveland Magazine
Cleveland News
Cleveland Plain Dealer
Cleveland Press
Elyria (Ohio) *Evening Telegram*
Lincoln (Nebraska) *Evening News*
Los Angeles Times
Mansfield (Ohio) *News*
Milwaukee Journal
New York Times
Pittsburgh Post-Gazette
Pittsburgh Press
Syracuse Herald
Washington Post
The Sporting News

Media Guides and Other Team Publications

Dunn Field Pointers, Cleveland Baseball
Club, 1921
League Park Day Souvenir Program, August
25, 1979
Indians Game Face Magazine, vol. 6, no. 3,
1992

Websites

ballparks.com
ballparksofbaseball.com
baseball-almanac.com
baseballhistorian.com
baseballlibrary.com
baseball-reference.com
blackbetsy.com
clevelandmemory.org
Indians.mlb.com
JohnnyKilbane.com
leaguepark.org
sabr.org
stlouisrams.com

Books and Articles

Alexander, Charles. *Ty Cobb*. New York:
Oxford University Press, 1984.
Bak, Richard. *Peach: Ty Cobb in His Time
and Ours*. Ann Arbor: Sports Media
Group, 2005.
Benson, Michael. *Ballparks of North Amer-
ica*. Jefferson, NC: McFarland, 1989.
Betzold, Michael, and Ethan Carey. *Queen
of Diamonds*. West Bloomfield, MI: Al-
twerger and Mandel, 1992.
Bevis, Charlie. *Sunday Baseball: The Major
Leagues' Struggle to Play Baseball on the
Lord's Day, 1876–1934*. Jefferson, NC:
McFarland, 2003.
Borsvold, David. *Cleveland Indians: The
Cleveland Press Years, 1920–1982*. Charle-
ston, SC: Arcadia,1993.
Boudreau, Lou, and Russell Schneider. *Lou
Boudreau: Covering All the Bases*. Cham-
paign, IL: Sagamore, 1993.
Bowman, Larry. *Before the World Series*.

Dekalb: Northern Illinois University Press, 2003.

Browning, Reed. *Cy Young: A Baseball Life*. Amherst: University of Massachusetts Press, 2000.

Buckley, Jr., James. *Classic Ballparks*. New York: Barnes & Noble, 2004.

_____. *Perfect: The Inside Story of Baseball's Sixteen Perfect Games*. Chicago: Triumph Books, 2002.

Coffey, Michael. *27 Men Out*. New York: Atria Books, 2004.

Cohen, Richard. *The Ohio State Football Scrapbook*. Indianapolis: Bobbs-Merrill, 1977.

Cope, Myron. *The Game That Was*. Cleveland: World, 1970.

Durso, Joseph. *DiMaggio: The Last American Knight*. Boston: Little, Brown, 1995.

Dyer, Bob. *Cleveland Sports Legends*. Cleveland: Gray, 2003.

Eckhouse, Morris. *Day by Day in Cleveland Indians History*. New York: Leisure Press, 1983.

_____. *Where Cleveland Played: Sports Shrines from League Park to Municipal Stadium*. Charleston, SC: History Press.

Eig, Jonathan. *Luckiest Man: The Life and Death of Lou Gehrig*. New York: Simon & Schuster, 2005.

Erickson, Hal. *The Baseball Filmography, 1915 through 2001*. Jefferson, NC: McFarland, 2002.

Felber, Bill. *Under Pallor, Under Shadow: The 1920 American League Pennant Race That Rattled and Rebuilt Baseball*. Lincoln: University of Nebraska Press, 2011.

Feller, Bob, and Burton Rocks. *Bob Feller's Little Black Book of Baseball Wisdom*. Chicago: Contemporary Books, 2001.

Fitch, Jerry. *Cleveland's Greatest Fighters of All Time*. Charleston, SC: Arcadia, 2002.

Fleitz, David. *Louis Sockalexis: The First Cleveland Indian*. Jefferson, NC: McFarland, 2001.

_____. *Shoeless: The Life and Times of Joe Jackson*. Jefferson, NC: McFarland, 2001.

Gavin, Donald. *John Carroll University: A Century of Service*. Kent, OH: Kent State University Press, 1985.

Gay, Timothy. *Tris Speaker: The Rough-and-Tumble Life of a Baseball Legend*. Lincoln: University of Nebraska Press, 2008.

Gershman, Michael. *Diamonds: The Evolution of the Ballpark*. New York: Houghton Mifflin, 1993.

Green, Stephen. *Wrigley Field*. New York: McGraw-Hill, 2003.

Ham, Eldon. *Larceny and Old Leather: The Mischievous Legacy of Major League Baseball*. Chicago: Academy Chicago, 2005.

Hauser, Christopher. *The Negro Leagues Chronology: Events in Organized Black Baseball, 1920–1948*. Jefferson, NC: McFarland, 2006.

Heidenry, Jack. *The Gashouse Gang*. New York: Public Affairs Press, 2007.

Hetrick, Thomas J. *Misfits! The Cleveland Spiders in 1899*. Jefferson, NC: McFarland, 1991.

Hickey, David, Kerry Keene and Raymond Sinabaldi. *The Babe in Red Stockings*. Champaign, IL: Sagamore, 1997.

Hittner, Arthur. *Honus Wagner: The Life of Baseball's "Flying Dutchman."* Jefferson, NC: McFarland, 1996.

Hodermarsky, Mark, ed. *The Cleveland Sports Legacy, 1900–1945*. Cleveland: Cleveland Landmarks Press, 1992.

Hudak, Timothy. *The Charity Game: The Story of Cleveland's Thanksgiving Day High School Football Classic*. Cleveland: Sports Heritage, 2002.

_____. *When the Lions Roared: The Story of Cathedral Latin School Football*. Cleveland: Sports Heritage, 2002.

Huhn, Rick. *The Sizzler: George Sisler, Baseball's Forgotten Great*. Columbia: University of Missouri Press, 2004.

Jedick, Peter. *League Park*. Cleveland: Peter Jedick Enterprises, 1978.

Johnson, Lloyd, and Miles Wolff, eds. *Encyclopedia of Minor League Baseball*, 3d ed. Durham: Baseball America, 2007.

Kaplan, Jim. *Lefty Grove: American Legend*. Cleveland: SABR, 2000.

Kohout, Martin. *Hal Chase: The Defiant Life and Turbulent Times of Baseball's Biggest Crook*. Jefferson, NC: McFarland, 2001.

Kuklick, Bruce. *To Every Thing a Season*.

Princeton: Princeton University Press, 1991.

Lanctot, Neil. *Negro League Baseball: The Rise and Ruin of a Black Institution.* Philadelphia: University of Pennsylvania Press, 2004.

Leventhal, Josh. *The World Series: An Illustrated Encyclopedia of the Fall Classic.* New York: Black Dog and Leventhal, 2001.L

Lewis, Franklin. *The Cleveland Indians.* New York: Van Rees Press, 1949.

Liscio, Stephanie. *Integrating Cleveland Baseball.* Jefferson, NC: McFarland, 2010.

Longert, Scott. *Addie Joss: King of Pitchers.* Cleveland: SABR, 1998.

Lovarro, Thom. *The Encyclopedia of Negro League Baseball.* New York: Checkmark Books, 2003.

Lowry, Phillip. *Green Cathedrals, The Ultimate Celebration of all 271 Major League and Negro League Ballparks Past and Present.* Boston: Addison Wesley, 1992.

Macht, Norman. *Connie Mack and the Early Years of Baseball.* Lincoln: University of Nebraska Press, 2007.

McCollister, John. *The Best Baseball Games Ever Played.* New York: Kensington, 2002.

McDonald, Brian. *Indian Summer.* New York: St. Martin's Press, 2003.

Miller, Carol Poh, and Robert Wheeler. *Cleveland: A Concise History, 1796–1996,* 2d ed. Bloomington: Indiana University Press, 1997.

Montville, Leigh. *The Big Bam.* New York: Doubleday Broadway, 2006.

Murphy, Cait. *"Crazy '08{in}: How a Cast of Cranks, Rogues, Boneheads, and Magnates Created the Greatest Year in Baseball.* New York: HarperCollins, 2007.

Nichols, Bill. *...And We Must Excel.* Cleveland: Davies Wing, 2001.

O'Karma, David. "The Forgotten Championship." *Cleveland Magazine,* May 2006.

Okkonen, Marc. *Baseball Memories, 1900–1909.* New York: Sterling, 1992.

Osborn Engineering Company. *A Century of Progress: Meeting the Challenges of the Times: A History of the Osborn Engineering Company, 1892–1992.* Cleveland: Osborn Engineering, 1992.

Paige, Leroy. *Maybe I'll Pitch Forever.* Lincoln: University of Nebraska Press, 1993.

Palacios, Oscar. *Ballpark Sourcebook, Diamond Diagrams.* Skokie, IL: Stats, 1998.

Park, Jack. *The Official Ohio State Football Encyclopedia.* [Columbus?]: Sports Publishing, 2003.

Piascik, Andy. *The Best Show in Football: The 1946–1955 Cleveland Browns.* Lanham, MD: Taylor Trade, 2007.

Pluto, Terry. *Browns Town 1964.* Cleveland: Gray, 1997.

_____. *Our Tribe.* New York: Simon & Schuster, 1999.

Rader, Benjamin. *Baseball, A History of America's Game.* Urbana: University of Illinois Press, 1992.

Reidenbaugh, Lowell. *The Sporting News Take Me Out to the Ballpark.* St. Louis: The Sporting News, 1983.

Reisler, Jim. *Babe Ruth, Launching the Legend.* New York: McGraw-Hill, 2004.

Ribowsky, Mark. *A Complete History of the Negro League, 1884–1955.* New York: Kensington, 1995.

Ritter, Lawrence. *Lost Ballparks: A Celebration of Baseball's Legendary Fields.* New York: Penguin, 1992.

Robertson, John. *The Babe Chases 60.* Jefferson, NC: McFarland, 1999.

Rose, William Gannon. *Cleveland: The Making of a City.* Cleveland: World, 1950.

Schneider, Russell. *The Cleveland Indians Encyclopedia,* 3d ed. Champaign: Sports Publishing, 2004.

_____. *Tribe Memories: The First Century.* Hinckley, OH: Moonlight, 2000.

Seidel, Michael. *Streak: Joe DiMaggio and the Summer of '41.* Lincoln: University of Nebraska Press, 1988.

Selter, Ronald. *Ballparks of the Deadball Era.* Jefferson, NC: McFarland, 2008.

Shannon, Bill, and George Kalinsky. *The Ballparks.* New York: Hawthorn Books, 1975.

Sickels, John. *Bob Feller.* Dulles, VA: Brassey's, 2004.

Smith, Curt. *Storied Stadiums: Baseball's History through its Ballparks.* New York: Carroll & Graf, 2001.

Smith, Robert. *Baseball in the Afternoon.* New York: Simon & Schuster, 1993.

Sowell, Mike. *The Pitch That Killed.* New York: Macmillan, 1989.

Stump, Al. *Cobb.* New York: Workman, 1994.

Sullivan, Brad, ed. *Batting Four Thousand: Baseball in the Western Reserve.* Cleveland: SABR, 2008.

Tye, Larry. *Satchel: The Life and Times of an American Legend.* New York: Random House, 2009.

Van Tassell, David, and John Grabowski. *The Encyclopedia of Cleveland History.* Bloomington: Indiana University Press, 1987.

Vecsey, George. *Baseball: A History of America's Favorite Game.* New York: Random House, 2006.

Veeck, Bill, and Ed Linn. *Veeck–As in Wreck.* New York: G.P. Putnam's Sons, 1962 [Chicago: University of Chicago Press, 2001].

White, G. Edward. *Creating the National Pastime: Baseball Transforms Itself 1903–1953.* Princeton: Princeton University Press, 1996.

Wilbert, Warren. *The Arrival of the American League.* Jefferson, NC: McFarland, 2007.

Index